# Beyond Justice as Fairness

# Beyond Justice as Fairness

*Rethinking Rawls from a Cross-Cultural Perspective*

Paul Nnodim

LEXINGTON BOOKS
Lanham • Boulder • New York • London

Published by Lexington Books
An imprint of The Rowman & Littlefield Publishing Group, Inc.
4501 Forbes Boulevard, Suite 200, Lanham, Maryland 20706
www.rowman.com

6 Tinworth Street, London SE11 5AL, United Kingdom

Copyright © 2020 by The Rowman & Littlefield Publishing Group, Inc.

*All rights reserved.* No part of this book may be reproduced in any form or by any electronic or mechanical means, including information storage and retrieval systems, without written permission from the publisher, except by a reviewer who may quote passages in a review.

British Library Cataloguing in Publication Information Available

**Library of Congress Cataloging-in-Publication Data**

Names: Nnodim, Paul, author.
Title: Beyond justice as fairness : rethinking Rawls from a cross-cultural perspective / Paul Nnodim.
Description: Lanham, Maryland: Lexington Books, 2020. | Includes bibliographical references and index. | Summary: "This book explores the three foundational topics in Rawls's theories of justice (social justice, multiculturalism, and global justice) while deconstructing ideas of democratic citizenship, public reason, and liberal individualism latent in his treatment of these subjects in order to uncover their cultural and historical underpinnings"— Provided by publisher.
Identifiers: LCCN 2020033335 (print) | LCCN 2020033336 (ebook) | ISBN 9781498558068 (cloth) | ISBN 9781498558075 (epub) | ISBN 9781498558082 (pbk)
Subjects: LCSH: Rawls, John, 1921–2002—Political and social views. | Justice. | Social justice. | Human rights. | Liberalism.
Classification: LCC JC578 .N66 2020 (print) | LCC JC578 (ebook) | DDC 320.01/1—dc23
LC record available at https://lccn.loc.gov/2020033335
LC ebook record available at https://lccn.loc.gov/2020033336

For

Mom and Dad—Felicia and Damian

Nelson and Chisim

Dom, Rafael, and Chineé

# Contents

| | |
|---|---|
| Acknowledgments | ix |
| Introduction | 1 |
| **Part I: Social Justice** | **7** |
| 1   The Question of Justice | 9 |
| 2   Why Utilitarianism Is Not the Best Option | 25 |
| **Part II: Pluralism, Public Reason, and Political Stability** | **39** |
| 3   The Departure from Classical Liberalism | 41 |
| 4   Justice as Fairness: A Reinterpretation | 65 |
| 5   Why Public Reason Is Not the "Public Use of Reason" | 85 |
| 6   Rawls's Idea of a Well-Ordered Society | 103 |
| **Part III: Rawls's Global Justice and the Non-Western World** | **127** |
| 7   Human Rights in *The Law of Peoples* | 129 |
| 8   Liberal Individualism and the Concept of the Person in African Philosophy: Implications for Rawls's Basic Human Rights | 149 |
| Epilogue | 161 |
| Bibliography | 163 |
| Index | 175 |
| About the Author | 179 |

# Acknowledgments

I am very thankful to Almighty God, who through His Divine Mercy continues to lead me on the path of more profound truth. My gratitude also goes to my colleagues at Massachusetts College of Liberal Arts, especially to Anthony Daly, David and Nicole Braden-Johnson, and Mike Birch. I am equally grateful to my students at MCLA; the student-assistant Kenny Olchowski, who helped with arranging the bibliography; and students of my Kant Seminar class of spring 2020, who were among the first to read the chapters. Thank you also to Austin Okigbo (University of Colorado, Boulder). I am deeply indebted to my beloved wife, MaryBlessing, for her unwavering support.

# Introduction

John Rawls was a professor of philosophy at Harvard University from 1962 until his death in 2002. He remains one of the most influential political thinkers of both the twentieth and the twenty-first centuries. I agree with Naomi Choi (2015) that "where liberal theory is concerned, John Rawls is routinely credited with single-handedly reviving political theory from its moribund post-World War state."[1] The Nobel Laureate Amartya Sen states in *The Idea of Justice* (2009) that "[m]oral and political philosophy took huge steps, under Rawls's leadership."[2] Rawls's notable works, *A Theory of Justice* (1971), *Political Liberalism* (1993, 1996), and *The Law of Peoples* (1999), rekindled and galvanized the discourse on justice in contemporary political philosophy. Today, his ideas continue to inspire debates across the disciplines, with notable impacts in academic fields such as economics, law, sociology, and politics.

Born in Baltimore, Maryland, on February 21, 1921, Rawls attended Princeton University for his undergraduate studies and majored in philosophy. He graduated with the highest honor in January 1943. Rawls served as a U.S. infantryman during World War II, first in New Guinea, where he won a Bronze Star, and later in the Philippines and Japan.[3] Rawls returned to Princeton at the end of the war to continue his studies in philosophy and received his PhD in 1950. After some years of teaching at Cornell University and the Massachusetts Institute of Technology, Rawls moved to Harvard University in 1962. Harvard named him the John Cowles Professor of Philosophy in 1975 and James Bryant Conant University Professor in 1979.

Rawls was married to Margaret Warfield Fox, with whom he had four children.[4] In an interview with the *Harvard Gazette* (2005), Margaret talked about Rawls's appearance on the day of their blind date in 1948: "He was an extremely handsome, almost penniless graduate student with an amazing smile and a significant stammer, who danced enthusiastically, but badly. What young girl could resist that combination?"[5]

The German philosopher Martin Heidegger once began a lecture series on Aristotle with this statement: "In the personality of a philosopher, there is only this interest: he was born at such and such a time, he worked, and he died."[6] Arguably, this was not the fate of Rawls. Although he was a gentle and quiet person, and, some would even say, reclusive and publicity-shy, when Rawls died on November 24, 2002, it was as, if in Shakespeare's words, "[t]he heavens themselves blaze forth the death of princes."[7] Major news organizations across the globe carried his obituary. The headline of the respectable and widely read German newspaper *DIE ZEIT* was no less striking: "*Ein Revolutionär der Gerechtigkeit: Zum Tod von John Rawls, einem der größten Anreger in der politischen Ideengeschichte des 20. Jahrhunderts.*"[8] (A revolutionary of justice: on the death of John Rawls, one of the greatest proponents of the political history of ideas of the twentieth century—translation mine.)

How did John Rawls become an intellectual rock star? One may argue that Rawls was not a public intellectual in the strictest sense of the term because he did not crisscross countries and continents delivering lectures to thousands of enthusiastic admirers. In fact, Rawls conscientiously rejected the image of a public figure and even declined some public honors. However, he accepted honorary degrees from Oxford, Princeton, Harvard, and a few other awards, such as the Rolf Schock Prize in Logic and Philosophy from the Swedish Academy of Sciences and the National Humanities Medal conferred by President Bill Clinton.[9] Nevertheless, *A Theory of Justice* did transform Rawls into one of the leading public scholars of modern times, with thousands of copies sold worldwide and published translations in twenty-three languages.[10]

In an exclusive interview he granted to three Harvard students ("John Rawls: For the Record" by Samuel R. Aybar, Joshua D. Harlan, and Won J. Lee) in 1991, Rawls attributed the popularity of *A Theory of Justice* to a conjunction of circumstances dogging two major political upheavals in the United States:

> It was during the Viet[n]am War and soon after the Civil Rights Movement. They dominated the politics of the day. And yet there was no recent book, no systematic treatise, you might say, on a conception of political justice. For a long time there had been a relative of dearth of political philosophy—both in political science and moral philosophy ... [s]o *Theory* was the first large work coming after this period of serious political conflict. And serious political conflict shows the need for political philosophy and normally calls it forth. (Aybar et al. 1991, 42)

Reading Rawls's works can be an overwhelming task because of his dense prose and style of presentation. One of my primary aims in *Beyond Justice as Fairness* is to make Rawls accessible to students, scholars, and anyone interested in the subject. Additionally, the book raises important philosophical questions about some of the contentious presuppositions of Rawls's works. While some readers may see these questions as a couched criticism of Rawls, the original intent is, nonetheless, to bring about a deeper understanding of his views by settling unresolved arguments, rather than undermining his core project. *Beyond Justice as Fairness* explores the three foundational topics in Rawls's theories of justice (social justice, multiculturalism, and global justice) while deconstructing ideas of democratic citizenship, public reason, and liberal individualism latent in his treatment of these subjects in order to uncover their cultural and historical underpinnings. Finally, I take up the question of how well these ideas fit with the concept of the person in a non-Western context.

*Beyond Justice as Fairness* has three parts. Part I contains two chapters on social justice. Chapter 1 examines the question of justice in the contexts of prejudice, meaning, and origin as it relates to Rawls's two principles of justice as fairness. Chapter 1 further investigates the theoretical value of Rawls's "original position" as a device of representation within the framework of the social contract theory. Here, the "veil of ignorance" serves the function of a phenomenological *epoché* or bracketing (*Einklammerung* in Husserlian terms) in an attempt to defend the principles of justice that fictive persons choose in a hypothetical or counterfactual, contractual situation.

Chapter 2 examines utilitarianism as a form of justice. In *A Theory of Justice*, Rawls identifies utilitarianism as the dominant moral theory of the twentieth century. However, utilitarianism framed as a system of justice, Rawls insists, does not address the overarching issues about fairness and equality. Additionally, Rawls assumes that utilitarianism could provide for proponents of unregulated capitalist aggrandizement of wealth and income the foundational principles to vindicate the social, economic, and institutional inequalities that exist in modern democracies. Therefore, he situates "justice as fairness" as a prevailing, alternative moral theory to utilitarianism. This chapter examines four significant points of distinction between classical utilitarianism and Rawls's justice as fairness.

Part II is on "Pluralism, Public Reason, and Political Stability," and its first two chapters constitute a discourse on multiculturalism and the features of the modern democratic state. Drawing from traditional classical liberalism (especially Kant), in *A Theory of Justice*, Rawls shows us how the liberal state ought to deal with the issue of distributive justice while ensuring the protection of citizens' fundamental liberties and rights. As a social theory of justice, his book became the target of some libertarian and right liberal-oriented scholars. One of Rawls's ardent critics is Robert Nozick, his colleague at Harvard and the author of *Anarchy, State, and Utopia* (1974). Rawls would later acknowledge that "Nozick had interesting and important objections. In part, they were based on misunderstandings, though in part they were very good points. Although I haven't done a whole article replying to him, I have replied to him at several points (although not by name) in an article I did in 1978. I now see things more clearly."[11]

As a meticulous and methodical scholar, Rawls considerably recast some of his original ideas in his later works. This change in perspective is the subject matter of chapter 4. It focuses on how a modern, liberal democratic society should deal with cultural, ethnic, religious, philosophical, or moral pluralism. Rawls's objective is to outline how a constitutional, democratic state could incorporate the different hopes, aspirations, and life prospects of its citizens into a coherent system of justice. So that people, although divided by different worldviews, may still unite in affirming a political conception of justice. Rawls calls his new project political liberalism, which is also the title of his second major work.

Chapter 5 is a comparative study of Rawls's "idea of public reason" and Kant's "public use of reason." The primary concern of Rawls's political liberalism is justice in a modern, multicultural, democratic society and the justification of political cohesion. For this reason, he describes justice as a political dialogue in which democratic deliberations rely on public reason—that is, on ideas entrenched in the public political culture of modern democratic societies. My aim in this chapter is to study the historical and philosophical foundations of the term "public reason" in political theory. I am particularly interested in examining the differences between Kant and Rawls in this regard, and in so doing, demonstrate that "public use of reason" is not the same thing as "public reason." Judging from Kant's riposte of 1784, *Beantwortung der Frage: Was ist Aufklärung?* ("An Answer to the Question: What is Enlightenment?"), "public use of reason" was a necessary condition for the advancement of the Enlightenment and philosophy within eighteenth-century Prussian society.

In contrast, Rawls's idea of public reason in *Political Liberalism* is only a formal mechanism for citizens of modern democracies to justify their public policies and government. The goal of Rawls's public reason is to enable citizens of today's heterogeneous, liberal democratic society to forge a sustainable basis for coexistence, despite their sharp and often conflicting ideological, cultural, and religious differences. Furthermore, while Rawls's idea of public reason satisfies the requirements set by the principle of political legitimacy (the normative and legal justification for the exercise of coercive political power by the government in the democratic state), Kant's public use of reason affirmed the moral autonomy of the individual in eighteenth-century Prussia.

Chapter 6 analyzes Rawls's political stability thesis. The foremost goal for Rawls in *Political Liberalism* is demonstrating that a well-ordered society, where most citizens endorse a set of ideologically neutral principles of justice, is achievable. Rawls poses two questions about stability in the well-ordered society. First, would citizens growing up under institutions regulated by justice as fairness acquire a sufficient sense of justice to support those systems freely? Second, given the fact that reasonable pluralism [12] characterizes modern democracies, would the political conception of justice be such that it can draw enough support from reasonable citizens?

Rawls answers the first political stability question with his notion of moral psychology, and the second political stability question with his "idea of an overlapping consensus." The developmental psychologies of Jean Piaget and Lawrence Kohlberg provide Rawls with the foundation for a theoretical analysis of how citizens of the well-ordered society acquire a sense of justice. To Rawls, the conception of justice naturally and psychologically suits human inclinations. He thinks that persons living under a just social system will develop behavioral traits robust enough to overcome the natural proclivities to commit injustice. Rawls presents the "idea of an overlapping consensus" in political liberalism to demonstrate that a well-ordered society of justice as fairness is attainable in our world. The "idea of an overlapping consensus" has an ecumenical feature. It is a consensus of reasonable, comprehensive worldviews on the political conception of justice as fairness. Thus, it is not merely a practical tool for the avoidance of conflict. Rawls argues that the stability achieved through his "idea of an overlapping consensus" is "stability for the right reasons," in contrast to a Hobbesian truce or a *modus vivendi*—a temporary cessation of violence.

The two chapters of part III discuss Rawls's idea of global justice, the opposition to his plan from the cosmopolitan wing of the global egalitarian movement, and the seeming normative problems created by his tampering with the articles of the Universal Declaration of Human Rights (UDHR)—a proclamation issued by the United Nations General Assembly in Paris on December 10, 1948.[13] In 1999, Rawls published *The Law of Peoples*, an extension of his views in *Political Liberalism* (1996). In recognition of the difficulty of espousing principles of global justice in the absence of a sovereign world state, Rawls considers his theory of international justice and relations a "realistic utopia." In chapter 7, I suggest that *The Law of Peoples* needs some restructuring to address effectively the issues of justice confronting our world today. Furthermore, Rawls insists that the existing international standard of human rights (UDHR) cannot achieve universal legitimacy because of its Western origins. As a departure from Rawls's position, I consider the prospects of a retrospective cultural-legitimacy argument for the UDHR norms, which attempts to secure informed appreciation for the articles of the declaration without bruising the sensitivities of the diverse peoples of the world.

Tolerating nonliberal peoples and truncating the list of internationally established articles of human rights are critical elements of Rawls's model of global justice. It can be argued that Rawls's position holds that non-Western concepts of personhood are incompatible with Western views about liberal individualism and democratic citizenship. The hierarchical societies of Rawls's *Law of Peoples*, which function as paradigms for nonliberal peoples, exhibit groupthink collectivism. For this reason, chapter 8 examines the concept of the person in a selected African community (the Igbo people of West Africa) and its implications for Rawls's theory of global justice.

My chosen area of research is not all encompassing, nor does it make broader claims about ideas of personhood across Africa. Nevertheless, it provides sufficient epistemological, moral, and metaphysical grounds for the discourse on the foundational properties of persons in a non-Western context. The goal is to demonstrate that "justice as fairness," as a moral theory rooted in human dignity, can apply in some form to all persons in the world irrespective of their geographical standpoints or positions in life. Therefore, while justice as fairness attempts to answer moral questions arising from the quiddity of persons, it should reflect as well the commonality of shared human conditions beyond the Western world.

## NOTES

1. Choi 2015, 244.
2. Sen 2009, 52.
3. See Military History Organization (www.military-history.org/articles/thinkers-at-war-john-rawls.htm).
4. See the *Harvard Gazette*, May 19, 2005 (https://news.harvard.edu/gazette/story/2005/05/john-rawls/).
5. Ibid.
6. See Large 2008, 3. For further reference, see also Martin Heidegger: *Grundbegriffe der Aristotelischen Philosophie*. Gesamtausgabe 18, Frankfurt am Main: Vittorio Klostermann Verlag, 2002, 5.
7. Shakespeare 2010, 44.
8. DIE ZEIT Nr. 49, November 28, 2002, 39.
9. See the *Harvard Gazette*, May 19, 2005 (https://news.harvard.edu/gazette/story/2005/05/john-rawls/).
10. This information is extracted from the back cover of the 1999 second edition of *A Theory of Justice* (Belknap Press).
11. Aybar et al. 1991.
12. The facts of reasonable pluralism are reasonable worldviews: religious, secular, cultural, moral, philosophical, and so forth. These are, broadly speaking, tolerable and acceptable views that characterize contemporary liberal societies. The facts of unreasonable pluralism are unreasonable worldviews that lead to fundamentalism, fanaticism, and extremism.
13. https://www.un.org/en/universal-declaration-human-rights/.

*Part I*

# Social Justice

*Chapter One*

# The Question of Justice

### IS IT IGNORANCE, PREJUDICE, OR INJUSTICE?

Someone can be willfully ignorant of the principles of justice and the context in which she judges or acts, in which case she is morally responsible for the consequences of her actions. Or she can be blissfully ignorant in both circumstances and therefore less culpable, but still causally implicated. As Thomas Jefferson once wrote, "Ignorance of the law is no excuse in any country. If it were, the laws would lose their effect, because it can always be pretended."[1] Here Jefferson's statement mirrors the legal principle of *ignorantia legis neminem excusat* (Ignorance of the law excuses no one), which derived from Roman law. While general knowledge of the law is not a requirement, ignorance of the law is not an excuse either in the administration of justice.

But what about immoral laws? Someone can be unaware of her participation in or propagation of structural injustices while successfully avoiding interpersonal injustice. Or, finally, she can be in full possession of the knowledge of justice and injustice, yet act unjustly as a consequentialist means to some higher end. Someone living under a brutal apartheid regime, who is complacent about its actions against marginalized groups, and who benefits consciously from the system, would fall into the above category.[2] These are some of the many scenarios that come to mind in the interplay of ignorance, prejudice, and injustice.

In the spring of 2010 and two years into the first term of the first African American president of the United States, Barack Obama, the Multicultural Resource Center at a New England liberal arts college kicked off a campus-wide, student-faculty interaction forum: Campus Conversation on Race (CCOR).[3] The objective of this meeting was to create awareness about the pervasive presence of racism and prejudice across college campuses in America. Pivotal to the program's success was getting students who had suffered some form of racial injustice to speak out. One personal account, in particular, initially irked many in the audience but eventually intrigued them. It was the narrative of a 22-year-old Ghanaian American student, Kofi Mensah,[4] an English major and aspiring foreign correspondent. He had just returned from a foreign-language immersion and study-abroad program in Germany. Overall, his study-abroad experience was positive, but there was one deplorable and remarkable incident. He had enrolled in one of the undergraduate courses taught in English, primarily to earn three additional credits and to find more space for expression without being restricted by his limited proficiency in German. The course was "Culture Studies II: The Native Americans," taught by Dr. Klutz, a professor from the American Studies Department.

On the first day of class, Dr. Klutz talked about his exploits at "Ole Miss" in 1962, where he pursued his undergraduate degree. He had marched alongside thousands of fellow segregationist white students, armed with axes, sticks, knives, and guns to protest the enrollment of James Meredith and to answer Governor Ross Barnett's call to arms: "We're getting ready to be invaded, we really want you as a Mississippian, a white Mississippian, to respond."[5] Mr. Meredith was the first African American student to gain admission to the University of Mississippi. In December 1961, he applied for admission to the University of Mississippi as an in-state transfer student and, despite meeting or even surpassing the university's standards, was denied access. Leaning on the Supreme Court's *Brown v. Board of Education* ruling of 1954, which made segregation in public schools unconstitutional, Mr. Meredith sued the university. He tenaciously pursued his admission for close to a year and a half. When he finally won his case, "[t]he town of Oxford erupted. It took some 30,000 U.S. troops, federal marshals and national guardsmen to get James Meredith to class after a violent campus uprising. Two people were killed and more than 300 injured."[6]

Beaming with an evocative smile, Dr. Klutz narrated with nostalgic delight the story of the "mini-civil war" that followed Meredith's admission, unperturbed by the apprehensive faces of two students of color sitting on the front row. Within the first couple of weeks of that semester, Kofi adjusted to Dr. Klutz's unapologetic and undiluted presentation of the so-called socio-anthropological facts about native peoples. However, the atmosphere became toxic the day Dr. Klutz described Navajo dance and song as "meaningless clatter of savage tongues." Kofi decried his professor's comment as cynical and suggested a less contemptuous characterization of Native American culture. Henceforth, Dr. Klutz made a habit of handing Kofi a special gift before class—a cluster of newspaper and journal clips of all variety of deleterious news about black people from around the world.

When the time came for the first quiz, and consistent with the German university system's tradition of fairness, Dr. Klutz distributed randomly assigned examination identification numbers to the students in place of names. Kofi scored 18.5 out of 20 points on the first quiz. A week later, Dr. Klutz, as if announcing the winner of a popularity contest, showered a shimmering approbation on the owner of the most impressive quiz grade in the class. Histrionically, he punctuated the four-digit number of the yet-to-be-identified outstanding student. When Kofi stood up to claim the grade, Dr. Klutz was both stunned and furious. There and then, he changed the rules: all subsequent exams must be completed with students' names written on the papers.

At the end of the semester, Kofi's cumulative grade was 93 percent, but Dr. Klutz decided to give him a C. Kofi took a couple of his fellow students to protest his grade at Dr. Klutz's office but had no success. "C is good for you," Dr. Klutz said. "But guess what? You can take your story to the University Senate if you like. But then again, before you do so, note that I'm a member of the Senate. You might not graduate if you bring a case against me," he threatened. In a country where students still revered university professors as demigods, Kofi and his friends walked away, feeling helpless. However, Kofi kept a record of his quiz papers, which he flipped over and over again before his listeners.

But what stirred Dr. Klutz to act undeservedly toward Kofi? If Kofi's story had ended at this point, perhaps we would not have found a definite answer to this question. During the last days of the subsequent semester, Dr. Klutz retired. However, one could still see him now and then hanging out alone at the cafeteria in the *Philosophicum*—the university's main humanities building. When he saw Kofi one day, he sprang up from his seat, abandoned his coffee, and rushed forward with the usual sinister grin. "Boy, I have retired. Are you happy now?" he asked. "Well, I'm here to tell you that although I may be physically gone, my spirit will still be around for a while, hovering like a bird in this hallway, to haunt you and folks like you." Kofi was too taken aback to give a coherent response. He only remembered muttering an "OK" in a muffled voice, wishing that the nightmare was only a fleeting dream.

Shortly before Kofi completed his study-abroad program, Dr. Klutz returned to campus looking for the young man. As usual, he waited at the cafeteria. What happened next was both bizarre and unexpected. Upon sighting Kofi, Dr. Klutz began to sob: "You must forgive me before I die. I was a stupid man, despite all my education," he said. He then went on to narrate the story of his recent journey to East Africa. His only child, a physician, had volunteered to work for *Médecins Sans Frontières* (Doctors Without Borders) in Uganda. Dr. Klutz and his wife had contrived every reason under the sky to persuade their daughter to cancel her plans, but they failed. Two weeks into their daughter's stay in the East African country, Dr. Klutz and his wife could no longer contain their disappointment. Therefore, they booked a flight to Uganda with the intention, when possible, of dragging their daughter back to Europe. On reaching Entebbe, Dr. Klutz was stunned to find the place and the people agreeable, courteous, and welcoming. Until then, he had lived a life replete with stereotypes, sweeping generalizations, and prejudices.ABrought himself spending three weeks with his family in Uganda, visiting strangers, making friends, and enjoying the landscape. He was a changed man.

Now Kofi added another twist to an already exciting story. He told the man point blank that he would not forgive him. Dr. Klutz begged all he could and even confessed his earlier unsuccessful attempts to change Kofi's grade from a C to an A with the help of a clandestine contact person in the office of the Dean of Academic Affairs. As Dr. Klutz was getting ready to walk away, Kofi, touched by the man's mental agony, said, "I forgave you on the day you gave me a C. Therefore, it would be redundant to forgive you a second time." Dr. Klutz looked at the young man remorsefully, yet visibly relieved, walked away in tears, and never returned.

Kofi admitted before his listeners that he had indeed forgiven Dr. Klutz from the depth of his heart long before the man resurfaced. But he would have also loved to keep this little secret to himself. It is undoubtedly heartwarming for the reader that a potentially explosive and ugly story has a happy ending. Dr. Klutz's journey to East Africa turned out to be an "aha" moment for him—a positively transformative learning experience leading to the perforation of his long-held prejudice against black people. But how should the victim, Kofi, or the reader categorize the behavior of Dr. Klutz? Is it ignorance, prejudice, or injustice? Should Kofi seek any form of restitution? The answer would lead us to a subject of both immense intrigue and confusion: justice. What is justice? Does it demand that we avoid holding preconceived opinions or making adverse judgments if we lack sufficient knowledge of a moral agent, a subject matter, or a situation? Does justice require us to be fair to all people or just to some?[7] If we reflect upon our common moral assumptions, then are some of our judgments of what is just or right not veiled forms of prejudice?

In *Justice: What's the Right Thing to Do?*, Michael Sandel (2009) reminds us that the question of justice calls for a moral reflection, which is "not a solitary pursuit but a public endeavor. It requires an interlocutor—a friend, a neighbor, a comrade, a fellow citizen. Sometimes the interlocutor can be imagined rather than real, as when we argue with ourselves. But we cannot discover the meaning of justice or the best way to live through introspection alone."[8] It is within this context that Rawls (1971) places the question of justice at the center of institutional morality. Just as epistemology, metaphysics, and other fields of both rational and empirical inquiries seek the truth, so also must social, economic, and political institutions of society seek justice.

## RAWLS'S JUSTICE AS FAIRNESS[9]

Rawls's *A Theory of Justice* (1971) has advanced the discourse on justice in modern-day political philosophy in ways no other works have done. Even Robert Nozick, Rawls's colleague and ardent critic, writes in *Anarchy, State, and Utopia* (1974) that "*A Theory of Justice* is a . . . systematic work in political and moral philosophy which has not seen its like since the writings of John Stuart Mill . . . political philosophers now must either work within Rawls's theory or explain why not."[10] But not everyone agrees with Nozick's claim. Choi (2015), for example, laments the pervasive presence of Rawls's theory in political philosophy. She remarks that "[t]he all too common narrative of Rawls as political theory's savior has rendered virtually invisible other notable ways in which political theory underwent 'reinvention' in the 20th century."[11] Additionally, Choi states that the dominant position of Rawls in modern political theory "has allowed the differences and similarities between Rawls and other prominent liberals to be obscured, and thus their relative strengths and weaknesses to be misdiagnosed."[12] Both supporters and detractors of Rawls attest to the importance of his works in political theory.

In *A Theory of Justice*, Rawls declares, "Justice is the first virtue of social institutions, as truth is of systems of thought. A theory, however elegant and economical, must be rejected or revised if it is untrue; likewise, laws and institutions no matter how efficient and well-arranged must be reformed or abolished if they are unjust."[13] His aim, he says, is to develop a sustainable conception of social justice implicit in the social contract tradition, which, however, "generalizes and carries to a higher level of abstraction the familiar theory of the social contract as found, say, in Locke, Rousseau, and Kant."[14]

Following the principle of liberal legitimacy, Rawls thinks that social, economic, or political cooperation must be predicated on the assumption that cooperating individuals freely consent to the terms of collaboration. Although he locates the ideals of justice in the classical tradition of virtue ethics, the principle of liberal legitimacy forms the moral basis for his contractarian approach—that is, "the liberal idea that the legitimacy of social rules and institutions depends on their being freely and publicly acceptable to all individuals bound by them."[15] Before the publication of *A Theory of Justice*, most political theorists considered the social contract theory obsolete, because prominent philosophers like David Hume (1711–1776) and Jeremy Bentham (1748–1832) had widely dismissed its method on account of counterfactuality.[16] A hypothetical contract, Ronald Dworkin (1977) adds, "is no contract at all."[17] By reviving the social contract tradition, Rawls's interest is not to "whip a dead horse." It appears that he is keen to develop a contract theory that is not only useful and relevant to contemporary political philosophy but also "not subject to the objections often thought fatal to contract views and one that is superior to the long-dominant tradition of utilitarianism in moral and political philosophy."[18]

In *A Theory of Justice*, Rawls presents democratic conceptions of person and society. Persons are free and equal citizens living in a society they see as a fair system of cooperation for their mutual benefit. In Rawls's human society, citizens practice "reciprocity of perspectives" by granting one another fair shares in the distribution of the benefits and burdens of socioeconomic cooperation. Given their nature as free and equal cooperating agents, citizens of Rawls's society must freely choose the principles of justice to regulate the basic structure of their society, because the basic structure determines to a great extent who succeeds and fails in society. For this reason, Rawls says that the basic structure (i.e., key institutions) of society is the primary subject of justice. He further elaborates on what the basic structure encompasses: "By major institutions I understand the political constitution and the principal economic and social arrangements."[19]

The conception of justice Rawls has in mind is unequivocally social—that is, social justice. To choose the principles of justice to govern the basic structure of society is serious business, which should not be left to an eccentric conjuring of intuitionist morals or to morality imposed from the outside. It is free citizens who should decide their fate. Samuel Freeman (2007a) reiterates this point:

> Rawls's parties conceive of themselves as free, not in the sense that they may act on any desire they happen to have but in the sense that they are able to control, revise, and take responsibility for their final ends and desires by acting on and from reasonable and rational principles. Recognizing the deep-seated effects of basic social institutions on these capacities and on their interests, they have a basic concern for how such institutions are designed. Not satisfied with the idea that these institutions answer to their desires for the accumulation of objects, Rawls's parties have a deeper interest in whether the institutions are structured so as to enable them to realize their reasoning capacities and whether the principles supporting these institutions can serve as a basis for the public justification among persons like themselves. (Freeman 2007a, 30)

The objectives of Rawls's contractarianism are not entirely new in political philosophy; many of his goals embody neo-Kantian features. For instance, in "The Contractual Basis for a Just Society," Immanuel Kant (1724–1804) writes that the lawful state must be grounded on three *a priori* principles: "1. The freedom of every member of society as a human being 2. the equality of each with all the others as a subject 3. the independence of each member of a commonwealth as a citizen."[20] Following Kant, Rawls explores conditions under which free and rational individuals would agree to uphold cooperative institutions that are mutually advantageous to everyone,[21] and thus find a moral foundation for the public justification of their political, social, and economic institutions. One way to articulate this arrangement is to design a hypothetical situation or thought experiment, which could then be applied to an actual society by using the method of "reflective equilibrium." This method consists of a dialectical back and forth between the original position and the real world: a deliberative process in which we reflect upon or revise our considered judgments about what is morally right or wrong.

Although Rawls's social contract doctrine does not presuppose the existence of an anthropological or historical condition, but rather a purely hypothetical one, it does involve the use of the veil of ignorance, which calls for some bracketing—*epoché* or *Einklammerung* in a phenomenological sense.[22] This can affect people's lives in a sense because, as Freeman (2007a) notes, "we do devise basic institutions"[23] in the real world. That is to say, "[w]e cooperatively decide, through laws and willing acceptance of social and legal conventions, how the constitution, the economy, property, and so on are designed and fit together into one social scheme."[24] The importance of Rawls's contractarian condition lies conclusively in the underlying phenomenological reductionism of the veil of ignorance, which enables citizens of modern democracy to express their moral autonomy and equality as rational and reasonable persons working together to design a just society by being fair to everyone. Accordingly, Rawls's hypothetical social contract theory, like Kantian contractarianism, has practical implications for the government of modern democracies. Like Rawls's idea, though Kant's original contract is purely an idea, it is nonetheless an idea with practical consequences. As Kant writes, "it can oblige every legislator to frame his laws in such a way that they could have been produced by the united will of a whole nation, and to regard each subject, insofar as he can claim citizenship, as if he had consented within the general will. This is the test of the rightfulness of every public law."[25]

For Rawls, if we are to think about justice as fairness, we must first immerse ourselves imaginatively in a condition of strict and primal equality where the decisions we make are free from the effects of prejudice and vested interest. For example, Rawls would want us to imagine, especially in this era of the Trump administration, a gathering of representatives of opposing parties or groups in front of the United States Capitol. These may include members of the major political parties—Republicans, Democrats, and Independents—as well as free marketers, trade war supporters and detractors, immigration law advocates and reformers, conservatives, liberals, socialists, and representatives of corporations. These parties have come to choose principles that would govern the collective interest and well-being of the American people. Given their conflicting and competing political, economic, and religious ideologies, which policies would the party representatives pursue?[26] It would be a complicated task for members of Congress to reach a nonpartisan agreement on laws regulating the life of every United States citizen, especially in this era of partisan polarization, populism, and political gridlock. Some lawmakers may favor one policy over another because of religion, gender, race, sexual orientation, or political ideology. For instance, some representatives (House members and senators) may oppose tax hikes on the wealthy because they represent conservative districts. In contrast, others may support increased social services for the poor because they represent constituencies with a high concentration of low income people or the working class. Even libertarians and their conservative friends may part ways on culturally divisive issues such as abortion and euthanasia.

Furthermore, some representatives of large financial corporations on Wall Street, such as Wells Fargo, JP Morgan Chase, Citigroup, and oil giants like Chevron and Halliburton, as well as dominant retailers like Walmart, Home Depot, and Amazon, might stick to some form of right-libertarianism, which promotes *laissez-faire*, free-market economy. At the same time, the social liberals representing "Main Street" would advocate for a government-regulated market economy. Bernie Sanders, the self-acclaimed socialist and senator from Vermont, may argue against what he sees as the reckless deregulatory practices and tax cuts for "Corporate America" by the Trump administration. However, sometimes in the political arena these representatives reach consensus on less contentious issues, such as those that relate to improving primary education for children.[27]

Now, imagine that the members of Congress and other representatives of the various interest groups were to pass through a famous dark tunnel known as the veil of ignorance before entering the Capitol, one that inflicts a form of temporary, dissociative amnesia on each party representative. Suddenly, they do not know any specific thing about themselves. They are no longer aware of their political affiliations, economic interests, race, gender, sexual orientation, position in society, religion, talents, psychological dispositions, advantages or disadvantages, and so on. All that the representatives now know is that they are members of Congress or representatives of interest groups choosing principles to govern a Western, democratic society—the United States. Rawls thinks that in this original position of equality, these representatives would only select principles of justice that further their rational interests since they do not know their real place in society. The veil of ignorance and its bracketing effects ensure that the representatives adopt a conservative attitude toward risk, and thus choose principles that allow the least undesirable conditions for the worst-off members of society. Rawls's engineered ignorance eliminates existent or natural biases and functions as a necessary phenomenological attitude for the development of certain conceptions of justice. Beyond this, the original position sets practical rules for the governance of modern democracies.

## THE TWO PRINCIPLES OF JUSTICE

Rawls calls principles chosen in the hypothetically strict condition of equality or original position, the "two principles of justice as fairness." These principles demand that:

> a. Each person has an equal claim to a fully adequate scheme of equal basic rights and liberties, which scheme is compatible with the same scheme for all; and in this scheme the equal political liberties, and only those liberties, are to be guaranteed their fair value.

> b. Social and economic inequalities are to satisfy two conditions: first, they are to be attached to positions of offices open to all under conditions of fair equality of opportunity, and second, they are to be to the greatest benefits of the least advantaged members of society. (Rawls 1996, 5–6)

The two principles of justice have implications for policymakers. The first (a) principle of justice, which is known as the equal basic liberty principle, ensures that under reasonably favorable conditions—that is, in a functioning society with enough resources to permit the full exercise of these liberties (e.g., in a country with a strong economy and a constitutional government)—citizens are guaranteed the same measure of basic liberties. As Freeman (2018) expounds:

> Rawls assumes that certain basic social institutions are necessary to sustain social life in any modern society and to guarantee the creation, distribution, and secure possession and enjoyment of these primary social goods. Basic social institutions include the political constitution, whose role is to make and enforce laws and adjudicate disputes; the legal institution of property, broadly conceived as rights and powers with respect to possession, use, and disposal of tangible and intangible things; the economic system of production, transfer, and distribution of goods and services; and the family, which is the primary institution for reproducing society from one generation to the next. (Freeman 2018, 108)

Rawls's basic liberties are in essence political liberties (though the list differs slightly in his later works): the right to vote and to be voted for, freedom of speech and assembly, liberty of conscience, freedom of person and the right to hold property, as well as freedom from arbitrary arrest.[28] The first principle of justice has lexical priority over the second principle. This means that in a society governed by justice as fairness, none of these basic principles can be traded off for other valued ends. As Cass R. Sunstein (1997) notes:

> We might treat equal liberty as a reflection of the foundational commitment to equal dignity and respect and believe that we do violence to the way we value that commitment if we allow it to be compromised for the sake of greater social and economic advantages. On this view, the lexical priority of equal liberty is structurally akin to the refusal to allow a child to be traded for cash. (Sunstein 1997, 96)

The basic liberties, for example, cannot be taken away from a social group, even if doing so promotes economic efficiency. The priority of the basic liberties, however, does not imply that these liberties cannot be limited in any form. Rawls asserts that the basic liberties can be restricted among themselves in order to achieve a coherent scheme of liberties for all citizens. In other words, if the basic liberties were to come into conflict with one another, then the institutional rules that define them would be adjusted to make the system of liberty, in general, more secure.[29] Therefore, one can be denied a basic liberty in society for the sake of other basic liberties, but not to promote, let us say, equality, the overall good of society, or economic efficiency. Basic liberty cannot be denied anyone in the interests of other public goods or valued ends, other than liberty itself. Rawls states that the first principle of justice also grants priority to the rights of individuals over the demands of the political majority: "the priority of the basic liberties implies that they cannot be justly denied to anyone, or any group of persons, or even to all citizens generally because such is the desire, or overwhelming preference, of an effective political majority, however strong and enduring."[30] In *Political Liberalism* (1993, 1996), Rawls seems to make the priorities of the basic liberties less narrow. To remain a robust system, especially in the face of reasonable pluralism, the basic liberties now include freedom from starvation or wanton neglect.[31]

The second principle of justice has two parts. The first part is the "fair equality of opportunity" principle, while the latter is known as the "difference principle." Again, between the second principles of justice, "fair equality of opportunity" has priority over the "difference principle." The fair equality of opportunity principle regulates, for instance, political offices, advertisements for jobs, and products for sale in society. It ensures that citizens with comparable talents have equal access to, for example, education and economic opportunities.

Furthermore, it mandates the government to demand that employers meet requirements of fairness and equality when advertising job openings. For example, advertised positions should not contain racist, sexist statements, words, or phrases that undermine fairness. The second principle of justice as fairness also allows the government to regulate firms in the advertisement of products, sales, and services by demanding that they engage in full disclosure of information regarding the goods and services being advertised. For the market to be efficient and competitive, consumers must be well informed about the goods and services offered by firms. This measure prevents, for instance, predatory lending or the covert marketing of potentially hazardous products to end-users.[32]

Some economists and political analysts consider the "difference principle" controversial because it calls for the toleration of some social and economic inequalities if doing so improves the situation of the worst off in society. In contrast, I think that the difference principle does not call for inequalities as such but instead recognizes the human condition in which through sheer brute luck and natural contingencies, social and economic disparities exist among citizens in modern societies. It looks for ways to remedy some of the effects of these inequalities. The underlying idea is that Rawls sees society as a system of cooperation, where citizens reciprocally share the burdens and benefits that result from this relationship. Rawls contends that a citizen's chances in life must not be entirely determined by either the social position in which she is born nor her natural talents (or lack thereof). Rather, society should see one's place of birth and the distribution of natural abilities as a matter of arbitrary contingency and, for that reason, mitigate their adverse effects on citizens' life prospects.

The unequal distribution of natural talents, which results in an uneven distribution of wealth and positions in society, is not going away. However, society can take advantage of natural inequality to restructure itself in favor of everyone and to the benefit of the least advantaged citizens. Thus, Rawls regards the distribution of natural talents as a collective societal asset because it is, by nature, accidental. We do not merit our place in the distribution of inborn endowments. "Who would deny it?" Rawls asks: "Do people really think that they (morally) deserved to be born more gifted than others? Do they think that they (morally) deserved to be born a man rather than a woman, or vice versa? Do they think that they really deserved to be born into a wealthier rather than into a poorer family? No."[33]

To see the distribution of natural talents as a shared asset does not mean that gifted people are not entitled to some of the benefits that come with their skills. Instead, the difference principle, as a principle of reciprocity, seeks ways to diminish the effects of this arbitrary distribution through regulating the basic structure of society. As a result, those who have many talents and those who have fewer complement each other in ways that benefit the whole society:

> Note that what is regarded as a common asset is the distribution of native endowments and not native endowments per se. It is not as if society owned individuals' endowments taken separately, looking at individuals one by one.

To the contrary, the question of the ownership of our endowments does not arise; and should it arise, it is persons themselves who own their endowments: the psychological and physical integrity of persons is already guaranteed by the basic rights and liberties that fall under the first principle of justice. (Rawls 2001, 75)

In practical terms, "common asset" represents the different talents and dispositions that cooperating individuals have. Irrespective of whether these differences are variations in talents of the same kind, they provide a balancing function in society reminiscent of the "principle of comparative advantage."[34] Consequently, justice as fairness as an egalitarian principle of justice could allow the government to tax very affluent individuals in order to alleviate the situation of the worst off if they are active and contributing members of society.

On the one hand, Rawls may have proposed an efficient distributive theory of economic justice, given that economic inequality in the United States is more widespread than in most Western countries. For example, a 2012 *Forbes* article by Alan Dunn reveals an enormous income disparity between the wealthiest 1 percent and the majority of the American population. There, he noted that "[a]ltogether, the top 1 percent control 43 percent of the wealth in the nation; the next 4 percent control an additional 29 percent. It's historically common for a powerful minority to control a majority of finances, but Americans haven't seen a disparity this wide since before the Great Depression—and it keeps growing."[35] A 2019 *Washington Post* report paints an even grimmer picture: Taylor Telford (2019) writes that "[i]ncome inequality in the United States has hit its highest level since the Census Bureau started tracking it more than five decades ago. . . . When the Census Bureau began studying income inequality in 1967, the Gini index was 0.397. In 2018, it climbed to 0.485. By comparison, no European nation had a score greater than 0.38 last year."[36] Such income inequality makes William A. Galston (2018) wonder in his recent book, *Antipluralism: The Populist Threat to Liberal Democracy*, whether societies in the West can be confident of the future, sustain broadly shared prosperity, or face a decline in living standards. He notes that "[p]rosperity is both the oil that lubricates the machinery of government and the glue that binds society together. Stagnation means a continuation of gridlocked, zero-sum politics and a turn away from the spirit of generosity that only a people confident of its future can sustain."[37]

On the other hand, Rawls's position is not welcomed by libertarian groups in America. Unlike Rawls, whose theory of justice seeks to diminish the inequality arising from nature, some libertarians argue that the fact of life is simple. In essence, life is naturally unfair, and any attempt to remedy this inherent inequity leads to infractions on the rights and liberties of individuals. In fact, Sandel (2009) observes that some libertarians think that inequality as a fact of life is a good thing and cites a passage from Milton and Rose Friedman's *Free to Choose* (1980) to bolster this claim: "Life is not fair. It is tempting to believe that government can rectify what nature has spawned. But it is also important to recognize how much we benefit from the very unfairness we deplore."[38] Against such libertarian views, Rawls's theory rejects the idea that it is wrong for the government to intervene in society by regulating the basic structure of society in ways that can lessen or even eliminate some of the undesirable effects of the unequal distribution of natural talents and other fortuities of life in society. Society does not have to be complacent about inherent inequalities in order to be fair. Most libertarians advocate for a minimal state. They see the deregulation of markets and loose governance mechanisms that result in unfettered markets as an expression of the fundamental rights of people to exercise total control over their property.[39] Robert Nozick, for example, thinks that Rawls's difference principle will stifle competition in a free market economy and usher in a welfare state with a significant proportion of "lazy folks."

In *Anarchy, State, and Utopia* (1974), Nozick worries that Rawls's difference principle favors the less endowed over the well endowed. He doubts that the rich and the gifted would have a strong incentive under a Rawlsian model to join the cooperative scheme. For Nozick, it is incontestable that "the difference principle presents terms on the basis of which those less well-endowed would be willing to cooperate (What better terms could they propose for themselves?)."[40] He then asks, "But is this a fair agreement on the basis of which those worse endowed could expect the willing cooperation of others?"[41]

Under his "entitlement theory," Nozick considers justice as fairness defective because it begins by looking at the outcomes or patterns of distribution of social and economic goods, or the patterns of this distribution over time, rather than considering whether the dealings that brought about those outcomes were just. Nozick believes that the distribution of economic or social goods is just only if everyone partaking in the arrangement is entitled to or merits her share.[42] An adequate scheme of distributive justice must meet two requirements—namely, the justice of initial holdings and the justice of transfer:

> The first asks if the resources you used to make your money were legitimately yours in the first place. (If you made a fortune selling stolen goods, you would not be entitled to the proceeds). . . . The second asks if you made your money either through free exchanges in the marketplace or from gifts voluntarily bestowed upon you by others. If the answer to both questions is yes, you're entitled to what you have, and the state may not take it without your consent. Provided no one starts out with ill-gotten gains, any distribution that results

from a free market is just, however equal or unequal it turns out to be. (Sandel 2009, 63)

Nozick's entitlement theory, however, does not reject the idea of restorative justice that remedies, let us say, past injustices brought about by colonialism or slavery. In such instances, the government may use taxation or other available methods to achieve justice.[43] Responding to Nozick and other critics, Rawls denies that justice as fairness will lead to the kind of welfare state they envision since, as Freeman (2007a) writes, "the 'least advantaged' under the difference principle are not the handicapped or the most depressed but rather the least skilled workers in the lowest income class. Handicaps and other disabilities are regarded as special needs, which a society is obligated to respond to under the natural duties of assistance and mutual aid."[44] Furthermore, Rawls says that the least advantaged should not be seen, under normal circumstances, as "the unfortunate and unlucky-objects of our charity and compassion, much less pity—but those to whom reciprocity is owed as a matter of political justice among those who are free and equal citizens along with everyone else."[45] The least advantaged are representative men and women, who are contributing actively to society in ways that are mutually advantageous and consistent with everyone's self-respect. The least advantaged, Rawls insists, "is not a rigid designator.... Rather, the worst off under any scheme of cooperation are simply the individuals who are worst off under that particular scheme. They may not be worst off in another."[46] The idea of "reciprocity of perspectives," which the difference principle embodies, is itself grounded in the notion that social cooperation is always a productive activity. Thus, if there is no cooperation, then nothing will be produced, and, consequently, there will be no benefits or burdens to be shared.[47]

Disagreeing with the suppositions of his critics, Rawls thinks that the kind of society resulting from justice as fairness would be a private-propertied market economy or "property-owning democracy," which is midway between *laissez-faire* capitalism and welfare socialism. He rejects *laissez-faire* capitalism because it secures only formal equality for citizens while denying the fair value of the equal political liberties and fair equality of opportunity. The goals of *laissez-faire* capitalism "are economic efficiency and growth constrained only by a rather social minimum."[48] Rawls also rejects welfare-state capitalism because it, too, does not guarantee the fair value of political liberties to citizens. As the name may suggest, welfare-state capitalism, according to Rawls, may provide some equality of opportunity, as well as satisfy a decent social minimum in welfare services. But it still allows substantial inequalities to occur in the area of the ownership of property, concentration of wealth, and the management of the economy, and it may keep the control of the government in the hands of a few.[49]

In contrast, the basic structure of a property-owning democracy allows for a wider distribution of assets and income and, in so doing, prevents a small segment of society from controlling the government and the economy. Rawls's new, paradigmatic, political society (property-owning democracy) does not achieve this sustained sharing of capital through the reallocation of income at the end of each year, let us say, by handing out stimulus checks. Instead, it does so "by ensuring the widespread ownership of productive assets and human capital (that is, education and training) at the beginning of each period, all this against a background of fair equality of opportunity."[50] A society that practices "justice as fairness," Rawls believes, will benefit both the rich and the poor. The rich will profit in the long run by living in a less antagonistic society. At the same time, the poor will benefit from the arrangement by having decent life prospects and by being in a better position than they would have been under an alternative constellation. With this argument, Rawls demonstrates that citizens of any society regulated by his two principles of justice as fairness will find the incentive to cooperate mutually with one another.

## NOTES

1. Jefferson 2018, 358.
2. Thanks to my colleague David Braden-Johnson for the exchange of ideas on the topic.
3. Although this story reflects a true-life encounter of the author, the names of individuals mentioned are pseudonyms, while the location and timing of some of the events are more or less a re-creation.
4. This is a pseudonym.
5. NPR, "Integrating Ole Miss: A Transformative, Deadly Riot," October 1, 2012: https://www.npr.org/2012/10/01/161573289/integrating-ole-miss-a-transformative-deadly-riot.
6. Ibid. See also Lambert 2010, 6.
7. I recognize the growing interest in animal and environmental ethics to extend legal and moral rights to both nonhuman animals and the environment. The limited scope of this book does not allow for a more elaborate conversation around those themes.
8. Sandel 2009, 28–29.
9. A modified, earlier version of this part of the chapter also appeared in Amaeshi et al. 2012.
10. Nozick 1974, 183.
11. Choi 2015, 249.
12. Ibid.
13. Rawls 1971, 3.
14. Ibid.
15. Freeman 2007a, 17.
16. Ibid., 8.
17. Dworkin 1977, 151.
18. Freeman 2007a, 3–4.
19. Rawls 1971, 7.
20. Sterba 2003, 102.
21. Freeman 2007a, 9.
22. Husserl's bracketing, or *Einklammerung* in German, is a phenomenological attitude that brackets most presuppositions of ordinary life in order to arrive at pure consciousness. This method is similar to Rawls's original position.

23. Freeman 2007a, 42.
24. Ibid.
25. Sterba 2003, 105.
26. See also Sandel 2009, 14–42.
27. Ibid.
28. Rawls 1971, 61.
29. Rawls 1996, 295.
30. Ibid., 365.
31. Ibid., 28–71. See also Sen 2009, 65.
32. Ibid., 36–65.
33. Rawls 2001, 7–5.
34. Ibid., 76.
35. http://www.forbes.com/sites/moneywisewomen/2012/03/21/average-america-vs-the-one-percent/#6fc2039d11a8.
36. Taylor Telford, "Income inequality in America is the highest it's been since Census Bureau started tracking it, data shows," *Washington Post*, September 26, 2019. https://www.washingtonpost.com/business/2019/09/26/income-inequality-america-highest-its-been-since-census-started-tracking-it-data-show/. Telford explains that "[t]he Gini index measures wealth distribution across a population, with zero representing total equality and 1 representing total inequality, where all wealth is concentrated in a single household."
37. Galston 2018, 32.
38. Sandel 2009, 165.
39. Ibid., 60.
40. Nozick 1974, 192.
41. Ibid.
42. See Blowfield and Murray 2008, 64.
43. Ibid., 63.
44. Freeman 2007a, 104–5.
45. Rawls 2001, 139.
46. Ibid., 59.
47. See Rawls 2001.
48. Ibid., 137.
49. Ibid., 13–38.
50. Ibid., 139.

*Chapter Two*

# Why Utilitarianism Is Not the Best Option

## CLASSICAL UTILITARIANISM

Classical utilitarianism is an aggregate-maximizing, hedonistic, consequentialist, and teleological ethical theory in which the goal of human conduct is happiness or subjective well-being, and the standards for differentiating between right and wrong actions are pleasure and pain. Although elements of utilitarianism can be found in the works of ancient Greek philosophers, such as Aristippus of Cyrene (c. 435–366 BC) and Epicurus (341–270 BC), as well as in those of the principal figures of the Scottish Enlightenment, such as Adam Smith (1723–1790) and David Hume (1711–1776), utilitarianism was, nevertheless, primarily an English affair.

According to Tim Mulgan (2014), the three most prominent early English proponents of utilitarianism "published their major works within a few years of one another: William Paley in 1785, Jeremy Bentham in 1789, and William Godwin in 1793."[1] Jeremy Bentham (1748–1832), who today is widely seen as the founder of the system and the foremost scholar to articulate the principles of the doctrine in a more systematic and explicit form, presents the canons of utilitarianism in *The Introduction to the Principles of Morals and Legislation* (printed in 1780 and first published in 1789):

> Nature has placed mankind under the governance of two sovereign masters, *pain* and *pleasure*. It is for them alone to point out what we ought to do, as well as to determine what we shall do. On the one hand the standard of right and wrong, on the other the chain of causes and effects, are fastened to their throne. They govern us in all we do, in all we say, in all we think: every effort we can make to throw off our subjection, will serve but to demonstrate and

confirm it. In words a man may pretend to abjure their empire: but in reality he will remain subject to it all the while. (Bentham 1970, 11)

As a system of ethics, utilitarianism often captivates the mind of rational, moral agents because of the straightforwardness of its methodology. An essential precept of utilitarianism is that "we should make the world as good as we can and that we can only do this by making the lives of people as good as we can. . . . It seems implausible to claim that we ought to do less good than we can and that the world is not made better if people are made better off."[2] This seems to say that morality is straightforward, uncomplicated, and that we all ought to seek and maximize the pleasurable while minimizing the unpleasurable. This pragmatic view "has certain virtues that make the idea that utilitarianism is the most rational way to assess the justice of society's basic institutional arrangement structure surprisingly compelling."[3]

Rawls (1971) says that "[i]t is natural to think that rationality is maximizing something and in morals it must be the good."[4] On this basis, classical utilitarianism draws the moral conclusion for both individual and societal ways of life: the calculation of the aggregate number of pleasurable experiences shared by citizens is possible, and "the greatest happiness for the greatest number" is the ultimate good. Society is just only when the aggregate pleasure of its citizens outweighs the aggregate of pain on the hedonistic scale. Furthermore, utilitarians can successfully arrive at such an inference without making any strong epistemic or metaphysical claims. The only necessary thing for the utilitarian to do is to recognize "that people have desires and interests and inclinations, together with a commitment to take everyone's desires and interests and inclinations into account."[5]

In *The Introduction to the Principles of Morals and Legislation*, Bentham expresses the underlying principles of utilitarianism as the foundation for the re-evaluation of all moral and social activities. Morality involves only the balancing of utility under the command of pain and pleasure, which are the sole motives governing individual human action. For this reason, personal pleasure and pain are not treated separately from the general happiness or well-being of society at large. The individual must promote the welfare of society for her rational self-interest. The moral goodness of an action is dependent on its utility in promoting the common good, alongside the personal benefit that an individual might obtain in the realization of the purpose of human life. Bentham defines utility as

> That principle which approves or disapproves of every action whatsoever, according to the tendency which it appears to have to augment or diminish the happiness of the party whose interest is in question: or, what is the same thing in other words, to promote or to oppose that happiness. I say of every action whatsoever; and therefore not only of every action of a private individual, but of every measure of government. By utility is meant that property in any

object, whereby it tends to produce benefits, advantage, pleasure, good, or happiness . . . or . . . to prevent the happening of mischief, pain, evil, or unhappiness to the party whose interest is considered: if that party be the community in general, then the happiness of the community: if a particular individual, then the happiness of that individual. (Bentham 1970, 12)

Bentham's utilitarianism chiefly concerns itself with the quantitative aspect of pleasure so that all acts are similarly good if they yield the same aggregate of pleasure. Thus, "[p]rejudice apart, the game of push-pin is of equal value with the arts and sciences of music and poetry."[6] The units of pain and pleasure can be calculated using a hedonistic calculus, which is mostly a catalog of various dimensions of pleasure and pain: intensity, duration, certainty or uncertainty, propinquity or remoteness, fecundity or fruitfulness, purity, and extent.[7] Goodness or rightness in Bentham's utilitarianism does not identify with any fixed conduct, but only with the quantity of pleasure measurable through the hedonistic calculus.[8]

John Stuart Mill's (1806–1873) utilitarianism does not disentangle itself from the collective egoism of Bentham's version. However, it does succeed in elevating the utilitarian ideal to a more sophisticated level. Bentham teaches that units of pleasure and pain are scientifically quantifiable, and for this reason makes no distinction between categories of pleasure; whereas Mill in *Utilitarianism* (1861) maintains that pleasures differ in quantity and quality. He makes a value judgment in favor of higher pleasures against lower pleasures, such that even a lesser amount of higher pleasure is preferable or more valuable than a greater amount of lower pleasure. For instance, the pleasures of the intellect (of mental state, imagination, and the moral sentiment) have a higher value than the pleasures of mere sensation.[9] Consequently, Mill makes his famed statement: "It is better to be a human being dissatisfied than a pig satisfied; better to be Socrates dissatisfied than a fool satisfied."[10] However, Mill's defense of this proposition is somewhat dependent on the aesthetical judgment of "sophisticated" individuals. He claims that every person of culture, who experiences both lower and higher pleasures, will know the qualitative differences between the two and would regard higher pleasures far more agreeable and superior to lower ones. For him, it ought to be the goal of human action and morality to secure for all humanity a life that is as free from pain as possible and as full of enjoyment as possible, in both quantity and quality.[11]

Historically, Henry Sidgwick (1838–1900) introduced the most significant modifications to utilitarianism. In the *Methods of Ethics* (1877), he sets out to develop ways and means of ethical inquiry, which he describes as a rational procedure aimed at determining "what individual human beings "ought" to do or what is "right" for them to do, or to seek to realise by voluntary action."[12] In the course of his investigation of the history of ethical theory, Sidgwick concludes that there are only three methods of ethics. The first is egoistic hedonism, which considers an act's tendency to benefit an agent. The other method is universalistic hedonism or utilitarianism, which he sees as the consideration of an act's tendency to benefit everyone affected by it. The third and last method is intuitionism, which appeals to self-evident moral axioms that hold without reference to consequences. Sidgwick considers all three methods defensible and viable. As a result, he unites the idea of intuitionism with utilitarianism. But in the final analysis, Sidgwick could not find irrefutable arguments to reconcile the uniformity of private interest (individual) and public interest (societal) in utilitarianism.[13]

In the forward for the seventh edition of *The Methods of Ethics* (1981), Rawls writes that the "classical doctrine holds that the ultimate end of social and individual action is the greatest net sum of the happiness of all sentient beings."[14] Rawls further explains this idea of happiness as "the net balance of pleasure over pain, or, as Sidgwick preferred to say, as the net balance of agreeable over disagreeable consciousness."[15] Rawls sees Sidgwick's *Methods of Ethics* as "the most philosophically profound of the strictly classical works," and the work which marks the end of the era of classical utilitarianism.

Since Sidgwick, utilitarianism continued to undergo modifications until the present day, and its effects in the area of politics, social, and economic affairs have been enormous. The type of utilitarianism that Rawls criticizes in *A Theory of Justice* is the classical utilitarianism that defines the good not only as pleasure or happiness but also as the satisfaction of rational desire (whatever this desire may be). In a society governed by classical utilitarianism, the appropriate terms of social cooperation are established by whatever in the circumstances will achieve the most significant sum of satisfaction of rational desires.[16]

## UTILITARIANISM AND SCAPEGOAT DILEMMAS[17]

Although utilitarianism promotes *prima facie* individual and societal well-being, critics of the system argue that it could permit gross injustice even if such acts produce the best consequences for the majority of the people. The assumption here is that utilitarianism oversimplifies morality by identifying the criterion for the morally good act only in consequentialist terms.[18] Thus, an act is good if it produces the best consequences for the greatest number of people, or, in other words, "the moral status of any bit of behavior is determined by the values of the consequences of the alternatives available to a moral agent."[19] To make evident the inherent weaknesses in the system, critics often employ scapegoat scenarios, as well as seek unconventional allies among fiction and nonfiction "scapegoat" writers.[20] As wide ranging as these storytellers might be in style and scope, they share one thing in common: their stories are disconcerting, gruesome, and, to the joy of their philosophical adopters, anti-utilitarian. Some of these detractors cite fictional works, such as Ursula Le Guin's "The Ones Who Walked Away from Omelas," Edgar Allan Poe's *The Narrative of Arthur Gordon Pym of Nantucket*, or a real-life story, such as that of the *Mignonette*, to illustrate the utilitarian jeopardy.[21]

## OMELAS

In Le Guin's short story, for example, Omelas is a sensational, idealistic, and tranquil utopian city: a place distinguished by its grandeur, magnificent buildings, and fairytale-like summer festivities. At first glance, everything seems to work impeccably well in this city. The inhabitants are lighthearted, wealthy, and gregarious. However, on closer examination, Omelas reveals a loathsome strangeness. In what appears to be the basement of the city hall lives a hungry, abandoned, and isolated child. This child, whose gender is not disclosed, used to cry for help but now only whimpers, its voice silenced by fatigue and despair.

The child sleeps on its excrement, and the sores all over its body have become septic. The cellar where the unfortunate child is kept is as foul smelling as a putrid pile of refuse. Folks know about the life of the miserable child, but no one is willing to help; otherwise, as they believe, their good fortunes go with the wind:

> It could be a boy or a girl. It looks about six, but actually is nearly ten. It is feeble-minded. Perhaps it was born defective or perhaps it has become imbecile through fear, malnutrition, and neglect. It picks its nose and occasionally fumbles vaguely with its toes or genitals, as it sits haunched in the corner farthest from the bucket and the two mops. It is afraid of the mops. It finds them horrible. It shuts its eyes, but it knows the mops are still standing there; and the door is locked; and nobody will come. The door is always locked; and nobody ever comes, except that sometimes—the child has no understanding of time or interval—sometimes the door rattles terribly and opens, and a person, or several people, are there. One of them may come and kick the child to make it stand up. The others never come close, but peer in at it with frightened, disgusted eyes. The food bowl and the water jug are hastily filled, the door is locked, the eyes disappear. The people at the door never say anything, but the child, who has not always lived in the tool room, and can remember sunlight and its mother's voice, sometimes speaks. "I will be good," it says. "Please let me out. I will be good!" They never answer. (Le Guin 2004, 281)

Sometimes a group of Omelas residents visits the gruesome cellar to inform themselves about the child's fate. Initially, they feel some disgust. But as time passes by, they adopt oblique stances to dampen any feelings of antipathy or any roiling of conscience. If we release the child from the cellar, they reason, it is already too degraded to know any real joy. It has been afraid for too long and would not rid itself of fear. Other times, a few sensible residents would visit the child and choose not to return home. They would walk through the main street of the city, pass the city gate, and head silently to some unknown place. "Each one goes alone, youth or girl, man or woman. . . . They leave Omelas, they walk ahead into the darkness, and they do not come back."[22] They are the ones that walk away from Omelas. Since classical utilitarianism seeks to maximize the aggregate utility (pleasure) of the largest number of people, it would seem morally permissible to abuse the rights of one innocent child, the scapegoat, for the greater happiness of the many.

## A TALE OF TWO RICHARDS

In Edgar Allan Poe's 1838 novel, *The Narrative of Arthur Gordon Pym of Nantucket*, the crewmen of a ship called Grampus find themselves cast away and starving to death. To survive, they will have to kill one of their members, eat his flesh, and drink his blood. They cast lots, and it falls on John Hunty Richard Parker,[23] a former mutineer. They quickly slaughter him, and the rest of the crew feeds on his body until rescue comes:

> I recovered from my swoon in time to behold the consummation of the tragedy in the death of him who had been chiefly instrumental in bringing it about. He made no resistance whatever, and was stabbed in the back by Peters, when he fell instantly dead . . . having in some measure appeased the raging thirst which consumed us by the blood of the victim . . . we devoured the rest of the body. (Poe 2013, 94–95)

In what appears to be one of the most bizarre coincidences in literature, forty-six years later and more than three decades after the death of Poe, a cabin boy, also named Richard Parker, became a victim of castaway cannibalism. But this time the story is real. In 1884, an English ship called the *Mignonette* sank in the South Atlantic, possibly on its way to Australia. The four Englishman crew survived treacherous days and nights at sea on a lifeboat. Within a couple of days, their meager rations ran out, and they were starving to death. The cabin boy, Richard Parker, who was an orphan, had fallen ill. The other crewmen conspired against poor Richard, murdered him, ate his flesh, and drank his blood. As the crew was anticipating whom next to kill for food, a passing boat found and rescued them. Upon their return to England, the men went on trial for murder. Two of them served minor sentences, while one even walked away free.[24] As Sandel notes, the most persuasive argument for their defense was a utilitarian one: "Given the dire circumstances, it was necessary to kill one person in order to save three. Had no one been killed and eaten, all four would likely have died. Parker, weakened and ill, was the logical candidate, since he would soon have died anyway . . . he had no dependents. His death deprived no one of support and left no grieving wife or children."[25]

The central idea of these stories is founded on a certain supposition. If we were offered a world in which the majority is kept enduringly happy on the condition that they deny some innocent citizens their inalienable rights, would it not be horrible conduct? Critics of classical utilitarianism and other forms of utilitarianism draw on such extreme suppositions to criticize the system. But would it not be clear to most rational and moral agents, including utilitarians, that torturing an innocent child or eating a sick cabin boy to maximize the aggregate pleasure of other people is a bad idea? As a normative ethical principle, utilitarianism may not defend itself successfully against such critics. Yet if we were to see utilitarianism as an applied ethical practice, then would marginal cases not constitute weak analogies against it? Rawls seems to have developed a more robust critique of classical utilitarianism.

## RAWLS'S OBJECTIONS TO UTILITARIANISM[26]

In Rawls, twentieth-century philosophical liberalism seemed to have found, at last, a champion to silence and replace utilitarianism with some form of neo-Kantianism.[27] For Rawls, moral theories at that time were moribund and had run out of ideas, except, of course, utilitarian ideas. For years, organizations, markets, and governments (especially in the United States) adopted a utilitarian calculus in the form of cost-benefit analysis, economic principles, and laws to shape public policies and organizational behaviors. In Rawls's view, although utilitarianism had been dominant, it not only failed to address critical issues of justice in the modern world but also served as the foundational principle for proponents of unfettered markets to vindicate and disastrously accelerate the social, economic, and institutional inequalities found in modern democracies.

For Rawls, the principles of utility are irreconcilable with the ideals of a well-ordered democratic society governed by the principles of justice as fairness, even though it appears "tempting to suppose that it is self-evident that things should be arranged so as to lead to the most good."[28] From the simple fact that everyone desires pleasure and happiness, and abhors pain and unhappiness, classical utilitarianism draws this conclusion: the moral issue of goodness can ultimately be understood in terms of the principle of the greatest happiness or good for the greatest number. The good is achieved in a society when the aggregate of pleasure outnumbers the sum total of pain. Therefore, in order to arrive at the right action in a society, the interests of the different individuals must be added together with the view of producing the greatest amount of happiness overall.

The contrast Rawls sees between his theory of social justice and classical utilitarianism is, in essence, a difference between a teleological theory and a deontological one. For teleological theories, "the good is defined independently from the right, and then the right is defined as that which maximizes the good."[29] Teleological doctrines, therefore, are consequentialist in nature. Classical utilitarianism is a consequentialist moral theory according to which the only value is the happiness of sentient beings, especially humans (although some utilitarians do not discount nonhuman suffering[30]). Consequentialism, as a form of ethics, states that the moral value of any action lies in its consequences. Thus, consequentialists judge actions that bring about desirable outcomes as good or as morally right, even if the connection between a moral agent and the value of her action is only instrumental.

The classical utilitarianism that Rawls focuses on is the type represented by Henry Sidgwick's *Methods of Ethics* (1907). As I said earlier, a fair interpretation of this contemporary form of classical utilitarianism defines the good as the satisfaction of rational desires. Society is correctly ordered and, therefore, fair when its major institutions are arranged in such a way that they bring about the greatest net balance of satisfaction of all the individuals belonging to it.[31] According to Rawls, utilitarianism as an aggregate-maximizing, economic principle sacrifices equality and social justice because it does not matter to utilitarians how "the sum of satisfactions is distributed among individuals. The correct distribution is whatever yields the maximum fulfillment."[32]

Also, utilitarians appeal to impartiality in order to extend a method of individual practical rationality to society as a whole.[33] Impartiality combined with sympathetic identification allows a hypothetical observer to experience the desires of others as if they were her own and to compare alternative courses of action according to their conduciveness to a single maxim, in addition to maintaining equal consideration and showing sympathy throughout the process. What is noteworthy here is that appeals to equal consideration have nothing to do with impartiality between persons. Rawls insists that what is given equal consideration in utilitarianism are the desires or experiences of separate individuals.[34]

Rawls develops his theory of social justice—justice as fairness—consciously in opposition to utilitarianism. Most of his criticisms of utilitarianism in *A Theory of Justice* are chiefly against classical utilitarianism. Much of the acclaimed dominance of utilitarianism in moral philosophy, according to Rawls, rests on the inability of previous theories of justice to stand up to the utilitarian challenge. Such theories owe their failure to the fact that they were more interested in pointing out the obscurities and apparent inconsistencies in utilitarian principles, rather than on constructing an alternative, workable, and systematic moral conception capable of posing a great challenge to utilitarianism. The result of the failure of these moral theories in combating the influence of utilitarianism, Rawls claims, leaves one with the choice of two extremes in moral theory: utilitarianism and an "incoherent jumble of ideas and principles"[35] known as intuitionism. He defines intuitionism as "the doctrine that there is an irreducible family of first principles, which have to be weighed against one another by asking ourselves which balance, in our considered judgment, is most just."[36] In "justice as fairness," which Rawls sees as a superior alternative to utilitarianism, the role of intuitionism is limited by the contractarian choice situation.[37] In demonstrating the failure of utilitarianism, Rawls compares it directly to justice as fairness on four major points.

## The Problem of Choice

Rawls takes us back to the hypothetical original position, where he places the principles of utility side by side with the two principles of justice as fairness. Here he takes utilitarianism to task for failing to pass the fairness test of his thought experiment. Rawls believes that the representatives in the original position, acting under the influence of the veil of ignorance, would rank the alternative principles available by their worst possible outcomes. Therefore, the representatives would eschew principles of justice that simply maximize aggregate utility (utilitarianism) or welfare in favor of those that guarantee basic liberties. The representatives would instead follow what Rawls calls the "maximin rule"[38] and choose principles that come with minimal risks: principles that guarantee everyone a decent life prospect, irrespective of the contingencies of birth or socioeconomic status. They would consider the principles of utility too precarious an option, since, in theory, no one in the original position would willingly risk sacrificing their basic liberties and an equal share of primary social goods for the possible maximization of the greater utility of others: "In this respect the two principles of justice have a definite advantage [over utilitarianism]. Not only do the parties protect their basic rights but they insure themselves against the worst eventualities."[39]

## The Notion of Justice as Impartiality

For Rawls, the violation of basic liberties cannot be justified on the basis of the assumption that such action promotes the general welfare of society. He claims that utilitarianism, by contrast, does not conceive of justice as independent of utility. Instead, as a teleological doctrine, utilitarianism defines the good (or utility) independently from the right, whereby it sees the good as the satisfaction of rational desire. Utilitarianism then identifies the right as whatever maximizes utility. Consequently, it considers rules, individual acts, or institutional undertakings as right, to the extent that they produce the most good or maximize utility.

Rawls's arguments against utilitarianism and its definition of utility as the satisfaction of rational desire stem from the question of distributive justice. Accordingly, a utilitarian society is just when it achieves the greatest aggregate of "satisfactions" or utility for most citizens, regardless of how these "satisfactions" are distributed among persons in society. Rawls believes that utilitarianism condones the violation of the liberty of a few for the greater utility of the many. In contrast to utilitarianism, justice as fairness accords priority to liberty and rights over an increase in aggregate utility. In a society regulated by justice as fairness, each citizen enjoys inviolable basic liberties and rights, which even the welfare of the majority (whether by way of political bargaining or the calculus of social interests) cannot override.[40]

Furthermore, Rawls derides the utilitarian conception of justice as impartiality. By so doing, he adds Adam Smith and David Hume to the list of the early proponents of classical utilitarianism.[41] Under the utilitarian view of justice as impartiality, a social system may be said to be right (or just) when an ideally impartial and sympathetic spectator approves it from a general point of view. This is someone who happens to have all the relevant knowledge of the circumstances and whose own interest is not at stake. The ideal spectator responds to each citizen's desires and aspirations one by one, as if they were her own, and approves each individual's desires sympathetically.

The ideal spectator makes each citizen's desires and satisfactions, when summed together, represent the most appropriate aggregate of utility in society: an act that defines justice as impartiality and benevolence.[42] If a just society is one meeting the approval of such an ideal, fictitious observer or person, then, in Rawls's view, utilitarianism clearly misconstrues impersonality as impartiality.[43] Therefore, the construct of ideal impartial, sympathetic spectator for defining justice would be implausible because such an ideal would only be realized in a society of perfect altruists. Since the original position guarantees impartiality, Rawls maintains that his justice as fairness proves to be superior to utilitarianism in defining justice as impartiality. The persons or parties in the original position are to choose the principles of justice under the veil of ignorance, creating a situation of impartiality.

## The Meaning of Society and the Integrity of Persons

Perhaps Rawls's most substantial criticism of utilitarianism lies in how utilitarians view persons and society. Rawls avows that one major flaw of utilitarianism is that it does not take the distinction between persons as integral selves seriously. Utilitarianism, he says, breaks down the differences between persons as citizens while aggregating human desires and interests into one giant conglomerate.[44] Thus, utilitarianism could permit gross inequalities if such acts produce the best consequences for the majority of people. John A. Simmons (2008) echoes Rawls's view when he writes:

> Utilitarians count happiness (and unhappiness) in their calculus regardless of the source of that happiness so in (say) determining the justice of slavery, the slaveholder's pleasure (including sadistic pleasures) would have to be weighed against the slaves' pains in the calculus. Even if utilitarian calculation reliably yielded the conclusion that slavery was unjust or wrong (since the slaves' pains always outweighed the slaveholder's pleasures), utilitarianism would have reached this conclusion for the wrong reasons, overlooking the facts that the slaves' lives and happiness are not simply counters to be tossed into and weighed against others in an impersonal calculus and that the pleasure the slaveholder takes in his slaves' suffering makes enslavement worse from the moral viewpoint, not better. (Simmons 2008, 74–75)

Utilitarians may counter Rawls's position with the claim that utilitarianism views individuals as moral equals, as Bentham and Mill once said: "everybody to count for one, nobody for more than one"[45] in the utilitarian calculus. However, this claim to formal equality still leaves room to bend everyone's happiness to the requirements of "social expediency."[46] Justice as fairness advocates for not just equal distribution of social goods but also the regulation of the basic structure of society in a way that allows for the fair treatment of individuals.[47] In the utilitarian society, the individual is subordinate to society. By contrast, justice as fairness regards citizens as distinctive persons, endowed with inviolable rights and basic liberties, which even the welfare of a majority cannot trump. In this sense, justice as fairness treats the individual in society as an end, rather than as a means to other people's ends. Besides, while utilitarianism views society as a fictitious body composed of individuals as its members, Rawls maintains that justice as fairness sees society as a system of cooperation that offers reciprocity of advantages to its members, neglecting neither the less nor the more favored members.

## The Social Bases of Self-Respect

Rawls thinks that people will find it difficult in a utilitarian society to become confident of their own worth, since they only have instrumental moral value. To regard persons as means to other persons' ends is to impose upon their lives an unequal (inferior) value. On the contrary, he claims, justice as fairness provides a social basis for self-respect. Persons in the original position express their respect for one another by choosing the two principles of justice.

Moreover, when persons publicly affirm these principles in the real world, they express their desire to treat one another not as means, but as ends in themselves. For Rawls, respect or self-respect is an essential primary social good without which a person's sense of self as a citizen is lost, and with that, "nothing may seem worth doing. . . . All desire and activity become empty and vain, and we sink into apathy and cynicism."[48]

In a utilitarian society, Rawls continues, people will experience loss of self-esteem, a weakening of their sense of motivation in pursuing their goals, since some must forgo their basic rights and liberties for the greater utility of others. As a result, a utilitarian society would not be stable for the right reasons because citizens, whose rights and liberties have been violated, would most likely develop a deep feeling of resentment, rather than a sense of identification with the greater social good.[49]

## NOTES

1. Mulgan 2014, 7.
2. Bykvist 2010, 16.
3. Kumar 2015, 858.
4. Rawls 1971, 24–25.
5. Norman 1998, 179–80.
6. Bentham 1825, 206.
7. Sprigge 1990, 10–11.
8. See also ibid.
9. See also Fagothey 1976, 66.
10. Mill 1968, 260.
11. Ibid.
12. Sidgwick 1981, 1.
13. See also Jones 1969, 389.
14. Sidgwick 1981, v.
15. Ibid.
16. See Rawls 1971, 25–26.
17. I published this portion of the chapter earlier in the MCLA Thesis XII Blogpost of May 2016 as "Utilitarian Dilemmas in the Literature of Scapegoats."
18. See also Slote 1985, 161.
19. Vessel 2010, 299.
20. The term "scapegoat" possibly has its origin in the Hebrew word עֲזָאזֵל (Azazel), found in the Pentateuch. The original meaning of Azazel is hard to figure out, but I'm willing to accept, if only momentarily, William Tyndale's 1530 translation of the Hebrew Bible. There, he seems to break the term into *ez* (the goat) and *azel* (that escapes)—hence, the [e]scapegoat: "And Aaron shall bring the goat upon which the Lord's lot fell and offer him for a sin offering. But the goat on which the lot fell to escape, he shall set alive before the Lord to reconcile with and to let him go free into the wilderness." The scapegoat then was a goat upon whose head the priest symbolically placed the sins of the people before letting the animal escape into the wilderness. This ritual was part of the Hebrew ceremony of Yom Kippur or the Day of Atonement. See also Leviticus, chapter 16, Tyndale's Old Testament, 1992 (Yale University Press; Modern Spelling edition), 172, and http://www.johnpratt.com/items/docs/lds/meridian/2009/scapegoat.html#fn2.
21. Both stories also can be found in Sandel 2009, 31–35, 40–41. See also *Illustrated London News*, September 20, 1884.
22. Ursula K. Le Guin, *The Wind's Twelve Quarters* (New York: Perennial, 2004), 283–84.

23. Edgar Allan Poe, *The Narrative of Arthur Gordon Pym of Nantucket* (2013), 55.
24. See Sandel 2009, 31–33, as well as Edgar Allan Poe, *The Narrative of Arthur Gordon Pym of Nantucket* (Wiley and Putnam, 1838), and the following link: http://mentalfloss.com/article/30093/edgar-allan-poes-eerie-richard-parker-coincidence.
25. Sandel 2009, 32.
26. I published a slightly modified version of this chapter in Amaeshi et al. 2012.
27. See also Weinstein 2007, 202.
28. Rawls 1971, 24–25.
29. Ibid., 24.
30. Peter Singer's 1975 classic, *Animal Liberation* (Harpercollins) is an excellent example of the utilitarian argument for minimizing pain among nonhuman sentient animals.
31. See Rawls 1971, 22.
32. Ibid., 26.
33. Ibid., 26–27.
34. Ibid., 61.
35. Kymlicka 1990, 50.
36. Rawls 1971, 34.
37. See Grcic 1980, 15.
38. Maximin rule is a conservative attitude toward risk or risk aversion (Rawls's lexicon).
39. Rawls 1971, 176.
40. Ibid., 28.
41. Sen 2009, 137.
42. Rawls 1971, 186.
43. Ibid., 183–92.
44. Ibid., 27.
45. Simmons 2008, 75.
46. Ibid.
47. Ibid.
48. Rawls 1971, 440.
49. Ibid., 183–92.

*Part II*

# Pluralism, Public Reason, and Political Stability

*Chapter Three*

# The Departure from Classical Liberalism

LIBERALISM IN HISTORICAL CONTEXT

Liberalism is a broad term. Judith Shklar (1989) recommends in her essay, "The Liberalism of Fear," that

> Before we can begin to analyze any specific form of liberalism we must surely state as clearly as possible what the word means. For in the course of so many years of ideological conflict it seems to have lost its identity completely. Overuse and overextension have rendered it so amorphous that it can now serve as an all-purpose word, whether of abuse or praise. To bring a modest degree of order into this state of confusion we might begin by insisting that liberalism refers to a political doctrine, not a philosophy of life such as has traditionally been provided by various forms of revealed religion and other comprehensive *Weltanschauungen*. Liberalism has only one overriding aim: to secure the political conditions that are necessary for the exercise of personal freedom. (Shklar 1989, 21)

By definition, a liberal is someone who believes in liberty. Liberals accord liberty a prime position in the hierarchy of political values. The philosophical term "liberal" is not synonymous with being a liberal in American politics. With this understanding in mind, we may consider a Democrat or a conservative Republican, liberal. For our purpose, liberalism is primarily a political philosophy, which Rawls calls a comprehensive philosophical and moral doctrine. Liberalism, in this sense, includes ethical theories of value such as utilitarianism, moral intuitionism, perfectionism, concepts of the person, and norms of behavior. Classical liberalism in the Western tradition comprises the political philosophies of Hobbes, Mill, Locke, Kant, Rousseau, and so on. Its principal idea revolves around individual freedom, equality, and the free consent of individuals to political arrangements. Beyond this broad focus, liberalism has some underlying, standard features. It presupposes the idea that humans are free, equal, and have moral worth, which in turn is the basis for human liberty and rights, private ownership of property, and the establishment of free markets. In *Liberalism and Distributive Justice*, Samuel Freeman (2018) writes:

> Liberalism is associated in political thought with non-authoritarianism, the rule of law, limited constitutional government, and the guarantee of civil and political liberties. A liberal society is tolerant of different religious, philosophical, and ethical views, and its citizens are free to express their views and their conflicting opinions on all subjects, as well as to live their lives according to their freely chosen life plans. In economic thought, liberalism is associated with a predominantly unplanned economy with free and competitive markets and, normally, private ownership and control of productive resources. In international relations, liberalism advocates freedom of trade and cultural relations, idealism instead of realism, international cooperation and institutions rather than isolationism, and the use of soft power instead of power politics. (Freeman 2018, 2)

Within the Western liberal tradition, the benchmark for justifying all forms of political cohesion depends on whether the exercise of political power respects human liberty and rights. For this reason, the social contract tradition expresses liberal ideals because it embraces the idea that humans are free and equal, even when the political reality of such contractarianism or contractualism may themselves contain unambiguously intolerant or even unfair features.[1]

As a philosophy that promotes individual freedom and rights, liberalism arose out of the historical circumstances that posed new philosophical and political questions about the nature of what constituted justice and the good. According to Bhikhu Parekh (1996), liberalism originated in the period between the Reformation and the French Revolution. As the European peoples' response to the sectarian wars arising from religious orthodoxy and political autocracy, liberalism propagated freedom of individual belief and dissent.[2] It sought to replace the conception of the good based on the authority of the church with a secular and humanist kind of moral understanding. Liberalism was a conscious effort to place humans (rather than God) at the center of human affairs. It identified with certain practices in the intellectual, social, and economic circles that promoted the freedom of humans from the supernatural, divine, and traditional ecclesiastical authorities. For this reason, liberalism was initially hostile to religious institutions, opposed authoritarianism in politics, advocated for the liberty of conscience, and abhorred sectarian violence. As Daniel A. Dombrowski (2001) puts it:

> One way to try to resolve this conflict . . . is to try to establish a basis of moral knowledge completely severed from ecclesiastical authority. Hume and Kant tried to do just this by insisting that morality be accessible to everyone (not just the clergy) who is morally reasonable and conscientious, that the moral order arises from human nature itself (rather than from God's intellect), and that we bring ourselves in line with morality without the need for external (divine or hellish) sanctions. (Dombrowski 2001, 5)

Dombrowski, for his part, lists three significant changes in the history of the West that ushered in liberalism. First is the Reformation in the sixteenth century, which fragmented the religious unity of the Middle Ages, made way for religious pluralism, and eventually encouraged other forms of pluralism. The development of religious tolerance was a noteworthy factor in the origin of liberalism, which explains the historical and conceptual relationships between liberalism and toleration in modern times. For this same reason, Kylimka Will (1995) states that liberalism cultivates a specific notion of toleration, which involves freedom of individual conscience and a commitment to autonomy (liberal toleration).[3] Second on Dombrowski's list of factors that precipitated the development of liberalism is the emergence of modern states and the middle class. And third is the rise in modern science in the seventeenth century, which brought about academic curiosity that required freedom of scientific inquiry.[4]

From John Gray's (2000) perspective, liberal toleration began in the West as a project of peaceful coexistence among Christians, whose rival claims to the "truth" and political power had ended in wars. It grew out of the divisions that existed between monocultures. Liberalism allowed individuals and communities, who did not share the same doctrinal beliefs, to reach some agreement on cultural values and be able to live together despite their sectarian differences.[5] Furthermore, Gray (2000) asserts that liberal toleration was an early modern adjustment of a Socratic Christian faith to the historical realities of intractable rivalry about the content of the best life or conception of the ideal good.[6] Nevertheless, liberal toleration was not a multicultural project. It was meant to foster coexistence among different forms of life, which people mutually acknowledged to be legitimate and worthwhile in a seemingly diverse society. It was one of restraint toward beliefs and practices.[7]

Liberal toleration, Gray (2000) notes, was toleration within the context of a consensus on the Christian culture—that is, a cultural agreement on shared European Christian values. Liberal toleration made moral disagreement within the European Christian culture permissible, while those who stood outside this culture were confined to unintelligibility and subjected to intolerance.[8] Accordingly, this early version of liberalism and liberal toleration were more or less a secularized form of Christianity. Parekh (1996) sees this account as responsible for the seamless synchronization of missionary activities with colonialism, as well as why the famous slogan of spreading civilization and

Christianity among the colonies during the dark era of European colonization of other parts of the world did not provoke any disapproval from either the church or the government.[9] It is hard to isolate the roots of liberalism in the West historically and culturally from European Christianity.

Liberalism promotes, among other things, the priority of the individual and her values, which include rational choice, independence of thought, and actions. The good life that liberalism presupposes must be autonomous, dynamic, animated, and opposed to the wastefulness of both natural and human resources.[10] Parekh states that in an attempt to define what constituted the good life, liberals set a standard for what qualified as the civilized life. From this standpoint, European liberalism considered other cultural values outside of the European Christian milieu as inferior, primitive, sometimes evil, and therefore, in need of improvement through colonization. This reason, Parekh claims, was responsible for many of the misdeeds of early liberalism, which included hostility, misjudgment, and mistrust of non-Western European cultures, as well as prejudiced representation of non-Western values in the works of prominent European philosophers such as John Locke (1632–1704), Immanuel Kant (1724–1804), and John Stuart Mill (1806–1873). Based on what constituted the good and civilized life, for example, Parekh notes that Locke condemned the culture and way of life of Native Americans:

> They were lazy, had minimal wants, and lacked rational discipline and a sense of individuality. They roamed free over the land, did not enclose it and lacked the institution of private property, the sine qua non of progress. . . . Since the Indians had no sense of private property, "their" land was really empty, free, vacant, and could be taken over without their consent. . . . God had given man land on condition that he should exploit it to the full, and he had given him reason in the expectation that he would lead a law-governed civil life and develop science and technology. Since the Indians did neither, they were in breach of God's commands and stood in need of discipline and education. English colonisation was indispensable to their transition to civilization, and hence fully justified. (Parekh 1996, 124–25)

The form of liberalism theorized by Locke considered cultures and values outside the absolute morality of Christianity unintelligible. Similarly, as Parekh (1996) further notes, John Stuart Mill thought that the right to the integrity of one's way of life only belonged to those capable of making use of it. For Mill, persons had reached the maturity of their human faculties and were capable of a self-chosen rational life and independent thought in the civilized European societies, while non-European nations were in a state of infancy, and therefore, in need of civilization from the outside. Likewise, Immanuel Kant assessed non-Europeans from a condescending and paternalistic angle. An excellent example to illustrate Kant's opinion can be found in his reply to Johann Gottfried Herder (1744–1803) in 1785, defending the then-current liberal distinction between civilized and uncivilized societies.[11] In his book *Ideen zur Philosophie der Geschichte der Menschheit*[12] (*Ideas for the Philosophy of Human History*—translation mine), Herder describes the general structure of the world and the place of humans in it and how history and the environment combine to shape the cultures of various groups.

The natural powers of humans (or what Herder calls genetic *Kraft*) sustain the species and prevent degeneration. The natural *Kraft*, combined with climatic elements, create the different individual cultures of the world's peoples. Indigenous cultures should be respected, and "each individual cultural expression is worthy in its own right."[13] Unlike the Enlightenment view, which considered human nature static, for Herder, the social environment of the individual helps to shape a person's human nature. Here, Herder calls into question the universalization of reason that the Enlightenment advocated. By so doing, he challenges the classification of non-European cultures as primitive. Herder's former teacher, Kant, rebuts in the *Allgemeine Literaturzeitung* (Jena 1785), justifying the colonization of the people of the Central Southern Pacific Ocean of Tahiti (known then as Otaheite) by the Europeans. He considers Herder's admiration of the happy temperament of the Tahitians preposterous:

> Does the author [Herder] really mean that, if the happy inhabitants of Tahiti, never visited by more civilized nations, were destined to live in their quiet indolence for thousands of centuries, one could give a satisfactory answer to the question of why they bothered to exist at all, and whether it would not have been just as well that this island should have been occupied by happy sheep and cattle as by happy men engaged in mere pleasure? (Berry 1982, 52)

Elsewhere, Kant states, "The world would not lose anything if Otaheite perished."[14]

For Kant, the Tahitians were neither rational nor industrious, and thus they were not capable of leading a self-chosen life. They were not morally disciplined and, as such, were not better than animals. The right of the Tahitians to independent existence or even to exist at all was a matter up for debate.[15] As Christopher J. Berry (1982) notes, "Here Kant's teleological conception with its "utilization" of the perspective of species to "place" or evaluate the Tahitians and their "uncivilized" order, is reminiscent of the Enlightenment's view (criticized by Herder) where history is seen in terms of the growth of reason, with ourselves as rational compared to the superstitious credulity of savages."[16] Since Kant never traveled far beyond Königsberg and its surrounding towns, it is evident that his anthropology of non-European cultures relied heavily on the travelers' literature circulating all over Europe in the eighteenth century, much of which was based on European curiosity about "otherness." It peddled "fake news" about people living in trees, having monkey-like tails, and gobbling up their fellow humans for dinner. For example, the Italian merchant, navigator, and explorer Amerigo Vespucci (ca. 1454–1512) wrote in 1502 about the Guarani tribe of Brazil, "they have no laws or faith. . . . The meat they eat commonly is human flesh."[17] Such bogus narratives about distant peoples must have inspired Kant in *Perpetual Peace* to ascribe cannibalism to the culture of Native Americans: "The chief difference between the European and American savages lies in the fact that many tribes of the latter have been eaten by their enemies, while the former know how to make better use of their conquered enemies than dine off them."[18] A similar unsubstantiated claim must have convinced Kant to believe that the Tahitians had no other useful purpose in life than to dance *ōte ʻa* and *hura*.[19]

In the nineteenth century, liberalism emphasized among its core doctrines the protection of property and the freedom to exchange goods and services as part of property rights. Willie Thompson (2011) points out that in both cases, liberalism benefited mostly those who controlled the means of economic production and sometimes condoned authoritarianism:

> Nineteenth-century liberalism sought to combine a doctrine of human emancipation with a central concern for the protection of property and the freedom of exchanging it, and clearly in both of these dimensions it represented an outlook favourable to economic actors—agricultural, industrial, commercial or financial—who relied on the unimpeded operation of market forces to promote their accumulation and profit. . . . It is important not to misunderstand: liberalism did not necessarily imply a humanitarian or cuddly outlook. On the contrary, depending upon how it was understood, liberalism left plenty of room for violence, racism, authoritarianism, lightly disguised slavery, even genocide. (Thompson 2011, 29)

In the twentieth century, liberalism began to extend its feelers to other fields of study and to gain meaning within important sectors of societal institutions. In response to the growing and multifaceted industrial economy, liberal theorists moved to support social welfare, which is the idea that the government should regulate capitalism and intervene when it threatens the self-worth and liberty of citizens. The government can do this by strengthening social security through affordable or free health care, taxation, unemployment benefits, food security, and so on, and to ensure the protection of citizens' inalienable rights and equality. Rawls's *Theory of Justice* (1971) was at the forefront of this type of liberalism. In that book, Rawls maps out how the liberal state should deal with the issue of distributive justice. His arguments draw from the traditional social contract theory of classical liberalism, the type of liberalism that Rawls now calls "comprehensive" in contrast to "political liberalism." This brings us to the questions of where the difference between comprehensive liberalism and political liberalism lies, and what the "political" stands for in Rawls's liberalism.

## POLITICAL LIBERALISM

It is ironic, Freeman (2018) observes, that American conservatism strongly resembles nineteenth-century classical liberalism, which provided the theoretical background for *laissez-faire* capitalism.[20] Yoram Hazony (2017) writes in his essay "Is Classical Liberalism Conservative?"[21] that the concept of classical liberalism "came into use in 20th century America to distinguish the supporters of old-school *laissez-faire* from the welfare-state liberalism. . . . Modern classical liberals, inheriting the rationalism of Hobbes and Locke, believe they can speak authoritatively to the political needs of every human society, everywhere."[22] One notable takeaway here is the belief of classical liberals regarding the feasibility of transplanting America's liberal individualism and free-market economy to the rest of the world and the moral justifiability of doing so. But Hazony (2017) contends that past, notable Anglo-American conservative thinkers were aware that the U.S. system of government, which is rooted in classical liberal principles, cannot be easily transplanted to countries around the world with different underlying, political cultures:

> The most important conservative figures—including John Fortescue, John Selden, Montesquieu, Edmund Burke and Alexander Hamilton—believed that different political arrangements would be fitting for different nations, each in keeping with the specific conditions it faces and traditions it inherits. What works in one country can't easily be transplanted. On that view, the U.S. Constitution worked so well because it preserved principles the American colonists had brought with them from England. The framework—the balance between the executive and legislative branches, the bicameral legislature, the jury trial and due process, the bill of rights—was already familiar from the English constitution. Attempts to transplant Anglo-American political institutions in places such as Mexico, Nigeria, Russia and Iraq have collapsed time and again, because the political traditions needed to maintain them did not exist. . . . China, Russia and large portions of the Muslim world resisted a "new world order" whose express purpose was to bring liberalism to their countries. The attempt to impose a classical-liberal regime in Iraq by force, followed by strong-arm tactics aimed at bringing democracy to Egypt and Libya, led to the meltdown of political order in these states as well as in Syria and Yemen. (Hazony 2017)

In *Political Liberalism* (1993), Rawls seems to buy into this conservative view that liberalism needs to be contextual rather than make sweeping universal claims. Thus, he distinguishes comprehensive or classical liberalism from political liberalism. Let us note right away that *Political Liberalism* is not only the title of Rawls's book but also a new development in political philosophy. Rawls rejects the notion of liberalism as a comprehensive philosophy for modern, pluralistic democracies in favor of liberalism that is purely political. Rawls attempts to replace traditional liberal toleration with the ideal of neutrality because he now thinks that the liberal morality of the classical theorists is not neutral toward the different conceptions of the good in society. Kant's or Locke's liberalism presupposes a particular way of life, precisely Western cultural values and ways of life. As such, classical liberalism does not represent the values that most people share in today's pluralistic societies. Therefore, Rawls's newfound liberalism adopts an ontologically neutral position in political debates about critical issues of justice that affect most people in society.[23] Donald Moon (1993) suggests that Rawls's eschewing of the metaphysics of human nature in *Political Liberalism* is a "strategy to achieve political community. . . . As a strategy to achieve political community in the face of moral pluralism, political liberalism, like other discourse-based theories, conceives of citizens as engaging in discussions with the aim of discovering norms they can accept."[24] Furthermore, Rawls also contrasts his avant-garde liberalism not only with classical liberalism in general but particularly with Enlightenment liberalism characterized by sharp antagonism toward orthodox Christianity. One of the tasks of political liberalism, he says, is to demonstrate that there is "no war between religion and democracy."[25]

This new development or shift away from classical liberalism in general, and Enlightenment liberalism in particular, is precisely what Rawls calls "political liberalism." Whereas liberal toleration addressed problems of religious conflict and helped achieve consensus on cultural values within European monocultures, political liberalism addresses the issues of modern liberal democratic societies, problems arising from the pluralism of the conception of the good, race, ethnicity, culture, gender, sexual orientation, religion, philosophical or moral doctrine, and so forth. In Rawls's opinion, comprehensive liberalism and its associated liberal toleration are ill suited to tackle the challenges of today's society. In the changing face of contemporary Western societies amidst the presence of multiculturalism, value pluralism is more of a reality than the figment of people's imagination about faraway, exotic cultures. Gray (2000) declares that "in late modern societies, value-pluralism has ceased to be a theory of ethics whose credentials come predominantly from historical instances or travelers' tales of distant cultures. It has become shared knowledge or a phenomenological commonplace."[26]

Rawls maintains that pluralism of reasonable comprehensive philosophical, moral, and religious doctrines characterizes modern liberal societies and that these doctrines sometimes come in conflict with one another. Thus, value pluralism calls for the recognition of the differences that exist between the various conceptions of the good in society. Another feature of the modern liberal, democratic society, Rawls notes, is that no single comprehensive doctrine commands the conformity of everyone in society. If we recognize all of these insights about modern liberal democratic societies, then it is implausible to expect that in the foreseeable future, all citizens of liberal democracy will affirm only one partially or fully comprehensive doctrine. For clarification purposes, Rawls says that a doctrine is fully comprehensive when it includes all recognized values within one precisely articulated system, and partially comprehensive when it consists of only a given number of nonpolitical values, which people articulate loosely.[27]

The existence of diverse, comprehensive doctrines in modern liberal societies, Rawls observes, is a result of the free exercise of human reason arising from the long history of free institutions and a culture of liberal democracy. Given this multiplicity of comprehensive doctrines, it would amount to indefensible sectarianism to base political decisions of governments or matters of justice on the comprehensive or classical liberalism of, for instance, Kant, Mill, or Locke. These doctrines incorporate the metaphysical theory of the person and avow a metaphysical or epistemological truth of certain moral values. Rawls now regards this kind of liberalism as a comprehensive moral view in a liberal democracy already inundated with similar thoughts. If such liberalism becomes the foundation of a democratic polity in modern times, it would be controversial, open to reasonable dispute among citizens, and cannot be justified politically or morally. Going by the standards of Rawls's political liberalism, a liberal democratic society that is chiefly regulated by comprehensive liberalism would cease to be liberal because its stability could only be sustained with the oppressive use of the power of the state. It would become more or less a police-state or an autocratic regime. The medieval Inquisition provides Rawls with an illustrative tool to buttress this point: "a continuing shared understanding on one comprehensive religious, philosophical, or moral doctrine can be maintained only by the oppressive use of state power. . . . A society united on a reasonable form of utilitarianism, or on the reasonable liberalism of Kant or Mill, would likewise require the sanctions of state power to remain so."[28]

Rawls thinks that those who lament the presence of pluralism of comprehensive doctrines in modern liberal democracies, as ill fated and therefore unfortunate, are mistaken. It is the culture of liberal democracies that brought about the pluralism that we now witness through the free exercise of human reason. Rawls enjoins citizens of liberal democracy to see reasonable pluralism from a somewhat positive viewpoint as an enrichment to a democracy, whose success hinges squarely on the acceptance of reasonable pluralism itself: "Indeed, the success of liberal constitutionalism came as a discovery of a new social possibility: the possibility of a reasonably harmonious and stable pluralist society. Before the successful and peaceful practice of toleration in societies with liberal institutions, there was no way of knowing of that possibility."[29]

In the absence of the toleration of reasonable pluralism in a liberal democracy, citizens will face what Rawls calls the "fact of oppression." Since the plurality of reasonable comprehensive doctrines is the inevitable outcome of the free exercise of human reason under free institutions, widespread social, economic, and political agreements in a pluralistic society cannot be reached on the basis of a single comprehensive doctrine, such as religion, except through the use of oppressive force by the state.

But when Rawls mentions pluralism here as the driving force for the success of liberal democracy, it is important to note that he does not regard all forms of pluralism as positive or favorable in the constitution of a harmonious and stable liberal state. Rawls distinguishes strictly between the "fact of reasonable pluralism" and the "fact of pluralism" in general from what he terms the "brute forces of the world."[30] The "fact of pluralism" is the idea that liberal institutions generate reasonable comprehensive worldviews, and that thoughtful citizens affirm such views, as opposed to a pluralism of narrow-minded worldviews stemming from people's unreasonableness or pure selfishness. Rawls thinks that for liberalism to serve as a basis for justice and become the focus of a political consensus in a modern society characterized by the existence of reasonable comprehensive worldviews, it must cease to be "comprehensive." That is to say, it must disentangle itself from controversial epistemological and metaphysical, moral considerations, and restrict itself, as much as possible, to a set of neutral political principles, capable of engendering acceptance from an overwhelming majority of citizens. Consequently, Rawls's political liberalism, having been distinguished from comprehensive or classical liberalism, adopts a "neutral" position vis-à-vis reasonable comprehensive worldviews. This is what Rawls designates as "liberal neutrality."

By assuming a neutral position in relation to reasonable comprehensive worldviews, political liberalism can impartially mediate disputes between reasonable comprehensive worldviews. This way, Rawls believes that his idea of political liberalism is unbiased toward the comprehensive doctrines found in today's liberal democracies. In this neutral position, political liberalism neither attempts to replace reasonable comprehensive doctrines nor seeks to pass judgment on their truth, falsity, or justification. What political liberalism does is unveil public reason in the public political discourse, leaving untouched questions of metaphysical, moral truth, or falsity to the judgment of comprehensive doctrines themselves. For instance, political liberalism does not consider the question of the divine revelation of the Judeo-Christian faith, nor does it require citizens to give up their religions in order to endorse the political conception of justice. It only obliges citizens to uphold the political conception of justice from within their comprehensive worldviews.

In other words, citizens can support the political conception of justice when they consider such an understanding compatible with their comprehensive worldviews. Political liberalism further points out to citizens the practical impossibility of reaching a political agreement on the "truth" of a particular comprehensive worldview or doctrine in a modern liberal democracy, given the "fact of reasonable pluralism."[31]

The primary concern of Rawls's political liberalism is justice in a pluralistic society and the justification of political cohesion. He conceptualizes justice in terms of political dialogue in which political discourse and democratic deliberation appeal only to public reason. Rawls describes public reason as reason latent in the public political culture of liberal democracy and distinguishes it from insights deriving from the transcendental theory of moral values or divine law.

## THE GOALS OF POLITICAL LIBERALISM

In the first edition of *Political Liberalism* (1993), Rawls declares that the main challenge facing his new theory is to answer the following question: How probable is it that there may exist, from one generation to another, a stable and fair society of free and equal citizens deeply divided by reasonable but compatible religious, philosophical, and moral doctrines?[32] Unfortunately, this question may lead one to believe that for the purpose of achieving stability, political liberalism simply plans to strike a balance between conflicting worldviews in a liberal democracy. If this were its goal, then Rawls's version of political liberalism would have been a redundant project in political philosophy because a Hobbesian truce, for example, is equally capable of achieving the same objective. In recognition of the ambiguous posture of the initial stability question, the 1996 edition of *Political Liberalism* has a slightly modified goal. The objectives of political liberalism, Rawls now says, are, first of all, to uncover what could reasonably and justifiably stand as the most reasonable basis for social unity in a liberal democracy given the "fact of reasonable pluralism." It investigates the conditions under which citizens, who are proponents of diverse belief systems, ideologies, and cultures, would support the political conception of justice without external cohesion and, in so doing, achieve political stability.[33]

The second aim of political liberalism is to conceptualize a well-ordered liberal democratic society in the face of not just conflicting reasonable, comprehensive worldviews but also contending liberal political conceptions of justice.[34] Rawls recognizes the existence of rival political conceptions of justice in the modern democratic state and the realization that citizens can employ the principles of such contending views of justice in political debates. These other political conceptions of justice also specify certain liberties, rights, and opportunities for citizens, as well as design political, economic, and social measures to reassure citizens of their freedom.[35] Rawls strongly believes that his justice as fairness is the most reasonable political conception of justice, among other competing liberal conceptions of justice.[36]

For society to have a reasonable and fair basis of social unity among citizens with some divisive and diverse worldviews, Rawls thinks that first, the basic structure of society has to be regulated by a political conception of justice and not by a comprehensive doctrine. Secondly, the political conception must be such that it can motivate diverse groups of people to build a consensus. Thirdly, the political conception must set the conditions for all public political debates involving matters of constitutional essentials and questions of basic justice. Thus, all such discussions can only rely on public reason, rather than on nonpublic reason.[37]

To summarize, Rawls's political liberalism makes the following assumptions, which are fundamental to understanding his new liberal theory. It assumes that today's democratic societies, especially in the Western context, are multicultural, multi-religious, and ideologically diverse. That is to say, citizens of such nations are proponents of various religious, moral, cultural, and ideological views. Political liberalism also assumes that the fact of reasonable pluralism in liberal democratic societies is a recent development. Furthermore, Rawls thinks that reasonable comprehensive worldviews in liberal democracies conflict with one another.[38] Finally, Rawls's political liberalism maintains that only a freestanding political conception of justice (not a comprehensive one) is capable of guaranteeing the stability of a genuinely liberal democratic society.[39]

## POLITICAL CONSTRUCTIVISM

In working out his political liberalism, Rawls utilizes the concept of "constructivism," an idea he believes philosophers seldom use, except perhaps in the philosophy of mathematics.[40] From this position, he develops a methodology for devising the principles of justice for modern democracies. He calls this technique "political constructivism." Michael Buckley (2010) defines constructivism in a way, I believe, captures the main features of Rawls's political constructivism:

> Constructivism is a metaethical theory about the objectivity and validity of moral or political principles and judgments. It attempts to balance the claim that moral principles depend on us especially on our concepts of persons and society together with certain facts about human relations with the claim that the proper combination of those concepts and facts generate objectively valid principles. It balances these claims by reversing our ordinary view of "truth"

as an accurate judgment about some "fact" existing independently of us. Instead, "true" political judgments and the "facts" to which they refer depend upon our having first constructed, through practical reason, objectively valid principles. (Buckley 2010, 673)

This method or approach, as it stands in political liberalism, appears to be the final stage in the development of Rawls's many years of work on constructivism, which he began in 1980 as part of a series of lectures titled "Construction and Objectivity."[41] The essay "Kantian Constructivism in Moral Theory" likewise emerged out of these lectures. In "Construction and Objectivity," Rawls exposes the essence of his constructivist approach in philosophy by showing the distinction between the methods of objectivity of Kantian constructivism in moral theory (e.g., justice as fairness) and moral realism (e.g., rational intuitionism) championed by scholars in the English tradition such as Samuel Clark, Richard Price, Henry Sidgwick, and W. D. Ross.[42]

In *Political Liberalism*, Rawls's political constructivism charts a new path by departing from both the canons of rational intuitionism and Kantian moral constructivism. This is necessary for Rawls to do in order to contrast political constructivism with moral constructivism, something absent in his previous work. The term "constructivism" suggests some architectonic inventiveness. It presupposes that something new is being made. But what is being constructed in Rawls's political liberalism? Rawls does not offer us a straightforward definition of political constructivism; instead, he provides a series of expositions and distinctions that highlight his constructivist approach in philosophy.

With political constructivism seen as a method of political theorizing, Rawls presents the principles of justice as the result of a procedure of construction that utilizes "pure" political concepts of the person and society to model an understanding of a just democratic society.[43] Rawls is clear about what is being constructed under political constructivism, and it is the conception of political justice: "We are here concerned with a constructivist conception of political justice and not with a comprehensive moral doctrine."[44] We can see that Rawls's political constructivism involves the erection of the structures and contents of the political conception of justice. Also, the fact of reasonable pluralism informs Rawls's political constructivism because he believes that the stability of the modern liberal society depends on a kind of consensus, on necessarily political values, rather than on comprehensive moral principles. Political constructivism is the process that Rawls hopes could provide justice as fairness the type of objectivity and justification needed to rally advocates of opposing comprehensive worldviews to achieve an overlapping consensus in society. Political constructivism, in this sense, is a method whose authority does not depend upon the acceptance of a particular metaphysical doctrine about the nature of moral values. It restricts itself to only political principles that are the outcome of procedural construction through the free exercise of human reason.[45]

Rawls claims that the features of political constructivism become more explicit once it is contrasted with rational intuitionism or Kant's moral constructivism. Accordingly, rational intuitionism consists of the belief that there is an independent order of moral values or principles, and that these values can be known through theoretical reason.[46] Rawls's political constructivism, in contrast, does not assume that the principles of political justice resulting from the constructivist procedure belong to an independent order of moral values or that human beings apperceive them by intuition through theoretical reasoning. Nevertheless, Rawls does not seek to engage rational intuitionism in a contentious debate about the affirmation or denial of the truth value of its doctrinal claims. Political constructivism only labels a doctrine or view as reasonable or unreasonable, but never as true or false. According to Rawls, rational intuitionism has four outstanding features from which political constructivism can be juxtaposed.

First, in rational intuitionism, moral first principles of judgments, when correct, are true statements about an independent order, and this independent order does not depend on or is not explained by the activity of any actual human mind, including the operation of reason.[47] For political constructivism, on the contrary, the principles of political justice are the outcome of a procedure of construction and do not derive from any given independent order, moral, or divine. Rawls writes:

> Consider again the idea of social cooperation. How are fair terms of cooperation to be determined? Are they to be simply laid down by some outside authority distinct from the persons cooperating, say by God's law? Or are these terms to be accepted by these persons as fair in view of their knowledge of an independent moral order? . . . We adopt, then, a constructivist view to specify the fair terms of social cooperation as given by the principles of justice agreed to by the representatives of free and equal citizens when fairly situated. (Rawls 1996, 97)

Secondly, in rational intuitionism, Rawls continues, moral first principles are known by theoretical reason, whereas in political constructivism, the procedure of construction that generates the principles of justice originates from practical reason. Relying on Kant's *Critique of Pure Reason*, Rawls distinguishes practical reason from theoretical reason as follows: "practical reason is concerned with the production of objects according to a conception of those objects—for example, the conception of a just constitutional regime taken as the aim of political endeavor—while theoretical reason is concerned with the knowledge of given objects."[48]

Thirdly, rational intuitionism as a form of moral realism, according to Rawls, does not make use of a substantive concept of the person, but rather utilizes a very thin idea. Rational intuitionism conceptualizes persons only in terms of the "self" as knower—that is, as capable of cognizing intuitive knowledge of first principles. The content of moral first principles is given by an independent order available to perception and intuition. Intuitionist principles are valid upon intuitive reflection of the rational agent, and to access these principles, persons only need to have the capacity for intuitive cognition. Therefore, persons as the knowers of intuitively given knowledge suffice for rational intuitionism, whereas political constructivism employs a more substantive concept of the person.[49] It conceives of a person as belonging to a political society seen as a fair system of cooperation over generations. For this reason, political liberalism ascribes to persons two moral powers: the capacity for a sense of justice and the conception of the good, which enables individuals to engage in social cooperation.[50]

Fourthly, rational intuitionism uses the notion of "truth" to represent objectivity, while political constructivism employs the concept of "reasonableness" as its standard of correctness in order to be neutral to conflicting worldviews that affirm the metaphysical or epistemological truth of moral judgment.

Rawls also distinguishes political constructivism from Kantian constructivism on the basis that Kant's constructivism is within the theoretical framework of what he now calls a comprehensive moral theory, as opposed to a purely political conception. Political constructivism concerns itself with the construction of the political conception of justice as fairness; a conception operational only in a domain Rawls calls the public political. Furthermore, Kantian transcendentalism maintains that the principles and conceptions of practical reason constitute the order of moral or political values. That is to say, the moral order, as understood by moral realism, does not create itself independently; instead, it is a result of the activity of human practical reason. Political constructivism departing from Kant does not claim that the principles of practical reason represent the order of values or that the principles of practical reason constitute the moral order itself.[51] It does, however, agree with Kant's view that the principles of practical reason originate in human moral consciousness.

Finally, Rawls distinguishes his justice as fairness as the outcome of a political-constructivist procedure from Kantianism in general because of the difference in the objectives of the two systems of thought. While justice as fairness aims to uncover a public basis for the justification of the broad issues of political justice, especially in the face of reasonable pluralism, Kant's philosophy generally speaking is an *apologia*, which Rawls calls the defense of reasonable faith:

> This [apologia] is not the older theological problem of showing the compatibility of faith and reason, but that of showing the coherence and unity of reason, both theoretical and practical, with itself; and how we are to view reason as the final court of appeal, as alone competent to settle all questions about the scope and limits of its own authority. . . . His view of philosophy as defense rejects any doctrine that undermines the unity and coherence of theoretical and practical reason; it opposes rationalism, empiricism and skepticism so far as they tend to that result. (Rawls 1996, 101)

By developing the conception of political justice by means of constructivism whose scope is restricted to the political as distinguished from a comprehensive conception, Rawls hopes to find neutral political principles that citizens of modern liberal democracies can endorse, despite their deep-rooted differences.

## LIBERAL NEUTRALITY AND IDEAS OF THE GOOD

Rawls articulates political liberalism in line with the tendency in postmodern liberal theory, sometimes, to identify the "political" with the "neutral." Thus, he sees the political or neutral in this sense as a platform on which conflicting interests, ideologies, or doctrines existing in modern democracies can find impartial arbitration. Noël O'Sullivan (1997) writes that

> A striking feature of contemporary political philosophy is the emergence of the nature of the political itself as a central theme of discussion. There are various reasons for this development, but all of them merely reinforce the problem posed in its most stark form by postmodern theory. This is the problem of determining what concept of the political, if any, can accommodate the extreme diversity that is the main feature of contemporary Western life. (O'Sullivan 1997, 39)

Given the problems posed by the pluralism of cultures, values, and doctrines in contemporary Western democracies, Rawls believes that political liberalism could provide citizens the foundation for social unity and cohesion, if only it can refrain from trying to regulate all spheres of life. When policymakers confine the application of liberalism to the political domain, its principles can then be said to be neutral toward comprehensive worldviews or conceptions of the good that govern citizens' nonpublic lives.

Consistent with the growing understanding of the term "political" as "neutral" among liberal theorists, Rawls states that political liberalism is neutral toward the ideals of the good life. He insists that the liberal state should be neutral toward the ideas of the good by abstaining from actions that favor a particular comprehensive doctrine, moral, philosophical, or religious, over others. Instead, the state should act as a neutral platform for citizens to pursue a variety of worldviews or conceptions of the good.[52] At the end of the preceding analysis, some questions come to mind. For example, what constitutes a conception of the good? Do the conceptions of the good that Rawls regards as "permissible ideas of the good" in political liberalism not undermine his notion of liberal neutrality?

A conception of the good is an understanding of what gives value and meaning to an individual's life. It is what constitutes a worthy life. Rawls calls the conception of the good "an ordered family of final ends and aims which specifies a person's conception of what is of value in human life or, alternatively, of what is regarded as a fully worthwhile life. The elements of such a conception are . . . interpreted by, certain comprehensive religious, philosophical, or moral doctrines in the light of which the various ends and aims are ordered and understood."[53] The conception of the good as embedded in comprehensive doctrines can mean different things to different people. For example, the conception of the good for a utilitarian may include the maximization of well-being, preference satisfaction, or pleasure. In other instances, it could mean the search for human perfection, self-realization, or the salvation of the human soul in the case of Christianity.[54] Liberal neutrality, as employed by Rawls, entails the idea that the pluralistic liberal state should not be modeled exclusively on a given conception of the good. According to Simon Caney (1995), Rawls thinks that the liberal democratic state is neutral between conceptions of the good when its legislation is not wholly dependent on the appraisal of the worth or value of any particular, personal ideal. This implies not only that all arms of government should be neutral in the above regard but also that when citizens of liberal democracies vote on public political issues, they ought to be indifferent to the conceptions of the good that they profess in their nonpublic lives. Their conception of the good should not influence the outcome of a political debate or an election.[55]

Rawls's reinforces his idea of liberal neutrality with the "priority of the right over the good," which conceives of individuals as concretely existing, independent persons, whose rights are not to be determined by the general or collective view of society about what constitutes the good life or well-being. Following the "priority of the right over the good," the liberal democratic state must protect citizens' right to follow their variously chosen conceptions of the good, as well as the right to revise or change these conceptions when they deem it necessary. Comprehensive worldviews that violate this right in the state are unreasonable and ought to be checked by policymakers. The state should, for example, prevent a comprehensive religious doctrine that sanctions the execution of heretics from violating the rights of other citizens.

Some critics, supposedly communitarians[56] (among them Michael Sandel and Alasdair MacIntyre), complain that Rawls's "priority of the right over the good" undercuts his principle of liberal neutrality. They argue that a liberal state, which subscribes to Rawls's ideal of the right, by so doing, already upholds a distinctively liberal conception of the good. According to Mulhall and Swift (1997), Rawls can only give justification to his "priority of the right over the good" by relying substantially on a distinctively liberal understanding of how people should live. For this reason, they conclude that Rawls's theory is not neutral to conceptions of the good.[57] Similarly, Sandel (1982) states that "[t]he ideal of a society governed by neutral principles is liberalism's false promise. It affirms individualistic values while pretending to a neutrality which can never be achieved."[58] Alasdair MacIntyre (1988) also mentions that "[l]iberalism while initially rejecting the claims of any overriding theory of the good, does, in fact, come to embody just such a theory."[59]

In *Political Liberalism*, Rawls makes it clear that his idea of neutrality does not exclude the acceptance of some conceptions of the good. He thinks that the total eschewal of the conception of the good is impossible for his political theory. Instead, his particular notion of liberal neutrality requires that the conceptions of the good used in political liberalism must be political ideas. That is to say, these ideas must only propose political values; they must be conceived in such a way as to meet restrictions imposed by the political conception of justice. Rawls lists five political conceptions of the good or ideas of the good in his 1988 paper, "The Priority of Right and Ideas of the Good," but extends the list to six in his 2001 book, *Justice as Fairness: A Restatement*. He mentions the sixth idea as "idea of the good of . . . society as the social union of social unions."[60]

To explain the meaning of "the idea of the good of society as a social union of social unions," one needs to consult Rawls's earlier treatment of the subject in *A Theory of Justice*, where he distinguishes the idea from a private society. He outlines the main features of a private society as follows:

> First that the persons comprising it, whether they are human individuals or associations, have their own private ends which are either competing or independent, but not in any case complimentary. And second, institutions are not thought to have any value in themselves, the activity of engaging in them not being counted as a good but if anything a burden. Thus each person assesses social arrangements solely as a means to his private aims. (Rawls 1971, 521–22)

The social union of social unions (in contrast to a private society) allows persons to share their talents, complement each other, and realize far greater potentials in the pursuit of shared ends:

> The social nature of mankind is best seen by contrast with the conception of private society. . . . The potentialities of each individual are greater than those he can hope to realize; and they fall far short of the powers among men generally . . . thus we may say following Humboldt that it is through social

union founded upon the needs and potentialities of its members that each person can participate in the total sum of the realized natural assets of others. (Rawls 1971, 522–23)

"The Idea of Goodness as Rationality . . . supposes that citizens of a liberal society have at least an intuitive plan of life in light of which they schedule their life endeavors and allocate their various resources so as rationally to pursue their conceptions of the good over a complete life."[61] The underlying assumption here is that human existence, its needs, and purposes are good, and that human rationality is necessary for political and social organization.

"The Idea of Primary Goods"—according to Rawls, the provision of adequate primary goods, as citizens' basic needs necessary for the realization of their goals, is a specific aim of justice as fairness. Primary goods include basic rights and liberties, freedom of movement, free choice of career, powers, and privileges of offices and positions of responsibility in the political and economic establishments of society, wages, and capital, and the social bases of self-respect.[62]

"The Idea of Permissible Conception of the Good"—under this idea, citizens are only allowed to pursue those conceptions of the good, which are compatible with the two principles of justice as fairness. Conceptions of the good falling outside this space are inadmissible in the scheme of things.[63]

"The Idea of Political Virtues"—the virtues that specify the ideal of good citizenship in a liberal democracy are "political." Their pursuit or promotion by the state, Rawls claims, does not violate his notion of liberal neutrality.[64]

"The Idea of the Political Good of Society Well-Ordered by the Principles of Justice as Fairness" characterizes citizens as having shared ends: the end of supporting just institutions and giving one another justice accordingly, and the ends accrued through fair social cooperation.[65]

Rawls considers all these ideas of the good compatible with his political conception of justice as fairness and its related notion of liberal neutrality.[66] The meanings of the "priority of the right over the good" and the idea of liberal neutrality imply, according to Rawls, that these conceptions of the good so far listed fit into the framework of the political conception of justice as fairness and that alone makes them permissible. Given the reality of reasonable pluralism in liberal democracies, these conceptions of the good must only be political ideas, applying specifically to public political issues, and only justifiable through public reason. Furthermore, they must be ideas shared by free and equal citizens generally and must not presuppose any particular comprehensive doctrine—neither philosophical, moral worldviews nor a religious belief.[67]

Despite Rawls's claim to neutrality, not everyone agrees with his ideas of the good as neutral principles. Rawls remarks that the political ideas of the good and "priority of the right over the good," as used in political liberalism, are not neutral in all circumstances, but rather represent a specific notion of liberal neutrality. For example, he makes clear that justice as fairness is not neutral in the sense that William Galston (1982) defines neutrality. In *Defending Liberalism* (1982),[68] Galston stresses that some forms of liberalism are neutral in the sense that they make no use of the ideas of the good at all, except purely instrumental ones. Rawls denies that justice as fairness is neutral in this sense.[69]

To be more distinct about his idea of liberal neutrality, Rawls discusses three meanings of neutrality of which justice as fairness is neutral only in one sense. The three are "procedural neutrality," "neutrality of effect," and "neutrality of aim." With "procedural neutrality," Rawls explains that a theory is procedurally neutral if it can be legitimate without appealing to any moral values at all, or if it appeals to otherwise neutral values such as impartiality, consistency in the application of principles to all reasonably related cases, and the value of equal opportunity.[70] Rawls maintains that justice as fairness, as a political conception, is not neutral in the procedural sense because it embodies principles of justice together with the conceptions of person and society, which express more than procedural values. The political conception of justice represents a public basis of justification for the basic structure of a liberal democratic society. To this effect, it draws from ideals that are central to the public political culture of liberal democracy. The political conception of justice as fairness seeks common grounds for justification, given the facts of reasonable pluralism, and this common ground is not procedurally neutral. In an "overlapping consensus," the political conception of justice as fairness seeks not to be grounded solely on, let us say, the value of impartiality or equal opportunity.[71]

Another meaning of neutrality, which Rawls political conception of justice does not subscribe to, is the "neutrality of effect." This form of neutrality demands that the state should not do anything that makes it more likely for individuals to prefer one particular conception of the good over another, unless the state takes measures to recompense affected citizens for the effects that the policies may have on them.[72] For Rawls, justice as fairness cannot possibly be neutral in this sense because it is practically impossible for the basic structure of a liberal democratic society not to have effects or influences, negative or positive, on citizens regarding which comprehensive moral, philosophical, and religious doctrines endure or cease to exist, gain or lose followers, over time. Rawls argues that "it is futile to try to counteract these effects and influences, or even to ascertain for political purposes how deep and pervasive they are."[73]

Justice as fairness, Rawls insists, cannot be neutral in the sense of preventing liberal institutions from influencing citizens or new immigrants. For instance, the promotion of certain political virtues by the liberal state may have effects on adult citizens or their children, who may be members of a religious sect, and this cannot be easily prevented. As Rawls says, "[e]ven though political liberalism seeks common ground and is neutral in aim, it is important to emphasize that it may still affirm the superiority of certain forms of moral character and encourage certain moral virtues . . . such as the virtues of civility and tolerance, of reasonableness and the sense of fairness."[74] Although justice as fairness is neutral regarding the way citizens make public political decisions via the use of public reason, nevertheless, it cannot hinder the effects such liberal choices may have on citizens. This issue, for Rawls, is the dilemma of political liberalism, which citizens have to live with. An excellent example of this dilemma is given by Kor-Chor Tan (1998):

> The liberal emphasis on civic education, which (for the political liberal) is justified solely on neutral political grounds (namely, the cultivation of traits and character necessary for equal and free citizenship), can have "liberalizing" consequences beyond the political sphere. . . . For the political liberal, this liberalizing effect is an unintended side effect of a neutrally justified public policy. . . . However, the fact that neutrally justified policies are not neutral in consequences allows the political liberal state to indirectly reform the internal arrangements of reasonable nonliberal groups, thereby protecting and promoting individual liberty (the liberal aspiration), without explicitly rejecting these group arrangements as inadmissible (the political liberal aspiration). (Tan 1988, 291–92)

Rawls's political liberalism does not prevent the basic structure or other institutions of liberal democracy from influencing nonliberal elements within the state. Instead, as Tan (1998) states, political liberalism utilizes such effects or consequences indirectly to reform tendencies it sees as nonliberal within the liberal state. Hence, Rawls's theory does not pretend to be neutral in the sense of "neutrality of effect."

A very different meaning of neutrality and one Rawls's political liberalism approves, is "neutrality of aim," which says that the state is to secure equal opportunity for all citizens to advance any permissible conception of the good. In this case, depending on how the meaning of equal opportunity is to be understood, Rawls's political liberalism can be said to be neutral in aim.[75] This implies that while justice as fairness, as a political conception, seeks to provide impartial grounds for comprehensive worldviews to thrive, and also, in return, strives for validation or support from comprehensive worldviews, it nonetheless ensures that basic institutions and public policies are not made to favor any given comprehensive worldview, and that such institutions and policies themselves are not the outcomes of a given comprehensive worldview.

By employing liberal neutrality, Rawls's political liberalism aims to persuade citizens of the liberal democratic state to pursue freely whatever conceptions of the good they may prefer, as long as they are compatible with the political conception of justice. That said, critics see Rawls's idea of liberal neutrality as deceitful rhetoric and a circular argument. Parekh (1996), for example, insists that Rawls's liberalism embodies a specific liberal conception of the good, despite his claims to neutrality:

> The tendency not to prescribe a substantive vision of the good life and yet to do so by means of apparently formal principles is to be found in almost all liberal writers from Hobbes onwards, albeit more pronounced in some than in others. John Rawls's insistence on the priority of right over the good is the most recent example of this. He says that individuals may entertain whatever conception of the good they prefer so long as these conform to certain general principles of right. Since these principles embody a liberal conception of the good, Rawls says in effect that all "reasonable" conceptions of the good should be little more than variations on the liberal. . . . His reasonable pluralism is pluralism within the limits of liberalism, and excludes a wide variety of ways of life while claiming to remain neutral. In him as in many other liberal writers, liberalism is both a specific vision of the good life and the arbiter of all others, both a moral currency and the measure of all others, both a player and an umpire, and is open to the charge at best of circularity and at worst of bad faith. (Parekh 1996, 124)

## NOTES

1. See *The Stanford Encyclopedia of Philosophy*, https://plato.stanford.edu/entries/liberalism/.
2. Parekh, 1996, 122.
3. See Kymlicka 1995, 55, 158.
4. See Dombrowski 2001, 4.
5. See Gray 2000, 323.
6. Ibid.
7. Ibid., 323–24.
8. Ibid., 324.
9. See Parekh 1996, 122.
10. See also Parekh 1996, 123; Ingram 1996, 154.
11. See J. G. Herder, *Ideen zur Philosophie der Geschichte der Menschheit* (Darmstadt: Joseph Melzer Vrlag, 1966).
12. Herder's *Ideen zur Philosophie der Geschichte der Menschheit* was originally published in parts between 1784 and 1791 at Riga und Leipzig by Johann Friedrich Hartknoch Press.
13. See Berry 1982, 52.
14. Ibid.
15. See Parekh 1996, 125–26.
16. Berry 1982, 52.
17. Ibid., 8.
18. Immanuel Kant, *Perpetual Peace*. In Sterba 1998, 286.
19. Two traditional dance forms of Tahiti.
20. Freeman 2018, 1.
21. Hazony 2017.

22. Ibid.
23. See also Gray 2000, 323.
24. Moon 1993, 98.
25. Rawls 1997a, 804.
26. Gray 2000, 325.
27. Rawls 1996, 13.
28. Ibid., 37.
29. Ibid., xxvii.
30. Ibid., 37.
31. Ibid., xxi–xxii, 63.
32. Ibid., xx.
33. Ibid., xxxix–xl.
34. Ibid., xlviii.
35. Ibid.
36. Ibid., xlviii–xlix.
37. Ibid., 44.
38. See also Höffe 1998, 274.
39. Ibid.
40. See Rawls 1996, 89–129.
41. *Journal of Philosophy*, 1980, Vol. lxxvii, No. 9, 515–72.
42. See Rawls 1980, 557.
43. See also Mulhall and Swift 1997, 180.
44. Rawls 1996, 90.
45. Ibid., 180.
46. See Dombrowski 2001, 81.
47. Rawls 1996, 21.
48. Ibid., 93.
49. Ibid., 92.
50. Ibid., 94.
51. Ibid., 99–100, 125.
52. Rawls 1996, 193; Kymlicka 1989, 883.
53. Rawls 2001, 19.
54. See also Clarke 1999, 627–28.
55. Caney 1995, 250–51.
56. *The Stanford Encyclopedia of Philosophy* states that modern-day communitarianism is mostly an Anglo-American movement, whose origin appears to be a direct reaction to Rawls's propositions in *A Theory of Justice* (1971): "Modern-day communitarianism began in the upper reaches of Anglo-American academia in the form of a critical reaction to John Rawls's landmark 1971 book *A Theory of Justice* (Rawls 1971). Drawing primarily upon the insights of Aristotle and Hegel, political philosophers such as Alasdair MacIntyre, Michael Sandel, Charles Taylor and Michael Walzer disputed Rawls's assumption that the principal task of government is to secure and distribute fairly the liberties and economic resources individuals need to lead freely chosen lives. These critics of liberal theory never did identify themselves with the communitarian movement (the communitarian label was pinned on them by others, usually critics), much less offer a grand communitarian theory as a systematic alternative to liberalism. Nonetheless, certain core arguments meant to contrast with liberalism's devaluation of community recur in the works of the four theorists named above" (https://plato.stanford.edu/entries/communitarianism/).
57. Mulhall and Swift 1997, 218.
58. Sandel 1982, 11.
59. MacIntyre 1988, 345.
60. Rawls 2001, 142.
61. Ibid., 141.
62. Ibid.
63. Ibid.
64. Ibid., 142.

65. Ibid.
66. See also Rawls 1988, 251–76.
67. See also Mulhall and Swift 1997, 222; Rawls 2001, 142.
68. See Galston 1982, 622.
69. Rawls 1996, 191.
70. Ibid., 191–92.
71. Ibid., 192.
72. Ibid., 193.
73. Ibid.
74. Ibid., 194.
75. Ibid., 193.

*Chapter Four*

# Justice as Fairness: A Reinterpretation

## REWORKING THE ORIGINAL CONCEPTION OF JUSTICE

In reinterpreting justice as fairness, Rawls defines justice only in procedural terms, while avoiding strong metaphysical, abstract universalistic statements, or any claims to normative universalism. Justice is fairness engendered by "reciprocity of perspectives" or putting ourselves in other people's shoes. In other words, rather than treating each case similarly in, let us say, a utilitarian sense, justice as fairness expresses both empathy and sympathy in the evaluation of the relevant circumstances that provide the backdrop for the determination of justice. In all situations of social justice, justice as fairness emphasizes the distinctiveness of the individual. It demands that the unique circumstances of an issue of justice be given priority over considerations of moral universalism.

For this reason, justice as fairness considers the concretely existing individual as the primary subject of social justice instead of a conceptually abstract entity. Thus, any reasonable agreements among citizens in a pluralistic, democratic regime can only be reached through a constructivist approach in discourse ethics. Rawls does not presume any longer that the normative principles of *A Theory of Justice* are valid for all persons in the world, and must override the cultural, religious, or historical circumstances of individuals. However, this is not the end of normative universalism, but rather the recognition of both the presence and the influence of reasonable pluralism in political liberalism.

We are here concerned with the interpretation and reinterpretation of Rawls's monumental work, *A Theory of Justice* (1971), and the system of justice that it advocates. A decade after its publication, Rawls began in a series of scholarly papers the project of recasting some of the views he expressed in the book. Some of these articles include "Kantian Constructivism in Moral Theory" (1980), "The Basic Liberties and their Priorities" (1982), "Justice as Fairness: Political not Metaphysical" (1985), "The Idea of an Overlapping Consensus" (1987), and so forth. Some of these academic papers became chapters in the compendium, *Political Liberalism* (1993), which Rawls later republished with some addenda in 1996. Furthermore, a year before his death in 2002, Rawls took more steps to make his views more transparent in *Justice as Fairness: A Restatement* (2001), edited by Erin Kelly.

This reworking of justice as fairness, in my view, calls for a new hermeneutics of Rawls's theory in general, which is pivotal to understanding his overall thesis today. While some of Rawls's critics may see themselves as the instigators of his new ideas, the man himself has a different opinion. In the 1991 interview "John Rawls: For the Record," Rawls has this to say:

HRP: Are most of those articles responses to criticisms from other people?

John Rawls: Well, I don't think so really. I have responded to people, certainly, so there are responses; but what I am mainly doing in these articles, as I now understand having written them—you don't always understand what you're doing until after it has happened—is to work out my view so that it is no[t] longer internally inconsistent. To explain: to work out justice as fairness the book [*Justice as Fairness: A Briefer Restatement*, an unpublished manuscript] uses throughout an idea of a well-ordered society which supposes that everybody in that society accepts the same comprehensive view, as I say now. I came to think that that simply can never be the case in a democratic society, the kind of society the principles of the book itself require. That's the internal inconsistency. So I had to change that account of the well ordered society and this led to the idea of overlapping consensus and related ideas. That is really what the later articles are about. Beginning with the three lectures in the *Journal of Philosophy*, that's what they are doing. So I don't see these articles mainly as replies to other people's objections, although I do make replies to important objections here and there, and in footnotes. People deserve to be answered if their objections make valuable points and can be dealt with reasonably. That's part of one's obligation when one engages in these things. But the main aim is to develop this other part of the view and then bring it together with the view of *A Theory of Justice*. As I see it, the development is from within—that is, I came to see there was something wrong, therefore I had to correct it. . . . In some cases there were things that were unclear; in other cases, there were just plain errors. (Aybar et al. 1991, 41)

The recasting of *A Theory of Justice* and the publication of *Political Liberalism* warrant a dual categorization of Rawls's theory: the early Rawls and the later Rawls. According to Dombrowski (2001), much of the controversy associated with Rawls's work is attributable to the relationship between the early and later Rawls. There is a great deal of continuity and discontinuity between his first two major works. The following issues are at the heart of the recast:

i. The lack of distinction between a "comprehensive doctrine" and a "political conception" in *A Theory of Justice* (1971)

Rawls considers his failure to establish a clear distinction between what he calls a comprehensive doctrine and a political conception in A *Theory of Justice* as a grave mistake. In *Political Liberalism*, he now classifies the "justice as fairness" of *A Theory of Justice* as a comprehensive or partially comprehensive doctrine. To this end, he expounds that "[a]lthough the distinction between a political conception of justice and a comprehensive philosophical doctrine is not discussed in *Theory*, once the question is raised, it is clear, I think, that the text regards justice as fairness and utilitarianism as comprehensive, or partially comprehensive, doctrines."[1]

Justice as fairness, reinterpreted, is no longer a comprehensive moral or philosophical doctrine, but rather a political conception. As Rawls explains, the political is not to be distinguished from the moral in the reinterpretation of justice as fairness. Preferably, Rawls wants us to see the political as a subset of the moral, and what makes the political a subcategory is the fact that its range of operation is very limited. This implies that while justice as fairness remains a moral conception even after the reinterpretation, it is a moral conception carved out precisely for a political purpose. We may take, for instance, the reinterpretation of the original position, which is an integral part of justice as fairness to illustrate Rawls's transition from a comprehensive philosophical or moral doctrine to a purely political conception. In *A Theory of Justice*, Rawls models the original position after Kantian moral philosophy, expressing the moral autonomy of persons, the capacity for rational choice, and the conception of persons as noumenal selves (or as Rawls would prefer to say: free persons equally situated). In *Political Liberalism*, however, the original position is reinterpreted in the light of the political conception, where Rawls now conceptualizes the autonomy of persons only as a political value, expressible in the public political sphere, instead of being a moral view that covers all areas of life. The original position now expresses a pluralistic notion of justice.

ii. The difference in the aims of the two books

Another discontinuity recorded between the early Rawls of *A Theory of Justice* and the later Rawls of *Political Liberalism* is the difference in the objectives of the two books. While contractarianism is the medium for presenting his system of justice as a superior alternative to utilitarianism in *A Theory of Justice*, the later Rawls of *Political Liberalism* has no such ambition:

> The aims of *Theory* [1971] ... were to generalize and carry to a higher order of abstraction the traditional doctrine of the social contract. I wanted to show that this doctrine was not open to the more obvious objections often thought fatal to it. I hoped to work out more clearly the chief structural features of this conception—which I called "justice as fairness"—and to develop it as an alternative systematic account of justice that is superior to utilitarianism. (Rawls 1996, xvii)

Instead, Rawls's *Political Liberalism* assumes a neutral position toward reasonable comprehensive worldviews, while simultaneously seeking their endorsement through an "overlapping consensus." One goal of the later Rawls is to achieve justice and stability in modern democracies that already have divisions along ideological lines.

### iii. The unrealistic account of stability in the well-ordered society of *A Theory of Justice*

The later Rawls admits that another error within his previous project is that the idea of stability and the conception of the well-ordered society of justice as fairness in *A Theory of Justice* were unrealistic. He regrets that these two conceptions were worked out without adequate consideration of the current sources of conflict in modern democracies—namely, the fact of reasonable pluralism of worldviews. As presented in *A Theory of Justice*, the main reason behind the conception of the well-ordered society is that citizens of any democratic society governed by justice as fairness, as much as possible, would endorse a comprehensive, liberal system of justice. The later Rawls, however, now thinks that his previous project would be quite improbable to achieve. He believes that the well-ordered society would typically be characterized by a plurality of incommensurable but reasonable doctrines and that justice as fairness, as a comprehensive moral or philosophical view, would have been one among such doctrines.

The later Rawls's epiphany stems from his realization that reasonable pluralism is a permanent feature of today's democratic societies. Citizens of liberal democracies will always be proponents of diverse, comprehensive worldviews, and there will never be a unitary comprehensive conception of the good, which all free citizens of these societies will endorse as long as the free exercise of human reason remains unhindered. Rawls is convinced that citizens of modern democracies will always pursue diverse life goals and aspirations, as well as devise different plans regarding how to realize their conceptions of the good. These citizens will also lay legitimate claims on their government in order to realize their distinct objectives. For the later Rawls, the fact of reasonable pluralism of worldviews makes it unreasonable and illegitimate to base the liberal state on one comprehensive conception of an ideal life such as utilitarianism, Judaism, Christianity, or Islam. The role of justice as fairness in *Political Liberalism*, as a political conception of justice, is to try to see whether the comprehensive worldviews in society can reach an agreement on political matters in a fair, just, and publicly justifiable manner.[2] As Elizabeth Frazer and Nicola Lacey (1995) put it, the task of the citizens of the well-ordered society of the later Rawls, a social order characterized by reasonable pluralism, is to find the proper justification for their political coercion of one another, in particular, those members of society who they believe embrace unreasonable doctrines.[3]

iv. Rawls's apparent shift from developing a universal theory of justice to a more contextual one

Another significant discontinuity from *A Theory of Justice* is Rawls's sudden shift from promoting an egalitarian theory of justice with universal overreach to one that is limited in scope. The underlying theoretical structure of justice as fairness in *A Theory of Justice* is the social contract theory. For the fact that social contract theories traditionally abstract from non-historical, universal standpoints, one can say that justice of fairness of the early Rawls exhibited normative universalism. Although the contents of *A Theory of Justice* point to a comprehensive model of constitutional democracy, it is, nevertheless, an ideal intended to serve as an excellent reference point upon which the rest of the world ought to weigh their justices. As William A. Galston (1989) remarks, "Rawls's 'ideal theory' abstracted from the empirical contingencies that differentiated existing political orders, was designated to judge and (when possible) to improve them. And he contended, his theory was neither produced by specific historical and social circumstances nor intended to defend any existing order."[4] The principles of justice available for choice to the contracting parties in the original position are without a doubt universally applicable: "Thus, to understand these principles should not require a knowledge of contingent particulars. . . . Next, principles are to be universal in application. They must hold for everyone in virtue of their being moral persons."[5]

Although it is not Rawls's intent that the principles of justice apply under every situation, nonetheless, his original plan is that societies across the globe should be able to adopt those principles wherever and whenever certain favorable conditions obtain or where and when such conditions develop.[6] Again, justice as fairness in *A Theory of Justice* has a universal undercurrent because Rawls claims to have developed its principles impartially and with the human situation in view, not only from a social outlook but also from all temporal perspectives.[7] The early Rawls conceives justice as fairness as *sub specie aeternitatis*, or under the aspect of eternity, which is another way of saying that the principles of justice as fairness are universally and eternally true, independent of any temporal aspects of reality. Rawls states:

> Thus what we are doing is to combine into one conception the totality of conditions that we are ready upon due reflection to recognize as reasonable in our conduct with regard to one another.... Without conflating all persons into one but recognizing them as distinct and separate, it enables us to be impartial, even between persons who are not contemporaries but who belong to many generations. Thus, to see our place in society from the perspective of this position is to see it *sub specie aeternitatis*: it is to regard the human situation not only from all social but also from all temporal points of view. (Rawls 1971, 587)

In *A Theory of Justice*, the early Rawls presents justice as fairness in line with his previous understanding of the task of political philosophy as the construction of an archetypical ideal society, grounded normatively on principles of justice, and with universal implications. In *Political Liberalism*, Rawls sees the task of political philosophy differently. Political philosophy no longer aims to search for epistemologically and ontologically truth-based normative principles of justice that are universally applicable. Rawls now tells us that the practical task of political philosophy, as part of society's public political culture, is, among other things, to proffer solutions to problems within a particular society or group of societies. Political philosophy does this by first examining the social and historical conditions under which it intends to operate and by appealing to some underlying ideas in the public political culture of society, as well as proposing principles agreeable with the essential beliefs and historical traditions of modern liberal democracies.[8] O'Sullivan (1997) observes that the "obvious departure from Rawls's original quest for a universal, non-contextual foundation for rational principles of justice specifically, the quest for rational grounds for justice is replaced by the seemingly more modest claims that he is merely eliciting the implications of intentions that are implicit in the public morality of a modern ... constitutional democracy."[9] But what prompted Rawls to shift from the search for a universally and normatively grounded principles of justice to a narrow one that owes its objectivity to the invocation of commonsense thoughts, deep-rooted in the political culture of liberal democracies? What are the implications of this change for Rawls's theory as a whole? According to Frazer and Lacey (1995), Rawls's move from universalism to a more contextual setting is merely a response to criticisms. In their view, *A Theory of Justice* was criticized on two main issues. First, it held that we could assume societies to be equally subject to a core conception of rationality, which goes above and beyond cultural specificities.

Second, *A Theory of Justice* presumed that all members of any society could be expected to consent to this rationally based values and principles, which the authors refer to as internal, societal homogeneity.[10] Frazer and Lacey seem to say that Rawls, as a liberal theorist, was willing to make political decisions for the entire world on liberal principles, irrespective of whether everyone will ever accept those principles. *A Theory of Justice* is precisely wrong in being a universal moral theory in this sense. Those who criticize Rawls on this basis think that moral values other than liberal ones ought to be considered when presenting morals with universal undertone and consequence. The later Rawls of *Political Liberalism* makes amends for this oversight by being overly context bound: "Rawlsian constructivism avoids the assumption that a theoretical schema is applicable beyond the domain in which it was built."[11]

But if Rawls's move from universality to particularity in *Political Liberalism* evades one group of critics, it galvanizes another. For Jürgen Habermas (1994), Rawls's eschewing of truth-based, normatively established, universal principles of justice in *Political Liberalism* relegates the task of political philosophy to mere eliciting of ideas from the public political culture of liberal democracies. He calls into question, once again, the normative foundation of Rawls's theory as a whole.[12]

## THE POLITICAL CONCEPTION OF JUSTICE

Although there is general agreement on the existence of some discontinuity as Rawls shifts focus from his first monumental work to his second, there is also, in some sense, a perceptible degree of continuity. *Political Liberalism* anticipates and expands some of Rawls's original ideas. Dombrowski (2001) asserts that "[t]he continuity thesis is enhanced when it is realized that the phrase 'justice as fairness' (as well as the original position, the veil of ignorance, the priority of the right to the good, and the two principles of justice) is retained in the later Rawls under the umbrella term political liberalism."[13] While *Political Liberalism* retains these terms, Rawls nevertheless gives them new meanings. Justice as fairness is now a political conception of justice. To unravel the meaning of this political conception of justice requires an in-depth study of its features:

i. The scope of a political conception

The range of application of the political conception of justice does not go further than the basic structure of society. Rawls is clear about this when he writes that "[i]n particular, it applies to what I shall call the 'basic structure' of society, which for our present purpose I take to be a modern constitutional democracy."[14] Thus, the area of influence of Rawls's political conception of justice includes only the political, social, and economic institutions of modern democracies. Unlike the "justice as fairness" of the early Rawls's project, whose scope was comprehensive or broad; the political conception of justice is very restricted. For example, the two principles of justice (equal basic liberties, equality of opportunity, and the difference principle) now apply specifically to the basic structure of society. Therefore, justice as fairness is not responsible for instructing citizens about what justice demands in all situations. It does not tell citizens how to organize the other institutions of society outside the basic structure to meet the criteria of fairness. For instance, justice as fairness, as a political conception, does not directly regulate the affairs of churches, sports clubs, or other social organizations. Although justice as fairness, as a political conception, concerns itself with how the operations of social or ecclesiastical organizations align with the requirements of the two principles of justice (so that, for instance, the liberty of conscience prevails among religious groups), the particular goals or interests of such groups are not the subject matter of the reinterpreted justice as fairness.

ii. The status of the political conception

Justice as fairness as a political conception is, according to Rawls, freestanding: "This means that it can be presented without saying, or knowing, or hazarding a conjecture about, what such doctrines it may belong to, or be supported by."[15] That justice as fairness is unattached means that it does not suffer the encumbrances of epistemological or metaphysical assumptions, or truth arising from comprehensive liberalism.[16] It further means that justice as fairness understood as a political conception does not derive from any specifically given moral, philosophical, religious, or classical theory of the good life. For Rawls, only a freestanding justice as fairness can serve as a point of consensus for deeply divided and conflicting worldviews, and for the citizens who are their proponents. By being freestanding, it is easy to distinguish justice as fairness from classical liberalism, whose emphasis on human freedom embodies some ontological and autonomous concept of the person, endowed with rationality and will. In Rawls's opinion, to base institutions of modern pluralistic societies on the normative principles of the classical liberalism of Kant, Mill, Hobbes, or Locke, would be highly divisive, conceivably unjust, and citizens who reject such truth-affirming moral and philosophical doctrines have the right to protest their imposition.[17] The central idea behind justice as fairness being freestanding, according to Rawls, is the fact that political liberalism operates only within the domain of the "political" and leaves philosophy as a whole just as it is. It leaves untouched all kinds of doctrines: religious, moral, and so on. Justice as fairness, Rawls insists, operates independently of such theories and, therefore, does not look up to comprehensive worldviews for the justification of its existence.[18]

Rawls thinks that justice as fairness, as a political conception, would be politically untenable if it were not freestanding. If all that justice as fairness, as a political conception, cares about were just how to achieve political stability at all costs in modern democracies, then it would have been a failed project. Again, if the primary intent of the political conception of justice as fairness were producing a workable compromise between the various political and vested interests in society by judiciously studying the constellation of comprehensive doctrines and then positioning itself to win their allegiance, it would have been a deceitful scheme.[19] Rawls maintains that justice as fairness is neither a hodgepodge of reasonable comprehensive doctrines nor a comprehensive doctrine in its own right.

### iii. The source of the political conception

A third distinctive feature of justice as fairness, as a political conception, is its source or origin. Rawls upholds that the content of justice as fairness expresses fundamentally intuitive ideas that are implicit in the public political culture of a liberal democratic society. These are the ideas that citizens of liberal democracies consider commonsensical and shared elements of political life. The public political culture comprises the political institutions of liberal democracy, the interpretations given to such institutions, as well as the history and constitutional documents that support them. Besides these sources that make up the public political culture of modern democracies, Rawls adds another—namely, the concept of society as a fair system of cooperation from one generation to the next.[20]

Although Rawls's view concerning the origin of the political conception of justice may be unproblematic, that does not disentangle it entirely from the features of classical or comprehensive liberalism. The challenge for Rawls is to demonstrate how the public political culture and its accompanying ideas escape the tag of a comprehensive doctrine, especially when we consider the fact that the history and institutional practices of liberal democracies themselves owe their origin to classical liberalism. This problem remains, in my opinion, a gray area in *Political Liberalism*.

Another issue of concern is Rawls's claim that the fundamental ideas in the public political culture of liberal democracies, which function as the substratum for justice as fairness, are shared elements of the political life of citizens.[21] By implication, citizens of liberal democracies generally must accept these fundamental ideas as inherent democratic values irrespective of their ideological differences. But Norman Daniels (2000) thinks that it is a shared set of institutions, practices, and history that give rise to Rawls's public political culture, not the fundamental ideas themselves.[22] The public political culture, serving as the reason for why the political conception of justice is freestanding, leaves such an all-important political conception of justice on a shaky foundation. Michael Buckley (2010) echoes this view:

> The difficulty facing Political Liberalism's justificatory strategy is significant, for if the choice procedure reflects ideas implicit in the political culture of society, then the principles derived from it cannot serve as independent criteria against which those ideas, and the practices they support, are assessed. In other

words, the procedure reflects a conception of the good, and therefore cannot serve as a neutral device for generating principles of right that constrain conceptions of the good. (Buckley 2010, 670)

iv. The political conception of person

The transformation of justice as fairness from a comprehensive doctrine to a political conception, as we have seen so far, requires a corresponding notion of person to avoid contradictions. Thus, from the idea of society as a fair system of cooperation from one generation to the next, an idea which is fundamental to political liberalism, Rawls works out a political conception of person. This new notion of person drops the neo-Kantian concept of *A Theory of Justice*—that is, the conception of persons as free and equal citizens. Some critics of *A Theory of Justice*, especially those that we appropriately or mistakenly identify as communitarians (since they themselves tend to treat this tag like a smudge of impropriety), such as MacIntyre (1981, 1984) and Sandel (1984), complain about what they see as Rawls's neo-Kantian liberalism. This form of liberalism, implicit in Rawls's work, they say, presents the "self" as prior to its ends by asserting "the priority of the right over the good" in ways that undermine the *telos* of the political community. Rawls's neo-Kantian liberalism does this, they claim, by detaching the individual from the burden of history, culture, tradition, and communal ties. This is precisely the type of individual that Sandel (1984) calls the unencumbered self:

> The liberal ethic asserts the priority of right, and seeks principles of justice that do not presuppose any particular conception of the good. This is what Kant means by the supremacy of the moral law, and what Rawls means when he writes that justice is the first virtue of institutions. For the unencumbered self, what matters above, what is most essential to our personhood, are not the ends we choose but our capacity to choose them. . . . Only if the self is prior to its ends can the right be prior to the good. Only if my identity is never tied to the aims and interests I may have at any moment can I think of myself as a free and independent agent, capable of choice. . . . The unencumbered self and the ethic it inspires, taken together, hold out a liberating vision. Freed from the dictates of nature and the sanction of social roles, the human subject is installed as sovereign, cast as the author of the only moral meanings there are. . . . And as actual individual selves, we are free to choose our purposes and ends unbound by such an order, or by custom or tradition or inherited status. . . . We are, in Rawls' words, "self-originating sources of valid claims. . . ." Can we make sense of our moral and political life by the light of the self-image it requires? I do not think we can. (Sandel 1984, 83–87)

Communitarian criticisms of Rawls's *A Theory Justice* are precipitated by a specific interpretation of the underlying features of liberalism, which they claim places individual persons, as rational agents, ontologically prior to their community. For Alasdair MacIntyre (1984), this liberalism misses a whole dimension of moral and political life, obligations of membership, loyalty, and solidarity when it separates the individual from the community. He counters liberalism with what he calls "the narrative conception of the self." According to this idea, human beings are essentially storytelling creatures because, as MacIntyre states, "the story of my life is always embedded in the story of those communities from which I derive my identity. I am born with a past: and to try to cut myself off from that past, in the individualist mode, is to deform my present relationships."[23]

According to Susan Mendus (1989), liberalism historically has always been committed to the autonomy of the moral person—that is, the notion that individuals are free to assess and revise their existing ends at will.[24] In Rawls's defense, his communitarian critics may have been ideologically biased, too, since they tend to give priority to the community at perhaps the expense of individual autonomy. Behind these communitarian criticisms, according to Dieter Sturma (2000), is the fear that Rawls's *A Theory of Justice* could liberate the self in a way that leads to some form of estrangement.[25] From the perspective of the later Rawls of *Political Liberalism*, his appropriation of Kantian autonomy in *A Theory of Justice* makes his early work unsuitable for modern liberal democracies characterized by a pluralism of comprehensive moral, philosophical, and religious doctrines.[26]

The later Rawls laments his failure in *A Theory of Justice* to make a clear distinction between political and moral autonomy. While the concept of the person in *A Theory of Justice* is a moral, neo-Kantian conception,[27] *Political Liberalism* stresses that this moral conception is different from a political one. The political conception of person covers only the political autonomy of persons.[28] Rawls now argues that Kantian autonomy or moral autonomy of *A Theory of Justice* would be sectarian if it were to be adopted as a basis for understanding persons as citizens in a pluralistic liberal democracy because such a moral conception would invoke ideals and values that are not generally accepted by all citizens.[29]

Rawls's approach to solving the problem that a neo-Kantian moral autonomy might generate in a pluralistic modern democracy is not to abandon the idea of moral autonomy entirely. Instead, he introduces a new way of looking at moral autonomy, one which can be said to accommodate communitarian objections because its scope begins and ends with the political conception of justice. Rawls now makes use of this notion of autonomy only in the public political sphere, while eschewing the use of the concept to cover other areas of nonpublic life. Will Kymlicka (2000) highlights this change:

> The idea that we can form and revise our conception of the good is, he [Rawls] now says, strictly a "political conception" of the person, adopted solely for the purposes of determining our public rights and responsibilities. It is not, he insists, intended as a general account of the relationship between the self and

its ends applicable to all areas of life, or as an accurate portrayal of our deepest self-understandings. On the contrary, in private life it is quite possible and likely that our personal identity is bound to particular ends in such a way as to preclude rational revision. (Kymlicka 2000, 159)

The issue of recognizing the autonomy of persons in the public political sphere of life, but with no need for such identification in other areas (what Kymlicka [2000] refers to as "private life"), evidently suggests a dual conception of self. If we follow Rawls's logic to its conclusion, we may break down the identity of persons into the public political or institutional concept of self and the nonpublic self-identification.[30] This dualism is vital to Rawls's political conception of person. One of the consequences of the duality of self is that the later Rawls no longer supports the idea that people's nonpolitical allegiances are sovereign choices. Rawls's political conception of person now asserts that nonpolitical commitments may be indispensable to people's identity because they may not be able to stand back from such ends, so as to reassess or revise them.

Nevertheless, citizens of modern liberal democracies are expected to put aside their attachments to nonpolitical ends, religious, philosophical, or moral, when they engage in public political debates. They should see themselves as citizens with the highest order interest in their capacity for autonomy, even if they lack such independence in their nonpublic lives. This dual conception of self of citizens depicts their pragmatic disposition for reaching political agreements on contentious issues. It derives from Rawls's efforts to provide a compelling argument for the public justification of political cohesion in the face of reasonable pluralism:

> Political liberalism incorporates a model of generalized discourse, in which participants seek to abstract from their particular—and conflicting—identities and aspirations, in order to discover bases of agreement with others that "bracket" the particular issues that divide them. The process of bracketing or abstracting from particular identities protects individuals against demands for unreasonable self-disclosure, while at the same time discovering bases on which mutually acceptable norms of justice can be developed. (Moon 1993, 98–99)

Since the conception of self (other than the political) is comprehensive and, as such, involves "truth" about the metaphysical doctrine of person, Rawls thinks that it would be sectarian and, therefore, unjustified to appeal to such truths in the public sphere.

Furthermore, if, for example, citizenship requires a particular religious test, then oppressive regimes could use force to foist a specific comprehensive doctrine on citizens, and this cannot be publicly justified in a genuinely democratic system. Rawls's political conception of person regards persons as free and equal citizens. This understanding, Rawls claims, derives from the public political culture of liberal democracies and stands free of any particular metaphysical or psychological affiliations. Rawls says that the political conception of person is a normative one; it is neither metaphysical nor psychological. Should there be any metaphysical assumptions inherent in his conception of person, Rawls says, they would be so broad that citizens would not be able to pinpoint whether they relate to realism, idealism, materialism, Cartesian, Leibnizian, or Kantian metaphysical concept of the person.[31]

The scope of the political conception of person is limited to the domain of the political. It applies only to persons as citizens of modern democracies and as cooperative members of the political society. It ceases to be operative in persons' nonpolitical spheres of life, which fall within the domain of the comprehensive understanding of self. According to Rawls, while this self-understanding can thrive in the contexts of the nonpublic or nonpolitical sphere—for example, in social clubs or associations, churches, and so on—such modes of self-understanding are not allowed, for instance, in a congressional debate of important matters of justice or the constitution.

Rawls's dualism of self is also the basis for the explanation of the freedom persons have as moral agents. Rawls views citizens as free persons in three respects. First, citizens are free in the sense of possessing the moral power to form, revise, and rationally pursue a conception of the good.[32] It does not follow from the political conception of person that citizens regard themselves as inseparably tied to a given conception of the good. Rather, citizens conceive of themselves as capable of evaluating and possibly changing their conception of the good at any time if and when reason prompts such an undertaking. Thus, according to Rawls, citizens as free persons have the right to view themselves as independent from any comprehensive conception of the good life. As free persons and citizens, Rawls maintains that when citizens make changes in their conception of the good, such as when they convert from one religion to another, their public political identities are in no way altered, although their nonpublic identity may be seriously affected.[33]

Second, Rawls says that citizens are free persons in the sense of being "self-authenticating sources of valid claims" against their government. This means that citizens can view themselves as empowered to make demands on their government in pursuant of their conception of the good or in their demand for good governance. These claims that citizens make are valid, according to Rawls, because they derive from the duties and obligations that the political conception of justice specifies.[34]

Third, Rawls considers persons as free citizens in the sense of being capable of assuming responsibility for the actions that they take toward achieving their life goals. From the standpoint of society as a fair system of cooperation, Rawls also thinks of citizens of liberal democracies as free persons because they are capable of adjusting their aims and aspirations to align with the behaviors of a people that see their society as a system of social cooperation. In Rawls's political liberalism, the political conception of person demands that citizens stick to their public identity when debating political matters or other issues of public interest. That is to say, citizens remember that they are first and foremost free and equal persons, sharing a fair system of social cooperation, and therefore exclude as much as possible from public consideration any issues originating from their comprehensive worldviews. Even if comprehensive doctrines constitute the meaning or essence of life for some citizens, they are, nevertheless, to be relegated to the background in the debate of public political matters.[35]

Rawls sees no difficulties with the dual conception of self. That citizens have dual identities, for him, does not mean that they have dual personalities. A change in a person's conception of the good, for Rawls, does not imply a change in personhood.[36] He cites the story of Saul's conversion to Paul on the way to Damascus in the Acts of the Apostles to illustrate this point: "I assume, that for the purpose of public life, Saul of Tarsus and St. Paul the Apostle are the same person. Conversion is irrelevant to our public or institutional identity."[37] For Rawls, the unexpected change in the conception of the good, the conversion of Saul of Tarsus to St. Paul the Apostle, the transformation from persecutor to the persecuted, significant as it may be, neither involved the alteration of his personhood nor affected his public political identity. This argument would lead Rawls to conclude that a majority of the citizens of liberal democracies will endorse his political conception of justice through an overlapping consensus. Although these citizens may be adherents of various worldviews, they still hold firmly to their public political identity as free citizens.

If we take a closer look at the story of Saul's transformation through his encounter with the light from heaven, Jesus Christ, one wonders whether people will give priority to their public identity over their nonpublic identity in matters of public significance. For example, the conversion of Saul brought about a sudden change in his conception of the good. Saul, the persecutor of followers of the new faith that would later be called Christianity, became a Christian himself. While such a change did not utterly rewrite the foundational properties of St. Paul's personhood, it undoubtedly influenced his public political identity and his idea of moral or religious truth. His political opinions about some core Jewish practices, such as male circumcision and interaction with the Gentiles, did change.

Therefore, it is difficult to see how most citizens of liberal democracies would justify political decisions in a way that violates their moral, religious, and nonpublic identity for the sake of their public political identity. It would be difficult for citizens to invalidate their comprehensive conception of what constitutes a good life and their religious, epistemological, or metaphysical standards of what constitutes a sound moral judgment for the sake of "political correctness." If Rawls's claim about the primacy of citizens' public identity over other identities were valid, some critics like Daniels (2000) and Mulhall and Swift (1997) think that Rawls's citizens will be diagnosed with moral schizophrenia or multiple personality disorder.[38]

v. Political conception of society

In the context of Rawls's political liberalism, modern democracies are multi-religious and multi-ideological because their citizens are proponents of diverse worldviews. Given this deep-rooted heterogeneity of faith, culture, and ideology, Rawls views society as a fair system of cooperation over time, from one generation to the next. Society conceived in this sense is fundamental to the understanding of the political conception of justice as fairness. Reasonable pluralism, as a characteristic feature of modern liberal democracy, makes it unreasonable to define citizenship in the liberal state along the lines of ideologies or religion. Rawls claims that "[i]n their political thought, and in the discussion of political questions, citizens do not view the social order as a fixed natural order, or as an institutional hierarchy justified by religious or Aristocratic values."[39] Thus, Rawls's idea of society can be distinguished from an association or a religious community, where membership may be based on some particular comprehensive moral values or a profession of faith. One noteworthy contention that communitarians have with *A Theory of Justice* is the claim that "the priority of the right over the good" makes society look more or less like the outcome of an agreement (social contract) between distinctive individuals or distinctive associations, cooperating mainly for the purpose of pursuing their pre-social, individual, or associational advantages, and without having any final common ends.[40]

Communitarians accuse Rawls's theory of undermining the importance of society primarily understood as a community. This goes hand in hand with other charges, such as the denial of the generally accepted fact that people's conceptions of the good and themselves are dependent upon a social matrix.[41] From a communitarian perspective, the social contract theory and its hypothetical original position of the early Rawls presuppose the assumption that people form their conception of the good and set the aims of the political society independently of society and through negotiation with other individuals.[42]

The later Rawls realigns his liberal theory to accommodate some communitarian objections, even as he claims that such criticisms are mostly motivated by a misreading and a misinterpretation of both *A Theory of Justice* and what the hypothetical original position stands for in the book. He emphasizes that "the original position is a device of representation whose function is to dramatize and articulate a particular substantive conception of the person."[43] Therefore, it does not make any explicit substantive claims about the priority of the individual over the community.

Rawls, in both his early and his later works, does not deny the fact that political society has effects on individuals. In *A Theory of Justice* as well as *Political Liberalism*, Rawls outlines various ways in which political society could influence the individual as a citizen, in shaping how one conceives of oneself, values, and esteems oneself and others, and what roles society could play in enabling citizens to realize their life prospects. Nevertheless, justice as fairness in its new form as a political conception does not promote the ideals of a community as communitarians would want it. Justice as fairness does not see the political society as a community united under one comprehensive religious, moral, or philosophical doctrine. Such an idea of social unity is an anathema for the political conception of justice because of the fact of reasonable pluralism. For Rawls, a liberal democracy based on communitarian ideals would lead to a denial of the basic liberties and rights of citizens and to the oppressive use of the state-legal force to maintain a system of communitarian justice.[44] Any efforts by anyone or group to impose such communal values on all citizens of liberal democracy is, in Rawls's view, divisive and subject to reasonable objection by citizens. The goods of the community, as promoted by communitarians, Rawls thinks, are reasonable goods which should be realized communally, rather than politically. For this reason, Rawls reminds us that "justice as fairness assumes, as other liberal political views also do, that the values of the community are not only essential but realizable, first in the various associations that carry on their life within the framework of the basic structure, and second in those associations that extend across the boundaries of political societies, such as churches and scientific societies."[45]

Contrary to the communitarian objections, Rawls argues that the political conception of justice as fairness embodies a conception of society that involves a commitment to shared common aims pursued by citizens, which is an integral part of citizens' nonpublic identity. Furthermore, Rawls asserts that his political conception of society requires that citizens affirm the political conception of justice as fairness, which equally implies that citizens share one primary political end—namely, the goal of supporting just institutions and granting justice to one another, besides the other goals they would realize through their political arrangement. Nevertheless, this common aim should not be misread, Rawls reiterates, to mean a conception of the good.[46]

vi. The morally true versus the reasonable

In *Political Liberalism*, Rawls makes use of the idea of the "reasonable" as a qualifying adjective for some key concepts in his recast theory. Such terms include reasonable pluralism, reasonable doctrines, reasonable peoples, and so forth. However, my primary concern in this section is limited to the context in which Rawls employs the term "reasonable" to establish the objectivity of justice as fairness as a political conception, and how he further utilizes the reasonable to justify the conditions for social cooperation. As I mentioned previously, Rawls's political constructivism adopts a method of political theorizing, which allows his liberal theory to be objectively evaluated not in terms of being true or false in any epistemological or metaphysical sense, but rather in terms of being reasonable. What does it then mean to say that a liberal theory is neither true nor false, but yet reasonable?

For Rawls, the question of moral truth or falsehood is irrelevant to justice as fairness because he does not present the political conception of justice as a morally true principle of justice in an ontological sense, but instead, as a conception that could become the basis for informed and workable agreement between reasonable parties. He insists that philosophy, as a search for the truth about independent moral or metaphysical order, cannot provide a justifiable foundation for a political conception of justice in a liberal society. That is to say, a political conception of justice whose principles espouse, for example, metaphysical, moral truth would cease to be a political conception and cannot be a focal point for an overlapping consensus. It would instead be another comprehensive, sectarian, and controversial doctrine. Rawls states that "[h]olding a political conception as true, and for that reason alone the one suitable basis of public reason, is exclusive, even sectarian and so likely to foster public division."[47] By employing the reasonable and shunning the use of moral truth, Rawls thinks that his political conception of justice is "neutral" to the comprehensive worldviews found in modern liberal democracies and can win their support in the form of an overlapping consensus.

However, Rawls's approach here is not without some philosophical objections, especially as it may seem that his political liberalism is willing to sacrifice established metaphysical or epistemological truths for the sake of a consensus. Furthermore, it would also seem that without the morally true, Rawls's political liberalism may have exposed itself to a new set of criticisms associated with value relativism, value skepticism, or even the "sin" of equating the reasonable with "truth." Habermas (1995), for example, raises some of these objections:

> But for Rawls, both moral realism and value skepticism are equally unacceptable. He wants to secure for normative statements—and for the theory of justice as a whole—a form of rational obligatoriness founded on justified intersubjective recognition, but without according them an epistemic meaning. For this reason, he introduces the predicate "reasonable" as a complementary concept of "true." The difficulty here is in specifying in what sense the one is a "complementary concept" to the other. Two alternative interpretations suggest themselves. Either we understand "reasonable" in the sense of practical reason as synonymous with "morally true," that is, as a validity concept analogous to truth and on the same plane as propositional truth. . . . Or we understand "reasonable" in more or less the same sense as "thoughtfulness" in dealing with debatable views whose truth is for the present undecided; then "reason-

able" is employed as a higher-level predicate concerned more with "reasonable disagreements" and hence with the fallibilistic consciousness and civil demeanor of persons, than with the validity of their assertions. (Habermas 1995, 123)

Habermas criticizes Rawls for his evasion in the use of the term "truth," a word which he assumes Rawls complements or replaces with "reasonable." In contrast to Rawls's claims, Habermas contends that political liberalism cannot be appropriately theorized without truth.

In response to Habermas, Rawls (1995) categorically states that the concept of the reasonable, as he uses it, calls for neither value skepticism nor some form of subjectivism in relation to the truth of moral values. He rejects any possible assumption that the idea of the reasonable is analogous to moral truth. For Rawls, while his political liberalism designates an objective judgment as reasonable, comprehensive doctrines see valid and objective judgments as true. The reasonable, he says, expresses a reflective attitude toward toleration because it invokes the "burdens of judgment"—that is, the idea that citizens of modern liberal democracies can have reasonable disagreements and yet obey the constraints of public reason.[48] Rawls's idea of reasonableness originates from his insistence that no citizen of modern democracy can be legitimately coerced to abide by specific political arrangements, except if such requirements can be justified by public reason, irrespective of whether the majority judges the citizen's worldviews as morally true or false.[49] Rawls's position is, in this sense, compatible with moral realism rather than with moral relativism or skepticism. Donald J. Moon (1993) buttresses this point:

> Political liberalism does *not* hold that morality is subjective; instead, it insists that there are a plurality of moral and religious positions that are rationally defensible, that there is no "best" way to live that is rationally warranted. Far from denying the importance of rational assessment in moral and political matters, political liberalism insists on it, for political liberalism is rooted in the belief that it is through rational discourse that such questions must be settled. What it does deny is that such discourse is capable of producing uniquely correct answers to these questions. Political liberalism is committed to pluralism, not skepticism or relativism. . . . Political liberalism insists upon fallibilism and pluralism, but neither of these positions is incompatible with realism. (Moon 1993, 102–3)

*Political Liberalism*'s use of the term "reasonable" instead of "morally true" is a progressive stance toward "otherness." It signifies the importance of liberal toleration for Rawls vis-à-vis the achievement of peace and stability in modern democracies, especially in the West, whose history had its share of bloody sectarian violence and religious wars.

## NOTES

1. Rawls 1996, xviii.
2. See also Beem 1998, 16.
3. Frazer and Lacey 1995, 234.
4. Galston 1989, 722–23.
5. Rawls 1971, 131–32.
6. See Rawls 1971, 542.
7. See also Galston 1989, 723.
8. See Rawls 2001, 1–4; Ingram 1996, 148; and Galston 1989, 723.
9. O'Sullivan 1997, 742.
10. Frazer and Lacey 1995, 236.
11. Ibid.
12. Habermas 1994, 82.
13. Dombrowski 2001, viii.
14. Rawls 1996, 11.
15. Ibid., 12–13.
16. See also Habermas 1999, 274.
17. See also Audard 1996, 171.
18. Rawls 1996, 134.
19. Rawls 2001, 188.
20. Rawls 1996, 14.
21. See Daniels 2000, 130.
22. Ibid., 130–32.
23. MacIntyre 1984, 221.
24. Mendus 1989, 56.
25. See Sturma 2000, 270.
26. See also Kymlicka 2000, 158–59.
27. Rawls 1971, 40, 70, 86.
28. Rawls 1996, xliii.
29. Rawls 1987, 6, 24; see also Kymlicka 2000, 163–64.
30. Rawls 1996, 30–32.
31. See Rawls 1996, 29; Frazer and Lacey 1995, 237.
32. Rawls 1996, 72.
33. Ibid., 30.
34. Ibid., 32.
35. See also Mulhall and Swift 1997, 197.
36. Rawls 1996, 31.
37. Ibid., 32.
38. See Daniels 2000, 129; Mulhall and Swift 1997, 197.
39. Rawls 1996, 15.
40. See Mulhall and Swift 1997, 203.
41. Ibid., 198, 203.
42. Ibid., 198, 203. See also Rawls 1996, 201.
43. Mulhall and Swift 1997, 198–99.
44. Rawls 1996, 146.
45. Ibid.
46. Ibid., 146, 202.
47. Ibid., 129.
48. Ibid., 149–50.
49. See also Estlund 1998, 253.

*Chapter Five*

# Why Public Reason Is Not the "Public Use of Reason"

## THE MEANING OF PUBLIC REASON[1]

Public reason in contemporary political philosophy presupposes the idea that democracy, as Amartya Sen (2009) describes it, is best seen as "government by discussion."[2] John Rawls reinforces this view when he writes in *Political Liberalism* that "[t]he definitive idea for deliberative democracy is the idea of deliberation itself. When citizens deliberate, they exchange views and debate their supporting reasons concerning public political questions."[3] My objectives in this chapter are twofold. In the first place, I would like to examine in more detail Rawls's use of the term "public reason" in political liberalism. Second, in claiming that Rawls's idea of public reason does not qualify as Kant's "public use of reason" and is, in fact, different in several ways from this Kantian concept, I argue against what has become conventional wisdom among contemporary social and political theorists in the Anglo-American tradition.

In this in-depth study of the distinction between the German philosopher, Immanuel Kant's (1724–1804) "public use of reason" (*der öffentliche Gebrauch der Vernunft*) and Rawls's "idea of public reason," I argue that whereas Kant viewed the public use of reason as a necessary condition for the advancement of the Enlightenment movement and philosophy within eighteenth-century Prussian society, Rawls sees public reason in *Political Liberalism* (1996) as a formal mechanism for citizens of modern democracies to justify their polity. The goal of Rawls's idea of public reason is to enable citizens of today's pluralistic, liberal democratic society to unearth a sustainable basis for coexistence, despite their sharp and often conflicting ideological, cultural, and religious differences. Furthermore, while Rawls's idea of public reason satisfies the requirements set by the principle of political legitimacy[4]—that is, the normative and political justification of the exercise of coercive, political power by the government in modern democracies—Kant's concept of the public use of reason affirmed the moral autonomy of the individual. As a comparative analysis of Kant's "public use of reason" (*der öffentliche Gebrauch der Vernunft*) and Rawls's "public reason" (which when translated into German is *die öffentliche Vernunft*), this chapter aims to bring some clarity to the debate about the origin, meaning, forum, and content of public reason in political theory.

But what constitutes public reasoning? Among contemporary political philosophers, the idea of public reason has no single, unified meaning. Rather, the term "public reason" is associated with a profusion of often conflicting interpretations attributable to the contentious debates among philosophers, political scientists, and other scholars in related fields about what qualifies as public reason. For some political philosophers, though, the answer is quite simple: public reason is identical with secular reason, as opposed to "public political"[5] arguments emanating from religious viewpoints.[6]

For Rawls, however, the answer is different. In *Political Liberalism*, Rawls construes public reason in terms of shared reasonability among citizens of modern, liberal democratic societies. Rawls states that "[p]ublic reason is characteristic of a democratic people: it is the reason of its citizens, of those sharing the status of equal citizenship. The subject of their reason is the good of the public: what the political conception of justice requires of society's basic structure of institutions, and of the purposes and ends they are to serve."[7] Yet shared reasonability for Rawls does not mean common reasonability understood as the reason people simply share in common in a given society. If that were the case, Freeman (2007b) reasons,

> Any society has a conception of public reason. In this sense the basis for public reason in a theocracy might be the Bible, the Koran, or some other religious text. But for Rawls the idea of public reason is essentially a feature of a democratic society . . . simply because people in a society commonly accept and reason in terms of a common religion does not make that doctrine part of public reason. . . . Differences among comprehensive views supply the background for Rawls's idea of public reason. (Freeman 2007b, 383)

Public reason for Rawls is reason implicit in modern democracy characterized by a plurality of possibly irreconcilable religious, philosophical, and moral doctrines. Rawls does not claim any originality in his use of the term "public reason" in political liberalism.[8] Instead, he attributes the source of this standard liberal concept to Kant: "This title [The Idea of Public Reason] is suggested by Kant's distinction between public and private reason in 'What is Enlightenment?' (1784), although his distinction is different from the one used here."[9] Rawls's allusion to Kant in relation to public reason in *Political Liberalism* (1996) warrants a substantial analysis of the concept. Such inquiry is necessary because there are other distinguished scholars who share Rawls's view of Kant as the first philosopher in the Western tradition to set a seminal conception of public reason in liberal theory.[10]

## KANT ON THE PUBLIC USE OF REASON

In his article "What Is Enlightenment?" (1784), Kant presents an astonishing distinction between the "public use of reason" (*der öffentliche Gebrauch der Vernunft*) and the "private use of reason" (*der Privatgebrauch der Vernunft*). He defines both terms in reference to the ongoing debate at the time about what constituted Enlightenment among the eighteenth-century Prussian educated public. Kant, in this article, defines Enlightenment—*die Aufklärung*—in the most provocative sense as emancipation from a self-incurred minority (*die Unmündigkeit*). The word *Unmündigkeit* (as Kant uses it in the text) signifies immaturity of the individual in the form of *"geistige Unselbstständigkeit,"* or lack of independence in the exercise of the faculty of reason:

> Enlightenment is man's exit from his self-incurred minority. Minority is the incapacity to use one's intelligence without the guidance of another. Such minority is self-incurred if it is not caused by lack of intelligence, but by lack of determination and courage to use one's intelligence without being guided by another. Sapere Aude! Have the courage to use your own intelligence! is therefore the motto of the Enlightenment. (Wood 2001, 135)

Kant may not have envisioned his article, which some experts cite as the reference point and historical groundwork for the discourse on deliberative democracy, to be anything more than an incendiary answer (rather than a philosophical treatise of immense importance) to a rhetorical question. Kant's "What Is Enlightenment," which appeared in the December edition of the journal, *Berlinische Monatsschrift* of 1784, was a response to a periphrastic question posed by a Lutheran pastor working in Berlin, Johann Friedrich Zöllner (1753–1804),[11] in the same journal a year earlier. In his article, *"Ist es rathsam, das Ehebuendniss nicht ferner durch die Religion zu sanciren?"*[12]—"Is it Advisable to Keep Validating Marital Alliance through Religion?" (translation mine)—Zöllner was antipathetic to the idea of making ecclesiastically instituted marriage redundant in the wake of the Enlightenment. His stance against validating marriage only through the courts was provoked by an anonymous article published in the September edition of the *Berlinische Monatsschrift* of 1783, which, he thought, hypothesized that church marriage undermined the Enlightenment. The anonymous piece, it turned out, was written by Johann Erich Biester (1749–1816), who with Friedrich Gedike (1754–1803) served as editor of the *Berlinische Monatschrift*. Both men had close ties to Zöllner because they all belonged to the same secret society, the *Mittwochsgesellschaft* (Wednesday society), also known as "Friends of the Enlightenment."[13] James Schmidt (1989) elucidates:

> Biester had argued that the presence of the clergy led the "unenlightened citizen" to feel that the marriage contract was unique in that it was made with God himself, while other contracts "are only made with men, and are therefore less meaningful." Because of this tendency to underestimate the importance of contracts which did not require clerical participation, Biester concluded that a purely civil wedding ceremony would be appropriate not only for the "enlightened citizen," who "can do without all of the ceremonies" but also for the unenlightened citizen, who would thus learn that all laws and contracts are to be equally respected. (Schmidt 1989, 271)

Zöllner in his rebuttal defended the sanctity of holy matrimony against the arguments of some people (a seeming jab at some famous philosophers) who, he claimed, confused the hearts and minds of people in the name of Enlightenment.[14] He insisted that in a time when religion had already taken enough beating from the so-called Enlightenment, the issue raised by Biester was ill-conceived; the family stood in grave need of support, especially that support which the traditional religious denominations provided (Schmidt 1989, 272)

As a footnote, Zöllner then asked in a sarcastic fashion, *"Was ist Aüfkalärung? Diese frage, die beinah so wichtig ist als: was ist Wahrheit, sollte doch wohl beantwortet werden, ehe man aufzuklären anfinge! Und doch habe ich sie nirgends beantwortet gefunden!"*[15]—"What is Enlightenment? A question that is nearly as important as: 'What is truth?' Should be answered first before one even begins to enlighten. However, I have never found anyone with the answer" (translation mine). Ironically, Zöllner's footnote generated a multitude of responses and stretched the debate about Enlightenment in Prussia a little further.[16]

Responding to Zöllner, Kant further claims in "What Is Enlightenment?" that the habit of self-incurred tutelage or immaturity (*Unmündigkeit*) is progressively becoming an accepted nature of humanity:

> Through laziness and cowardice a large part of mankind, even after nature has freed them from alien guidance, gladly remain in minority.... It is so comfortable to be a minor! If I have a book which provides meaning for me, a pastor who has conscience for me, a doctor who will judge my diet for me and so on, then I do not need exert myself. I do not have any need to think; if I can pay, others will take over the tedious job for me. (Wood 2001, 135)

Although Kant considers the question of self-liberation from this form of complacency a difficult task for the solitary individual, he nevertheless foresees a more fruitful approach toward emancipation in the collective effort of a reasoning public.[17] Kant views the public use of one's reason as a necessary condition for the Enlightenment movement: "Which restriction is hampering enlightenment, and which does not, or even promotes it? I answer: The public use of a man's reason must be free at all times, and this alone can bring enlightenment among men."[18]

The public use of reason calls for freedom from institutional constraints on the powers of the human intellect. Such limitations hinder independent, rational activities through the enactment of restrictive laws. Public reason also demands freedom from ecclesiastical authorities that substitute intellectual inquiries with dogmas. For Kant, the public use of reason necessitates the intellectual freedom of the "self" from any form of alien authority.[19] The public use of one's reason requires an inner ability and an act of radical courage to take up the task of thinking for oneself in public.[20]

Kant designates the use of reason by scholars—*die Gehlerte*—whose freedom of communication through writing and publishing enables the dissemination of scholarly information or opinions to transcend the confines of their immediate society, as an example of the public use of reason. The scholars or learned persons, through their writings, address the entire reading world—*die Leserwelt*—at large and are in the service of the authority of their consciences alone. In Kant's view, people working for civil and ecclesiastical establishments, who must obey orders from these authorities when communicating with the public, are exercising the private use of reason.[21]

Here, Kant conceptualizes the public use of reason in relation to the world at large as an unlimited audience.[22] The private use of reason, by contrast, is an act of communication addressed to a defined and limited audience. It is a form of reasoning directed by a superimposed authority for specified purposes. For example, government officials, priests in church services, and military officers in the service of the state exercise the private use of reason when contrasted with the public use of reason. Therefore, the private use of reason as an act of communication is neither free nor complete, since the agents engaged in this kind of reasoning act on orders which are not originating from their free will, but rather from the will of others.[23] In this case, the term "private" does not connote individual or private affairs in ordinary parlance, but rather points to circumstances in which a person gives up his or her freedom to embark on the service of some given ends set by an alien authority:[24] "In one's private use of reason, one behaves 'passively,' as 'part of a machine,' bound by an 'artificial accord' (*künstliche Einhelligkeit*) to promote certain 'public ends.' In this context it is 'impermissible to argue.'"[25]

From Kant's standpoint, the private use of reason, unlike the public use of reason, could be limited and censored without endangering the progress of the Enlightenment spirit—that is, the pursuit of universal rational truth by means of pure reason:[26]

> Thus a soldier may not quarrel with the orders given by his superiors, and a clergyman may not question the doctrines of his church in the course of performing his official duties. But both may argue against these same things (or say anything they like about the army or the church) in a published article or treatise addressed universally to the learned public. (Wood 2001, 307)

A necessary condition for the Enlightenment, however, is the freedom to reason independently and publicly without institutional fetters: "In one's public use of reason, one acts as 'a member of the complete commonwealth [*ganzes gemeinen Wesen*] or even of a cosmopolitan society [*Weltbürgergesellschaft*].' Here an individual 'may indeed argue without harming the affairs in which he is employed in part in a private capacity.'"[27] The sense in which Kant distinguishes the public use of reason (*der öffentliche Gebrauch der Vernunft*) from the "private" use of reason (*der Privatgebrauch der Vernunft*) discloses the role of philosophy and its associated freedom of reasoning in society, as well as the tension that exists between the free exercise of reason and the exercise of authority.[28] Underlying Kant's distinction between the public use of reason and the private use of reason is the meaning associated with the word "public"—*die Öffentlichkeit* or *das Publikum*—in eighteenth-century Prussia. On the one hand, the word public referred to the bourgeoisie, the state, or whatever was open and accessible to everyone. On the other hand, the term "public" stood for the learned public: *die literarische Öffentlichkeit*.[29]

Kant uses the term "public" in "What Is Enlightenment?" in reference to the learned public. He sees the "public use of reason" and the Enlightenment movement, first and foremost, as a matter for scholars (*die Gelehrte*) or philosophers, who engage with the principles of pure reason. Later on, according to Habermas (1989), Kant broadened the scope of who can be or should be enlightened to encompass anyone who understood how to make use of his or her reason publicly, which comprised both scholars and ordinary citizens. Accordingly, "[e]ach person was called to be a 'publicist,' a scholar whose writings speak to his public, the world."[30] Moreover, "public" in eighteenth-century Prussia had a definite meaning in relation to public discourse. Expressing one's view in public was synonymous with moral uprightness and justice,[31] whereas whatever could not be expressed in public was treated with some degree of circumspection.[32]

On further examination, Kant's distinction between the public use of reason and the private use of reason in "What Is Enlightenment?" reveals that what he refers to as "private" concerning the use of reason (civil, military, and ecclesiastical office holders) was generally considered as "public" in eighteenth-century Prussia. Kant's puzzling substitution of the meanings of the terms "public" and "private" in the use of reason exhibits a critical but politically subversive undertone.[33] Kant's critique points to the fact that institutional restrictions imposed on citizens by totalitarian or absolutist regimes, including perhaps the censorship of the "enlightened" king, Friedrich the Great II (1712–1786), constituted the greatest hindrances to the progress of the Enlightenment.[34]

## THE CONTENT OF RAWLS'S PUBLIC REASON

Modern liberal democracies are characterized by what Rawls calls the fact of reasonable pluralism. Thus, citizens of such democracies profess diverse religious, moral, and philosophical doctrines, which sometimes conflict with one another. Rawls's concept of public reason is an aspect of practical, deliberative democracy, which addresses the fact of reasonable pluralism. In this sense, public reason may be described as a discourse procedure or exercise in reasonable public dialogue designed to avert a possible political impasse in modern liberal democracies. Public reason enables citizens of the pluralistic, democratic society, who are proponents of diverse and often conflicting worldviews to reach a mutually engendered consensus (the idea of an overlapping consensus) on fundamental political issues, despite their trenchant differences. Also, public reason fulfills the requirements set by the principle of political legitimacy.

According to Rawls, a broadly liberal political conception of justice provides content for public reason. Such an understanding of justice must incorporate the following:

> First, it specifies certain basic rights, liberties, and opportunities (of the kind familiar from constitutional democratic regimes); second, it assigns a special priority to these rights, liberties, and opportunities, especially with respect to claims of the general good and of perfectionist values; and third, it affirms measures assuring all citizens adequate all-purpose means to make effective use of their basic liberties and opportunities. (Rawls 1996, 223)

A political conception of justice for any deliberative democracy will be incomplete, Rawls maintains, if it does not contain "guidelines of inquiry that specify ways of reasoning and criteria for the kinds of information relevant for political questions."[35] These guidelines of public inquiry found in the political conception of justice are, so to speak, the content of public reason. Rawls's guidelines of public deliberation enjoin citizens of modern liberal democracies to avoid making controversial claims in their debate of public political issues that concern what he calls "constitutional essentials" and "basic justice." Citizens should appeal neither to their religious, philosophical, or moral doctrines nor to contentious economic theories in such debates. Rather, they should appeal to plain or uncontroversial truths widely accepted by others and available to most citizens in a modern liberal democratic society. Such plain truths include claims originating from common sense, as well as assertions based on uncontroversial science.[36] Although the content of public reason is not a unitary set of information data or static form of political values, its variability is limited by the scope of the political conception of justice.[37]

It is necessary in Rawls's liberalism that citizens reason from within the confines set by the political conception of justice in order to realize the common good of the liberal-democratic society. When citizens adhere strongly to their divisive comprehensive worldviews, they usually tend to differ seriously on what constitutes the common good for all. For this reason, Rawls insists that in debating crucial public political issues, citizens of modern liberal democracies should exercise conversational constraints and refrain from imposing what they consider as the "whole truth" on fellow citizens. This is similar to the form of bracketing suggested earlier by Bruce Ackerman (1989) in his article "Why Dialogue?" In this way, divisive and irreconcilable issues emerging from citizens' comprehensive worldviews, which might otherwise threaten the basis of social cooperation, are excluded from the agenda of political debate:[38]

> When you and I learn that we disagree about one or another dimension of the moral truth, we should not search for some common value that will trump this disagreement; nor should we try to translate it into some putatively neutral framework; nor should we seek to transcend it by talking about how some unearthly creature might resolve it. We should simply say nothing at all about this disagreement and put the moral ideals that divide us off the conversational agenda of the liberal state. In restraining ourselves in this way, we need not lose the chance to talk to one another about our deepest moral disagreements in countless other, more private, contexts. We simply recognize that, while these ongoing debates continue, we will gain nothing of value by falsely asserting that the political community is of one mind on deeply contested matters. Doubtless the exercise of conversational restraint will prove extremely frustrating—for it will prevent each of us from justifying our political actions by appealing to many of the things we hold to be among the deepest and most revealing truths known to humanity. Nonetheless, our mutual act of conversational restraint allows all of us to win a priceless advantage: none of us will be obliged to say something in liberal conversation that seems affirmatively false. Having constrained the conversation in this way, we may instead use dialogue for pragmatically productive purposes: to identify normative premises all political participants find reasonable (or, at least, not unreasonable). (Ackerman 1989, 16–17)

At the core of this notion of conversational reticence is what Rawls terms the "criterion of reciprocity"—that is, the idea that reciprocity generates civic friendship in a liberal democracy. In showing reciprocity in public political discourse, citizens enter as equals into the public world of "others" and stand ready to propose or to accept, as the case may be, the fair terms of social cooperation. The "criterion of reciprocity" requires that decisions on issues touching on constitutional essentials and basic justice in the liberal state be made in terms each citizen believes the others could accept, even in the face of conflicting comprehensive worldviews.[39] Citizens' ability to explain to one another how the political values of public reason can sustain the policies they advocate or vote for, demonstrates fair-mindedness toward one another, which in turn engenders civic friendship and mutual respect.[40]

Furthermore, Rawls's "criterion of reciprocity" underscores the need for the justification of political power and cohesion in the liberal state. Like most liberal theorists, Rawls believes that political power in a modern liberal democracy is only justifiable when promulgated or exercised following the principle of political legitimacy. Accordingly, the state's coercive legal or political power is legitimate if, and only if, citizens themselves endorse it and if the principles governing such a state derive from the political values shared by most (if not all) citizens. Jeremy Waldron (1987) describes the principle of political legitimacy as follows:

> The liberal insists that intelligible justifications in social and political life must be available in principle for everyone, for society is to be understood by the mind, not by the tradition or sense of its community. Its legitimacy and the basis of social obligation must be made out to each individual. . . . If there is some individual to whom a justification cannot be given, then so far as he is concerned the social order had better be replaced by other arrangements, for the status quo has made out no claim to his allegiance. (Waldron 1987, 135)

Thus, citizens of the liberal state need to be on their guard at all times to make sure that parochial interests and factional doctrines do not pervade the principles governing their political system. The normative and political justification of power in the liberal state involves the search for political principles with self-supporting public morality, capable of generating broad acceptance among reasonable citizens of a pluralistic, liberal democratic society.[41] One way to derive such principles is through the use of public reason in public political discourses: "Public reasoning aims for public justification. We appeal to political conceptions of justice and to ascertainable evidence and facts open to public view, in order to reach conclusions about what we think are the most reasonable political institutions and policies.[42]

A modern, liberal democracy which grounds its public policies, institutions, and laws on a comprehensive worldview, has only succeeded in substituting public reason with a sectarian doctrine. In such a situation, Rawls says, the government would cease to be liberal, having demonstrated its willingness to coerce citizens on grounds opposed to their political conception of justice. That said, public justification of laws, government legislation, or political institutions does not imply that every individual citizen must be satisfied with every law or bill legislated by the government in a liberal democratic society, since a unanimous agreement on such matters by all citizens may be unrealistic. Instead, public justification requires that citizens be able to comprehend the processes and morally endorse the institutions from which government policies or legislations derive. As Tomasi (2002) elaborates:

> This liberal principle of legitimacy does not require that a person must agree with every particular rule, policy or court decision that is enforced by the liberal state. Rather, the ideal is that if many people agree to have some set of foundational principles regulate the basic structure of their society, including the process by which particular policies and laws will be arrived at, then they affirm the use of political coercion even regarding the particular outcomes they dislike. (Tomasi 2002, 4)

Thus, the liberal principle of legitimacy aims to resolve the tension that exists between the liberal conception of person as an autonomous agent and the normative justification of the state's use of its legal apparatus to coerce citizens.[43]

## THE FORUM OF RAWLS'S PUBLIC REASON

Rawls's concept of public reason addresses only a limited range of questions. Public reason, he maintains, does not cover all political issues and political debates in the public forum. It only applies to questions of public political matters of immense importance—that is, to "constitutional essentials" and "questions of basic justice." Taking the American political system as a starting point for what a liberal democratic society might look like, even though it may only represent an imperfect example, Rawls tells us what should count as constitutional essentials and questions of basic justice:

> Constitutional essentials concern questions about what political rights and liberties, say, may reasonably be included in a written constitution, when assuming the constitution may be interpreted by a Supreme Court or similar body. Matters of basic justice relate to the basic structure of society and so would concern questions of basic economic and social justice and other things not covered by a constitution. (Rawls 1996, 1)

In a more elaborate interpretation, constitutional essentials include the principles that specify the liberal democratic process and the structures of government. Constitutional essentials cover the basic rights and liberties of citizens in a liberal democracy. Such rights include, for example, the right to vote and be voted for, liberty of conscience, and freedom of association. Principles regulating social and economic inequalities may not count as constitutional essentials, but can be categorized as questions of basic justice.[44]

The limits set by public reason apply to public officials in a liberal democratic government, such as state legislators, Supreme Court judges, senators, and other officials in the service of the state, when they engage in public political debate. Public reason also regulates the activities of political parties and people engaging in political advocacy, when matters of constitutional essentials and basic justice are at stake.[45] Furthermore, public reason applies to ordinary citizens when they cast their votes on issues pertaining to constitutional essentials and questions of basic justice. Rawls is also keen to point out that there is a subtle difference between the idea of public reason and what he refers to as the ideal of public reason. Freeman (2007b) elaborates:

> The idea of public reason is the requirement in any democratic society that political power is exercised only pursuant to the political values of public reason when constitutional essentials and basic justice are at stake. The ideal of public reason is that of a well-ordered democratic society whose citizens generally accept a reasonable political conception of justice, which is regularly referred to in order to provide content to public reason and construe political values and their relative significance. (Freeman 2007b, 402)

For Rawls, the ideal of public reason is realized in the well-ordered democratic society when ordinary citizens cast their votes from the perspective of what each regards as an expression of the political conception of justice. Additionally, ordinary citizens achieve the ideal of public reason, when they conceive of themselves, reflectively and hypothetically, as public officeholders. Public reason demands that ordinary citizens review the laws and policies of the government. When necessary, ordinary citizens must denounce government officials who disregard the limits set by public reason.[46]

Ordinary citizens express the ideal of public reason through active participation in the electoral processes. However, this ideal is not a legal duty, but rather a moral obligation. The ideal of public reason does not call for the enactment of laws mandating ordinary citizens to vote against the impulse of their consciences or to stipulate the direction to which they should cast their votes on fundamental public political issues. Public reason allows for freedom of expression on such matters but imposes a moral obligation on citizens to honor the "duty of civility."[47]

Additionally, Rawls distinguishes his idea of public reason from the numerous forms of nonpublic reason in society. He avoids making a distinction between public reason and private reason. Private reason, strictly speaking, is incompatible with Rawls's political liberalism: "The idea of 'private reason' is a nonsense for Rawls, as reason always operates in a dialogical relation: it manifests itself as reasons that we present to others and express in a public, not a 'private' language."[48] The limitations imposed by Rawls's conception of public reason do not affect personal deliberations, reasoning within associations, religious groups, or independent organizations. Such proceedings take place within the domain of nonpublic reason: a sphere where comprehensive worldviews are properly operative and even required.[49] Dauenhauer (2000) provides a useful description of nonpublic reason: "The obvious example of an exercise of nonpublic reason is that which members of a church employ to establish norms for membership, to articulate church doctrine, and to determine what standards of conduct the doctrine calls for."[50]

Nonpublic reason, according to Rawls, may even have the status of public reason within the domain of background cultures. For instance, social organizations or religious groups may have specified rules and regulations, guidelines for deliberations or inquiries, which their members must honor in order to realize the particular aims of such groups or organizations. The criteria and methods of nonpublic reason vary because they are dependent on the specific objectives of each association or group, and on the conditions under which the group pursues these aims.[51]

## THE LIMITS OF RAWLS'S PUBLIC REASON

Initially, Rawls's idea of public reason was limited to what he framed as the exclusive view of public reason. The exclusive view of public reason in liberal theory, according to Weithman (1997), is remarkable for its tendency to exclude religion from the public political forum in the liberal state under the cloak of the separation of church and state. Weithman (1997), citing Carter (1993), writes, "The liberal tendency toward religion seems to generate a culture of disbelief, a situation in which religion has been relegated to the 'private sphere' and hence been trivialized."[52]

Rawls, apparently responding to charges of extreme exclusionism and excessive reticence, especially from religious groups, widens the scope of his idea of public reason originally propounded in the "Melden Lectures"[53] to douse the agitation of his critics. The revised idea of public reason, as found in *Political Liberalism* (1996), includes two additional views: the "inclusive view" and the "proviso" or "wide view." The inclusive view of public reason allows the introduction of religious or teleological arguments into public reason in situations of emergency, where true democracy is still far off. In such circumstances, arguments originating, for instance, from the Christian doctrine, and other comprehensive, religious doctrines may be freely employed to strengthen the existing form of public reason and to precipitate the emergence of just political order.[54]

The proviso or wide view of public reason allows citizens of a liberal democratic society to introduce into public reason, freely and at all times, arguments stemming from their reasonable, comprehensive religious, moral or philosophical doctrines, provided that "in due course" such arguments are replaced with those that reflect only the political values permitted by the political conception of justice. Arguments from comprehensive worldviews, when employed in public political deliberations, are only meant to support or complement the existing public reason. As Rawls warns, citizens of the liberal state should resist the temptation to replace public reason with secular or religious reason.[55]

The proviso, in the first instance, allows citizens debating serious public political issues to employ whatever arguments they believe complement the existing public reason, as long as they are willing to present only arguments from within the confines of their political conception when needed. These are reasons that their fellow citizens are willing to accept. Allowing citizens of the liberal state to introduce their comprehensive worldviews into public reason, Rawls insists, does not jeopardize the original aim of public reason or the public justification of political power in the liberal democratic state. Instead, Rawls argues, "citizens' allegiance to the democratic ideal of public reason is strengthened for the right reasons."[56]

In defending the use of comprehensive worldviews in public reason, Rawls argues that such views will provide additional evidence in support of public reason and thus motivate citizens to honor public reason.[57] Since the proviso is less restrictive than the exclusive view or inclusive view, Rawls believes that it will allow citizens of liberal democratic societies to explain to one another, from within their respective comprehensive worldviews, why they endorse the political conception of justice. In this way, citizens will come to have a deeper understanding of their different points of view, while at the same time affirming the same political conception of justice.[58]

By modifying his idea of public reason to accommodate comprehensive worldviews professed by citizens of the liberal democratic state, Rawls expresses respect for the reasonable, comprehensive worldviews existing in today's pluralistic, liberal democratic societies. It is also an acknowledgment of the fact that citizens of liberal democracies cannot readily abandon what gives meaning to their lives when participating actively in the political process. Furthermore, Rawls seems to have realized that appealing to shared political values alone may be insufficient in settling the fundamental issues of everyday politics in a liberal democratic society.

## PUBLIC REASON AND THE
## PUBLIC USE OF REASON RE-EXAMINED

A common attribute shared by Kant's "public use of reason" and Rawls's "public reason" is the importance of publicity. In both concepts, reason is a publicly exercised form of communication, subject to the scrutiny of the public. It is only by being publicly used that reason can have a normative force. Nonetheless, Kant and Rawls differ substantially on what reasoning publicly means and on what the term "public" stands for in relation to reason. For Kant, in contrast to Rawls, reason as a form of communication, which does not address the whole world at large but only a socially limited audience (for instance, a National Assembly or Congress), cannot count as the public use of reason. Though it may take place in a public forum and its audience may be numerically large, nevertheless, such a form of reasoning is incomplete.[59] The public use of reason transcends national and regional boundaries. It is a form of communication addressed to the entirety of reasoning humanity:

> The vindication of Kant's account of public reason lies in the thought that reasons be exchangeable among reasoners, hence that any reasons that are relevant for all cannot presuppose the contingencies of particular social or political formation. Universality is the heart of practical reason for Kant in that it is the model requirement that principles and standards be sharable by all even when not all can act on them successfully. (O'Neill 1997, 426)

In *Political Liberalism*, Rawls uses the term "public" in relation to the "political." Thus, his idea of public reason is purely a political concept.[60] The term "public political" in Rawls's *Political Liberalism* designates a separate domain, which is distinct from other spheres of social life. It is only within this distinctive sphere that public reason is operative. Also, unlike Kant, Rawls does not contrast "public reason" with "private reason," but rather with "nonpublic reason."[61] According to Frazer and Lacey (1995):

> He [Rawls] is presumably not prepared to say—as liberals frequently have said—that the public is the sphere of regulation while the private (whether this refers to sexual, familial or economic relations, or all three) is beyond regulation or intervention. That is, his use of the term "non-public" leaves open the possibility that certain aspects of non-public can and might be regulated. (Frazer and Lacey 1995, 242)

Rawls's public reason, unlike Kant's public use of reason, is directed at a politically defined and limited audience. It is reason targeted at a restricted range of fellow citizens in the liberal democratic state. For Kant, the public use of reason is a capacity common to all rational human beings, by which they search for universal truth; while Rawls views public reason as a form of reasoning constructed out of commonly accepted political values latent in the political culture of liberal democratic societies. Kant's public use of reason embraces the universal aspiration of liberating the whole of humanity from self-incurred immaturity. Rawls's concept of public reason is rather more contextual in nature.

The effective use of Rawls's idea of public reason depends largely on the shared sense of political identity and affinity among citizens of liberal democratic societies. In societies where such bonds of fellow citizenship do not exist or where political systems other than liberal democracy are in place, Rawls's public reason may not work.[62] From a Kantian perspective, political principles that fail to attract universal, moral support and validation by reasonable persons cannot be accorded the status of the public use of reason. Therefore, Rawls's idea of public reason does not qualify as the public use of reason in the Kantian sense. The regulated nature of Rawls's public reason attests to the specific role assigned to this form of reasoning in his political liberalism. It demonstrates that the question of political justification in Rawls's liberal theory is limited to domestic political issues within a given liberal democratic society. Consequently, Rawls's political liberalism does not consider investigating the internal structures of nonliberal societies or the organization of their basic structures as a primary area of interest.

Finally, Rawls thinks that public reason, as reason implicit in the public political culture of modern liberal democracies, must be commonsensical and noncontroversial. The principle of political legitimacy requires that citizens, who exercise coercive political power over one another, appeal to the reason that everyone can accept in the discussion of public political issues. The aim here is to enable citizens to achieve an overlapping consensus on the political conception of justice, even in the face of reasonable pluralism of conflicting comprehensive worldviews. Kant's public use of reason calls for a more radical approach to public reasoning, which does not shy away from controversies and ideological conflicts

## NOTES

1. An earlier version of this chapter was published as "Public Reason as a Form of Normative and Political Justification: A Study on Rawls's Idea of Public Reason and Kant's Notion of the Use of Public Reason in What is Enlightenment?" by Paul Nnodim in *South African Journal of Philosophy*, copyright © Philosophical Society of Southern Africa, reprinted by permission of Taylor & Francis Ltd, http://www.tandfonline.com on behalf of Philosophical Society of Southern Africa.
2. Sen 2009, 324.
3. Rawls 1999, 138.
4. In *Political Liberalism* (1996), Rawls sometimes refers to the principle of political legitimacy as the principle of liberal legitimacy or simply liberal legitimacy.

5. The "public political" is a special domain in Rawls's political liberalism. It is in this sphere that public reason is operational.
6. See also Audi and Wolterstorff 1997.
7. Rawls 1996, 213.
8. Political liberalism is a trend in political philosophy, as well as the title of Rawls's book, *Political Liberalism* (1993, 1996).
9. Rawls 1996, 213.
10. See O'Neill 1997, 411–28.
11. See also Heiner F. Klemme and Manfred Kuehn (eds.), *Bloomsbury dictionary of 18th century German philosophers* (New York: Bloomsbury Academic, 2016), 886.
12. See Frieder Lötzsch, *Philosophie der Neuzeit im Spiegel des Judentums* (Muenster: LIT Verlag, 2005), 117 / *Berlinische Monatsschrift* 1783, 509–16.
13. See Lötzsch 2005, 117. See also *Bloomsbury dictionary of 18th century German philosophers* (2016).
14. See Lötzsch 2005, 116–18.
15. Hölscher 1979, 99.
16. Besides Kant, Mendelson also wrote a rejoinder to Zoellner's article. See Lötzsch 2005, 116–31.
17. See O'Neill 1989, 32.
18. Wood 2001, 136.
19. Kant 1967, 58.
20. Sullivan 1989, 8.
21. See Kant 1967, 57.
22. O'Neill 1989, 32.
23. See Kauffmann 2000, 323.
24. See Clarke 1996, 148.
25. Schmidt 1989, 287.
26. See also O'Neill 1997, 424–25.
27. Schmidt 1989, 287–88.
28. See Clarke 1996, 140.
29. See also Hölscher 1979, 91–92, 103.
30. Habermas 1989, 106.
31. See Hölscher 1979, 99.
32. See also Kauffmann 2000, 321; Hölscher 1979, 103.
33. See Kaufmann 2000, 322–23.
34. Ibid.
35. Rawls 1996, 223.
36. See Rawls 1996, 224–25; Solum 1994, 218.
37. See also Hampton 1994, 202; Rawls 1996, 15.
38. See Rawls 1996, 157.
39. See also Reiman 2000, 108.
40. Weithman 1997, 4–5; Rawls 1996.
41. On a further interpretation, the liberal principle of liberal legitimacy enables citizens to review the legitimacy of their government, state policies, or laws. That is to say, citizens use the principle of legitimacy to ascertain whether their political system or government is worthy of their allegiance and loyalty, or illegitimate, and hence to be resisted or transformed by means of civil disobedience. See also D'Agostino 1996, 23; Macedo 1990, 280; George and Wolfe 2000, 2–3.
42. Rawls 1999, 155.
43. See Horton 2003, 5–23.
44. See also Greenawalt 1994, 674.
45. See Rawls 1999, 133; Solum 1994, 218.
46. See Rawls 1999, 56.
47. See also Quinn 1997, 146; Rawls 1999, 56.
48. Audard 2014, 208.
49. See Greenawalt 1994, 673.

50. Dauenhauer 2000, 210.
51. Rawls 1996, 221.
52. Weithman 1997, 1.
53. See Rawls 1996, 1999, 2001.
54. Rawls (1993) cites two prominent events in the history of the United States to exemplify this non-ideal situation: the movement for the abolition of slavery of the 1830s and the civil rights movement for the rights of the black ethnic minority of the 1960s led by Martin Luther King Jr.
55. Rawls 1996, lii; 1999, 152; 2001, 90. See also Greenawalt 1994, 685.
56. Rawls 1999, 153.
57. See also Dombrowski 2001, 115.
58. Rawls 2001, 90.
59. See also O'Neill 1997, 424.
60. See also Frazer and Lacey 1995, 242.
61. In *Political Liberalism* (1996), Rawls refers to Kant's distinction of "public use of reason" from "private use of reason" primarily to show how his idea of public reason differs from that of Kant.
62. Rawls 1996, 213; see also O'Neill 1997, 426.

*Chapter Six*

# Rawls's Idea of a Well-Ordered Society

## THE JUST AND FAIR SOCIETY

"Justice as fairness" is Rawls's theory of a just and fair liberal, democratic society. When teaching *Theories of Justice* to undergraduate students, I often solicit students' opinions on the prospects of realizing a Rawlsian model of society in the United States. The typical answer has always been that although the theory in itself is impressive, its implementation could become a wild goose chase because of the vested interests of corporate America and the few super-wealthy, influential citizens who impact public policies and public opinions.

In the previous chapters, I have extensively explored Rawls's idea of justice and, at various stages, presented elaborately much of the academic problems surrounding it. However, it remains for us to ask what the political landscape might look like for a society that practices Rawls's justice as fairness. For example, what system of government may be compatible with his two principles of justice? Rawls answers these questions in "The Idea of a Well-Ordered Society."[1] In both *A Theory of Justice* (1971) and *Political Liberalism* (1993, 1996), Rawls insists that a conception of justice is realistic only if it can model a stable, well-ordered society.[2] Therefore, the transition from potentiality to actuality or from theory to practice is undoubtedly for Rawls of primary importance. Otherwise, his entire treatise could only conjecture fanciful intellections with a utopian knack and nothing more. Nonetheless, it would not amount to a mistake if some scholars of political philosophy view Rawls's concept of the well-ordered society, at least *prima facie*, as an idealization.

As a liberal paradigm, the well-ordered society of Rawls may resemble any functioning, constitutional democracy, though its foundations do not derive from one particular, existing, democratic society. To bolster this claim, Rawls writes that "[e]xisting societies are of course seldom well-ordered in this sense, for what is just and unjust is usually in dispute. Men disagree about which principles should define the basic terms of their association."[3] Existing liberal societies may share to a large extent the essential elements of the well-ordered society, though they may not yet be perfectly well ordered in the Rawlsian sense. The well-ordered society is an ideal union of a particular kind because its status depends on the practical outcome of the extent to which justice as fairness can serve as a political conception of justice and a mutual basis for the governance of a just, fair, and stable society. The hope is that someday liberal democracies can model themselves after the Rawlsian ideal and, in so doing, realize justice as fairness.

The question of political stability is paramount for Rawls's idea of a well-ordered society. It revolves around the problem of political and social order and historically constitutes no less of a difficult task in political philosophy. For Thomas Hobbes (1588–1679), for example, the English Civil War (1642–1651) was a replay of the "State of Nature." As a staunch advocate of social and political order, he taught that unfettered exercise of repressive sovereign power would tame the "Leviathan" and bring about political stability. Classical political philosophers after Hobbes, such as John Locke (1632–1704), Jean Jacques Rousseau (1712–1778), and Emile Durkheim (1858–1917), took to a more egalitarian posture in their stability thesis by rejecting despotism as the solution to the problem of social and political stability, and pushing for some normative consensus among members of society instead.[4] Their propositions claimed that a social contract or a general agreement on a single conception of justice could be useful in resolving the issue of political and social order.[5] Rawls's stability thesis in *A Theory of Justice* is an offshoot of this tradition, except that he recognizes the futility of seeking the solution for social and political problems in contemporary times through a normative consensus on a single, comprehensive conception of justice. The current challenge, therefore, is to formulate a conception of justice that is appropriate for the complex and manifold pluralism of modern times.

As already discussed in chapters 3 and 4, the prompting factor for the justification of Rawls's substantial reworking of his earlier project was the unrealizable nature of the stability he envisioned for the well-ordered society. Rawls acknowledges in this context that the idea of justice as fairness, as he presented it earlier in *A Theory of Justice*, could not guarantee the stability of the well-ordered society because it was general in scope and not restricted to the domain of the political. Justice as fairness in *A Theory of Justice* was a comprehensive conception of justice, and as such, inappropriate for modern liberal societies characterized by the fact of reasonable pluralism of conceptions of the good.

What then has changed in Rawls's notion of a well-ordered society? How does Rawls present the stability of the well-ordered society in *Political Liberalism* that is patently different from *A Theory of Justice*? At the moment, stability for Rawls means not only that citizens follow the laws and rules that govern society but also that they freely approve the political conception of justice. Stability is predicated on the free allegiance of comprehensive worldviews to the political conception of justice. According to Rawls, any notion of justice that is unable to achieve this free and unconditional support from the majority of the politically active members of society is self-defeating and, therefore, incapable of serving as the basis for a well-ordered society. Incidentally, a stability thesis is workable only if a conception of justice appropriate for such purpose has been identified. To this end, Rawls adopts a two-stage approach in the recasting of justice as fairness in *Political Liberalism*:

> Justice as fairness is best presented in two stages. . . . In the first stage it is worked out as a freestanding political (but of course moral) conception for the basic structure of society. Only with this done and its content—its principles of justice and ideals—provisionally on hand do we take up in the second stage, the problem whether justice as fairness is sufficiently stable. Unless it is so, it is not a satisfactory political conception of justice and it must be in some way revised. (Rawls 1996, 140–41)

A well-ordered society, then, as theorized by Rawls, is a secure, stable, and fair deliberative form of liberal democracy, whose basic structures are regulated by the political conception of justice as fairness. Citizens of such a society, who are themselves reasonable persons endowed with a sense of justice, must see their polity reciprocally as a system of social cooperation:

> To say that a society is well-ordered conveys three things: first . . . it is a society in which everyone accepts, and knows that everyone else accepts, the same principles of justice; and second . . . its basic structure—that is, its main political and social institutions and how they fit together as one system of cooperation—is publicly known and with good reason believed to satisfy the principles. And third, its citizens have a normally effective sense of justice and so they generally comply with society's basic institutions, which they regard as just. (Rawls 1996, 35)

Upholding that every citizen in the well-ordered society accepts the same principles of justice implies that social cooperation between citizens must meet the "full publicity condition." Consequently, the basic structure of society—social, economic, and political institutions—must be sufficiently transparent to align with the publicity requirements, stand up to public scrutiny and accountability, and be publicly justified. To this end, the well-ordered society cannot be established on false or prejudiced ideology. Rawls says that "in a free society that all correctly recognize as just there is no need for illusions and delusions of ideology for society to work properly and for citizens to accept it willingly. In this sense a well-ordered society may lack ideological, or false consciousness."[6] The publicity condition that citizens abide by in the well-ordered society, which renders the knowledge of the principles of justice public and the acceptance of these principles mutual, institutes a shared basis for citizens to justify to each other their political judgments. From this perspective, citizens cooperate politically and socially on terms all can endorse as just.[7]

The well-ordered society, as Rawls intends, is a "complete" society in a sense unique to his theory. It is a self-sufficient society, providing an adequate means for the fulfillment of the purposes of human life. Setting the issues of immigration, emigration, and international relations aside, Rawls describes his archetypal society as a closed one: "entry into it is only by birth and exit from it is only by death. We have no prior identity before being in society."[8]

By being "closed," Rawls easily distinguishes the well-ordered society from an association, where membership is free or voluntary. Furthermore, the well-ordered society also goes beyond the ordinary concept of community because its basic structure is not arranged according to the values of one doctrine or group of comprehensive doctrines, but rather according to the values of the political conception of justice. While Rawls builds his well-ordered society around the meaning of a political conception of justice, the stability thesis for that society requires an additional idea: specifically, the idea of the reasonableness of persons who constitute the majority of its politically active citizens. The citizens of a well-ordered society are—if not altogether, then by a majority—reasonable persons. In addition to the capacity for reciprocity, good reasoning, inference, and judgment, reasonable persons also have two moral faculties—namely, the capacity for a sense of justice and the capacity for a conception of the good. The capacity for a sense of justice is the aptitude citizens need to be able to understand, apply, and act within the parameters of the principles of political justice, which specifies the fair terms of social cooperation.

The capacity for a conception of the good means the ability to pursue rationally what one considers the good and, when necessary, revise it.[9] According to Rawls, having these capacities, at least to a minimal degree, bestows on someone the status of equal citizenship and the competence for full, social cooperation. It also qualifies one as a "person" in an inimitably Rawlsian sense, which Rawls contrasts from the understanding of "human being" in both biology and psychology:

> This conception of the person is not to be mistaken for the conception of a human being (a member of the species homo sapiens) as the latter might be specified in biology or psychology without the use of normative concepts of

various kinds, including, for example, the concepts of the moral powers and of the moral and political virtues. (Rawls 2001, 24)

The sense of justice as a moral capacity stirs in citizens the desire and willingness to act reciprocally toward fellow citizens on fairgrounds acceptable to all and provides citizens with the motivation to honor the appropriate terms of social cooperation, to support liberal institutions, and the principles of justice. The absence of a sense of justice would only create a scenario of injustice and the collapse of law and order, expressing a major deficiency in what defines persons as moral beings. Rawls hypothesizes that "if men did not do what justice requires, not only would they not regard themselves as bound by the principles of justice, but they would be incapable of feeling resentment and indignation, and they would be without ties of friendship, and mutual trust. They would lack certain essential elements of humanity."[10] This capacity for the good enables citizens to acquire a reasonable understanding of the good commensurate with liberal democratic principles. It is a disposition that leads citizens to balance, revise, and abandon old conceptions of the good or to accept new ones. Furthermore, the capacity for the good allows for consistent ordering of the life goals and interests that people consider valuable. Reasonable people profess reasonable worldviews and honor the burdens of judgment, thereby creating room for tolerance.

## THE ACQUISITION OF THE SENSE OF JUSTICE

Rawls approaches the question of the stability of the well-ordered society from two perspectives. First, he asks whether citizens growing up under institutions regulated by the political conception of justice as fairness would develop a sufficient sense of justice to support those institutions. Secondly, given the fact that reasonable pluralism characterizes modern liberal societies, Rawls asks whether a political conception of justice is capable of achieving an unforced union of citizens' different worldviews and become a reference point for the adjudication of public policy issues, even though citizens profess diverse or even conflicting beliefs. Rawls answers the first question, which we may call the first stability question with his "moral psychology," and the second question with the "idea of an overlapping consensus."[11]

Rawls's moral psychology assumes that since persons have two moral capacities as citizens, they are also capable of being reasonable and rational. He postulates that under the conditions of certain psychological principles, citizens of the well-ordered society will naturally acquire a sense of justice and a reasoned allegiance to political and social institutions, as well as gain the motivation to honor the terms of social cooperation sufficient enough to render such a society stable. The conception of justice, according to Rawls, is naturally and psychologically suited to human inclinations, such that persons as citizens who have experienced life under a just government or a just social system will develop behavioral traits strong enough to overcome the usual tendencies toward injustice.[12]

If citizens are convinced that the institutions they live in and the social practices of daily life are just and fair, Rawls believes that they naturally would be willing to fulfill their duties in society, provided they are sufficiently assured that other members of the society would do their part. When others regularly and reliably perform their tasks in society, citizens develop confidence and trust in one another. Furthermore, Rawls thinks that this trust and confidence in one another would deepen if the fair system of cooperation is successfully managed and sustained over a long period, and if the institutions that guarantee fundamental rights and liberties are more willingly and consistently recognized in public political life.[13]

The development of children's morality and moral judgment provide Rawls the psychological basis to present a theoretical analysis for the acquisition of a sense of justice by the citizens of a well-ordered society, as well as explain how citizens become naturally disposed to act by such a view.[14] In presenting his moral psychology, Rawls tends to appropriate the behavioral, psychological perspectives of the rationalists' tradition over that of the social learning theorists. Rawls adopts the views of rationalist's tradition because they support the idea that the development of moral conception or the acquisition of moral judgment is not a set of *sui generis* dispositions forced onto an otherwise amoral child, but rather something that develops out of already existing natural (primitive) attitudes.[15] Rawls draws on Jean Piaget's (1896–1980) cognitive-developmental approach to morality and its interpretation by Lawrence Kohlberg (1927–1987).[16] In his approach, Rawls assumes that there are empirically verifiable stages of the child's moral development. Piaget's central thesis on moral development, on which Rawls grounds his "sense of justice," involves the possibility of unraveling a puzzle: How can individual, autonomous morality develop from the necessarily imposed (heteronomous) morality of the adult world (parent's authority)?[17]

To deal with this paradox, Piaget undertook empirical psychological analyses of children's behaviors, studying their interactions with parents and peers, and the changes in the evolution of interactive relationships over the years. For example, in the games with rules, he observed that children under the age of seven receive rules given by their parents or elders as "sacred" or of transcendent origin (from God or the State). Older children, by contrast, view rules as the result of mutual agreement among contemporaries and understand that rules can be changed on the basis of a democratically reached consensus. By the age of seven, Piaget noticed, children have developed a sense of justice that is often more important than obedience based on parental authority.[18]

Based on these observations, Piaget classified children's morality in two phases. These stages are divided into "the morality of constraint" and "the morality of cooperation." Piaget learned through his empirical research that the respect exhibited by the child moved from what he called unilateral respect for the authority of the parents to mutual respect among peers.[19] In *The Moral Judgement of the Child* (1934), Piaget notes that unilateral respect binds the inferior (the child) to a superior (the parent) and begets in the child a morality of obedience characterized by a heteronomy, which with time, and following social interaction with peers, declines and makes way for mutual respect characterized by autonomy.[20] Autonomy for Piaget is identical to the ethics of mutual respect. A person is thus morally independent if she is capable of making moral judgments free from external influences, particularly of grown-up authority or the moral decisions of adults around her. Semi-autonomy for Piaget is a transition toward obedience to the moral principle itself. Heteronomy, however, suggests the morality of duty in obedience to the adult.[21] Wright (1982) elaborates further:

> The young child first experiences relationships of unilateral respect with his parents. These induce in him a morality of duty, that is, a sense of obligation to keep parental rules and an understanding of those rules as authority based and therefore unchangeable (moral realism). Morality is heteronomous, that is, something external to be obeyed. Later, the child begins to experience relationships of mutual respect with peers; these make possible for the child the experience of co-operation and lead to the morality of aspiration and autonomy. Morality is internalized. The child originates moral judgments rather than applying parental judgments, and displays the cognitive signs of the morality of cooperation, such as taking account of intention and understanding rules as based upon mutual agreement. The basic formula is that morality is first heteronomous and subsequently autonomous. (Wright 1982, 213)

Following Piaget, Rawls declares that children who are growing up under just regimes, such as those regulated by justice as fairness, will pass through three psychological stages before acquiring a full sense of justice. As children, and later as adults, this sense will engender in these citizens sufficient motivation for allegiance to the conception of justice and democratic institutions, and thus bring about stability in the well-ordered society. These three stages, which in a sense correspond to Piaget's morality of constraint and morality of cooperation, Rawls designates as the morality of authority, the morality of association, and the morality of principles.[22]

## THE MORALITY OF AUTHORITY

The morality of authority is the first sequence in Rawls's developmental moral psychology. At this stage, children are entirely dependent on their parents and submit themselves to parental jurisdiction because of their utter helplessness and ulterior motives. At this stage, self-interest and instrumentally valued acts are the chief motivators for the child's obedience to her parents' orders. The child has a sustained desire for existence, protection, and guidance from her parents.[23] It is at this stage that Rawls proposes the first psychological law, which posits that if one accepts that the family is an integral part of the basic structure of society and, on that account, just, then the authority of the parents over the child is legitimate at this stage. If the parents love their child, she will in turn love and trust her parents: "In due course, the child comes to trust his parents and to have confidence in his surroundings; and this leads him to launch out and to test his maturing abilities, all the while supported by their affection and encouragement. . . . And this brings about his love for them."[24]

Rawls further argues that since children lack standards of criticism, they are unable to subject the injunctions of their parents to critical or rational evaluation. For this reason, parents at this stage can easily "program" their child to follow one belief or the other that they support. For the sake of love and trust, the child is eager to meet the demands of her parents. Since, at this stage, she still sees her parents' authority as a restriction, she will most likely explore her limits within the bounds of parental authority, and in so doing, violate her parents' precepts once in a while. When that happens, the child will develop a feeling of guilt and seek reconciliation through the love and trust of her parents. Children see their parents as role models, such that when the parents live exemplarily by fulfilling their share of demands, the children will strive to imitate their parents. Children will obey the parents' injunctions even in the absence of threats of punitive action, and even if they consider some of their parents' orders arbitrary or unfavorable to their natural inclinations. The development of the morality of authority by children, Rawls says, is only possible through the love and affection of parents: "In the absence of affection, example, and guidance, none of these processes can take place, and certainly not in loveless relationships disrupted by primitive threats and reprisals."[25] For this reason, Rawls considers the morality of authority transitory and subordinate to the principles of rights and justice, which can determine the moral merit of precepts independent of affections.[26]

## THE MORALITY OF ASSOCIATION

Here, just as in the first stage, the older child acquires, in addition to her parents, new role models through association. The child's association can be the school environment, the community, or an organization. Exemplary people within any of these segments of society can be role models to the child. These role models engender in the older child the desire to imitate or internalize the standards of the group and to establish bonds of friendship, confidence, and trust among associates.[27] At this stage, Rawls argues, the older child tends to fulfill her duty and obligation within the group once there is the evident intention that other members of the association are willing to do their share. The failure to fulfill her cooperative assignments produces in the older child (just like in the former stage) feelings of guilt toward her peers within the group and the desire to make right any wrongdoings through reparation. However, the failure of others, equals, and associates in the group to do their part by being dishonest or unfair generates in the older child the feeling of resentment and indignation.[28] Rawls further elucidates the morality of association through the second psychological law: "Thus once a person's capacity for fellow feeling has been realized by his acquiring attachments in accordance with the first psychological law, then as his associates with evident intention live up to their duties and obligations, he develops friendly feelings toward them, together with feelings of trust and confidence."[29]

## THE MORALITY OF PRINCIPLES

In this last stage, the child who is now a fully cooperating member of society develops a complete sense of justice. Progressing through the three phases, the child realizes that social cooperation based on mutual trust, confidence, and empathy for others is for the general good of society. The sense of morality acquired at the previous stage is taken to a higher level of generalization, which widens the range of cooperative arrangements by progressing from the affection of parents and the fellow-feeling of associates to a sense of justice expressed in the principles of justice governing society. McClennen (1999) expounds on this when he remarks:

> On Rawls's account, it is a perception that others are intending to act for our good (as exemplified, for example, in the loving care of our parents) that sets in motion the developmental process culminating in our having a sense of justice. But the primal capacity for a loving response is transformed into a sense of justice via the mediating effect of experiencing successively more abstract forms of association in which the perception of others as directly caring for us is replaced by a sense of others doing their part, and of institutions arranged, in ways that work to our own benefit. (McClennen 1999, 150)

For Piaget, as well as for Rawls, who adopts much of his theory, the central thesis appears to be that genuine morality or autonomous morality, which expresses the sense of justice, derives from cognitive abstractions acquired through social cooperation. Thus, Rawls maintains, that the sense of justice provokes in citizens the desire to uphold just institutions in which they and those they care about are the beneficiaries. Stability of the well-ordered society requires, in Rawls's view, that persons as citizens possess this sense of justice that he has been delineating, which is a natural motivation and desire to act in ways congruent with the principles of justice as fairness (as a political conception). Rawls's reliance on less controversial psychological claims goes a long way to demonstrate that a stable, liberal democratic society modeled after the well-ordered society of justice as fairness is a real possibility for humanity. Paul Weithman (2009) writes in support of this opinion:

> Why does the stability argument show that a just society is a "real possibility" rather than a merely logical one, coherent but remote and unlikely? The argument does not appeal to highly improbable claims about human motivation, nor is stability said to depend upon heroic or supererogatory action. Rather, both stages of the stability argument draw on what Rawls thought are plausible and reasonable psychological claims, together with claims about the educative effects of just institutions. It is therefore reasonable to suppose that creatures with our nature who grow up in a just society could sustain it. Because the argument draws on relatively weak psychological assumptions, it shows that such society is a "real possibility" for us and that we have a "moral nature" rather than a nature that is "unfriendly" to justice. (Weithman 2009, 119)

## RAWLS'S OVERLAPPING CONSENSUS

Rawls introduces the idea of an "overlapping consensus" in his political liberalism with the sole purpose of presenting his well-ordered society to the reader as a possible social world.[30] In *Political Liberalism*, he distinguishes stability for the right reasons based on the idea of an overlapping consensus on his political conception of justice from the mere balance of power among various groups in society. As a distinct notion of stability, an *overlapping consensus* is a consensus on the political conception of justice. It is an agreement that draws support from the diverse and sometimes conflicting doctrines, beliefs, and values that the citizens of modern liberal democracies profess. The fact that this consensus is a convergence of a plurality of conflicting views on the political conception of justice implies that the possibility of achieving lasting stability, through such an agreement, depends on the nature of the political conception of justice itself. According to Rawls, the political conception of justice is in a position to gain full acceptance from the conflicting pluralism of worldviews because its demands and conditions relate only to the basic structures of liberal societies.

The acceptability of the political conception of justice does not presuppose favoring a given reasonable comprehensive doctrine over others. Above all, the source or origin of the political conception lies within the public political culture of liberal democracy. For this reason, one can argue that citizens of liberal democracy are, somehow, vaguely conversant with the demands of the political conception of justice and where it stands in relation to their reasonable worldviews.[31] The overlapping consensus on the political conception of justice has an ecumenical character because it is not only an essential point of confluence for reasonable doctrines but also a place of fair adjudication for these doctrines when they conflict with one another. The overlapping consensus can assume this ecumenical posture because it is compatible with all reasonable, comprehensive doctrines that democratic citizens profess without compromising itself.

Habermas (1996), in his analysis of Rawls, affirms that political liberalism is a response to the challenges of pluralism and that its concern is a necessary political consensus that ensures equal freedoms for all citizens regardless of their cultural background, religious beliefs and individual lifestyles. Concerning the multiculturalism that political liberalism addresses, Habermas acknowledges that the desired consensus that such pluralism necessitates in a modern democracy can no longer be based on a traditionally accustomed ethos, on society as a whole, even as members of modern societies still share the expectation of cooperating fairly and non-violently with one another.[32]

According to Rawls, the overlapping consensus has three distinctive features:[33]

i. It is a consensus of reasonable doctrines on the political conception of justice, as opposed to unreasonable doctrines.
ii. The political conception on which the consensus builds is a freestanding view.
iii. An overlapping consensus is not a mere *modus vivendi*.

First, in addition to the political conception on which the consensus is grounded being "freestanding," Rawls maintains that the consensus is an agreement of reasonable worldviews and doctrines, an agreement backed by reasonable citizens, as opposed to a consensus of irrational beliefs or doctrines that are implemented by equally unreasonable individuals. This depends, of course, on Rawls's particular understanding of "reasonable."[34] The overlapping consensus is such that citizens' support for it is not based on selfishness or self-interest, but rather on the merits of the consensus alone or moral grounds. From this perspective, Rawls argues, that citizens who support the overlapping consensus, would continue to do so regardless of any possible shift in political power or regardless of whether the comprehensive view they endorse becomes central or loses significance in society. The overlapping consensus can come about in this sequence. First, comprehensive doctrines endorse the political conception, each from its vantage point. Second, when the majority of the politically active citizens, who are proponents of reasonable doctrines, endorse the political conception of justice, and when there is no obvious conflict between these doctrines and the political conception of justice, then there is political stability. This happens when the demands of justice do not clash intensely with citizens' foremost interests.[35]

For opposing worldviews to endorse the overlapping consensus successfully, citizens who profess these views must embed their personal, rational conceptions of the good into the political conception of justice. Rawls explains this process with an analogy from logic: "Since different premises may lead to the same conclusions, we simply suppose that the essential elements of the political conception, its principles, standards, and ideals, are theorems, as it were, at which the comprehensive doctrines in the consensus intersect or converge."[36] The central element uniting the various conflicting views on the political conception of justice is their supposed reasonableness. Though Rawls expects all the reasonable worldviews in society to endorse the political conception of justice, each, however, is to engage in this process independently and for different reasons. For instance, a religious person may endorse the political conception because her religious practices encourage toleration and support the basic liberties of a constitutional democracy, which the political conception of justice fully expresses. Another citizen, for example, may affirm the political conception based on her secular moral orientations following the comprehensive liberalism of, let us say, John Locke or Immanuel Kant. Yet another citizen may approve of the overlapping consensus for reasons other than religion or secularism. These reasons may include less systematically articulated views or long-held political values that resonate with the idea of justice as fairness. Furthermore, differing metaphysical positions may find common interests in Rawls's overlapping consensus. Moral realists, moral constructivists, and even skeptics can agree with the essential content of the overlapping consensus, and they can do this for very different reasons.[37]

Regarding comprehensive worldviews, Rawls's notion of reasonableness is a liberal concept, which reminds the reader that his political liberalism is for liberal democratic societies only. Therefore, certain worldviews which from the standpoint of Rawls's understanding might appear fundamentalist or irrational are not part of the overlapping consensus. From this liberal position, for example, right- and left-wing extremists, as well as religious fanatics, have no place in the overlapping consensus.[38] A surprising candidate for Rawls's overlapping consensus is utilitarianism, a puzzling inclusion, which critics regard as either a mistake or an inconsistency.[39] Let us recall that Rawls spent considerable time in *A Theory of Justice* (1971), exposing the flaws of utilitarianism among the systems of egalitarian justice.[40] Even more than a decade after the publication of that book, Rawls consistently ruled out utilitarianism as a possible candidate for the overlapping consensus, and even when he tinkered with that possibility, he was sure to add a stringent caveat: utilitarianism must recast its fundamental features.

In "The Idea of an Overlapping Consensus" (1987), for example, Rawls insists that utilitarianism is not part of the consensus:

> It seems that while some teleological conceptions can belong, others quite possibly cannot, for example, utilitarianism. Or at least this seems to be the case unless certain assumptions are made limiting the content of citizens' desires, preferences, or interests. Otherwise, there appears to be no assurance that restricting or suppressing the basic liberties of some may not be the best way to maximize the total (or average) social welfare. (Rawls 1987, 433)

By the mid-1990s, Rawls's view on the inclusion of utilitarianism in the overlapping consensus had changed. For example, in *Political Liberalism* (1996), he claims that the utilitarianism of Bentham and Sidgwick would not have rejected his political conception; instead, the utilitarian may rather see it as "perhaps even the best, workable approximation to what the principle of utility, all things tallied up, would require."[41]

Although the inclusion of utilitarianism in the overlapping consensus may serve to bolster the range of compatibility of the political conception of justice with reasonable comprehensive doctrines, it is nonetheless, as some critics contend, an inconsistency. Scheffler (1994), for example, argues that it would be self-destructive for utilitarians to support Rawl's conception of justice since the constructivist modeling of justice as fairness (as a political conception) derives from fundamental ideas of the public political culture of liberal democracies. The essential features of these ideas include the understanding that society is a fair system of social cooperation between free and equal persons and the fact that the principle of reciprocity is integral to this conception of society. Both ideas are definitely incompatible with the mainstream utilitarian thinking:

> Rawls emphasizes that an overlapping consensus is a consensus not just on principles of justice but also on the fundamental ideas implicit in the public political culture from which those principles are derivable. . . . Indeed, what makes an overlapping consensus on a political conception of justice possible is precisely the fact that the political conception is developed from shared ideas. Accordingly, the original position is now to be construed as modeling certain of those shared ideas, and Rawls's arguments to the effect that his principles would be chosen in the original position are to be interpreted as beginning from those ideas. Yet many of these arguments are explicitly directed against utilitarianism. If utilitarianism is said to be included in the overlapping consensus on Rawls's two principles, then are we to imagine that utilitarians endorse Rawls's arguments for the rejection of utilitarianism even as they continue to affirm that view? This seems incoherent. (Scheffler 1994, 9)

Rawls's inclusion of utilitarianism in the overlapping consensus may have given extra gravitas to his critics, who think that his argument for stability of the well-ordered society, powered by the idea of an overlapping consensus, is not defensible because, after all, comprehensive doctrines are very unlikely to endorse the political conception of justice. Rawls's argument to this regard is not less potent than that of his critics. He points out that in the discussion of a political and social agreement by means of an overlapping consensus that his critics are wrong to focus exclusively on committed partisans of fully articulated and reasonable comprehensive doctrines. In any case, the consensus in question is a consensus of persons as citizens and not of theories.[42] He insists that the overlapping consensus is achievable and draws empirical support from the history of liberal democracies, which attests that their basic institutions can and do attract the moral support of citizens. Rawls further argues that, in reality, most citizens of liberal democracies do not follow well-articulated or fully comprehensive moral doctrines, instead exhibiting a looseness (some room for inaccuracy or ambiguity) toward comprehensive doctrines. That is to say that citizens only follow a set of values at varying degrees of generality, whose implications for the political conception of justice are not clearly defined. In other words, Rawls assumes that on specific issues of political concern, citizens' comprehensive views may be silent.

For this reason, Rawls postulates that most citizens of liberal democracies would affirm the political conception of justice even if they do not see any particular connection between it and their worldviews.[43] Also, Rawls says that the overlapping consensus is feasible because the political values and virtues of social cooperation that it expresses are essential and have preeminence over citizens' nonpublic or nonpolitical ideals stemming from comprehensive conceptions of the good. Such important and overriding values include justice expressed by the two principles, which comprise the values of equal political and civil liberty, fair equality of opportunity, and the values of economic reciprocity that the difference principle embodies and the social basis of mutual respect, as well as public reason and its associated virtues of reasonableness and fair-mindedness. Rawls is confident that should a conflict arises between the political conception of justice and citizens' comprehensive worldviews, that citizens would subordinate their nonpublic and nonpolitical values to the political conception. He is confident that citizens would be ready and willing to revise their moral, religious, or philosophical doctrines, rather than reject the political conception of justice.[44] To act otherwise would amount to unreasonableness on the part of the citizen.[45]

## *MODUS VIVENDI* VERSUS STABILITY FOR THE RIGHT REASONS

Rawls's notion of stability, which is closely related to the idea of an overlapping consensus, represents a freely entered agreement of citizens. His concept of stability is not an enforced homogeneity. It is on this basis that the overlapping consensus sharply contrasts with another form of stability that Rawls calls a *modus vivendi* or balance of power. The stability that Rawls approves for the well-ordered society is "stability for the right reasons."[46] Rawls's view of stability in political liberalism is rooted in his desire to achieve justice first before considerations of political stability. Charles Larmore (1996), for example, stresses that "[s]tability is not the ultimate value by which a political system is to be judged. Justice is a more important political value, though stability is itself often a sign of justice."[47] Likewise, for Rawls, the problem of stability is not about forcing citizens who may reject the political conception of justice to accept it, as if the task of political liberalism was to impose a given notion of justice on citizens once convinced that such an understanding is sound. The political conception of justice, which is the focus of the overlapping consensus, must freely win the support of reasonable citizens.[48]

Moreover, Rawls maintains that the overlapping consensus is not merely a practical tool with the tactical aim of avoiding conflict or narrowing the gap between diverse conceptions of the good life by identifying whatever citizens of liberal democracy can agree to despite their profound differences.[49] The overlapping consensus is a consensus reached on moral grounds, affirmed by citizens on its merit. Unlike a *modus vivendi*, it is not an agreement based on accepting the directives of certain authorities or complying with certain institutions because of self-interest or group interest.[50]

For Rawls, citizens' affirmation of the overlapping consensus on moral grounds would lead to more enduring stability than a *modus vivendi*. Citizens in the well-ordered society, whose stability is established in the overlapping consensus, live with one another under a social arrangement founded on the principles of justice as fairness. It is not an enforced cohabitation made possible by a political compromise.[51]

Rawls is not alone in pointing out the inadequacy of a *modus vivendi* to guarantee lasting peace. In the book, *Kleinere Schriften zur Geschichtsphilosophie, Ethik und Politik* (*Basic Writings on Philosophy of History, Ethics, and Politics*—translation mine), Kant (1964) likens such an idea of stability to the fable of Mr. Swift's house, which was perfectly built by a master builder according to all laws of equilibrium, but when a sparrow sat on the structure, it immediately became clear to everyone that the house was a mere figment of the imagination.[52] A balance of power, Kant declares, may sound great in the theories of Abbe de Saint-Pierre (1658–1743) or Rousseau (1712–1778), but it is bound to fail when put into practice.[53]

Rawls, for his part, equates *modus vivendi* to a Hobbesian truce, a balance of power among contending views and values between groups or states engendered by self-interest. Thus, he writes that "[w]hen Hobbes addressed the contentious divisions of his day between religious sects, and between the crown, aristocracy, middle classes, the basis of his appeal was self-interest. . . . On this basis, he sought to justify obedience to an existing effective . . . sovereign."[54] An example of a *modus vivendi* between states in modern times is the historical period of the Cold War between the United States and the Soviet Union. Although the period of the Cold War was relatively stable, it was, nevertheless, stability based on a balance of power, informed by exhaustion and suspicion or "mutually assured destruction." Neither side was confident that its military capability would guarantee victory over the other; each side then sought to avoid direct conflict, while being filled with suspicion and animosity against the other. Political stability under the superpowers throughout that period was not based on mutual reasons, but rather on the fear of the other's capability to inflict harm.[55]

In his political liberalism, however, Rawls's primary concern is stability within a liberal democratic society. Thus, the *modus vivendi* he talks about refers to the stability that arises out of the balance between contending comprehensive worldviews in society. Something close to this idea might be the pact between Catholics and Protestants that ended the bloody religious wars in Europe following the Reformation in the sixteenth century. The Christianity of the Reformation period was a comprehensive religious doctrine of the good and a salvationist religion. However, the clash of gods was not the reason for the conflict that bedeviled that period. Rawls specifies that it was the interpretation given to the essential doctrinal teaching of the good, which originated from both the competing authorities of the Catholic Church and differing interpretations of the Bible that led to sectarian violence. There was no resolution between the Catholics and Protestants, since the opposing and conflicting transcendent elements within the two did not allow for a compromise.

Thus, only circumstance and exhaustion could end the bloody wars. Both Catholics and Protestants had exhausted all efforts to bring the other, either freely or by the use of force, to show allegiance to the others' confessional doctrine. Therefore, they had to sign a peace treaty (*modus vivendi*), a necessarily tenuous situation, which was motivated not by right moral reasons, but self-interest.[56] As such, a *modus vivendi* is a precarious situation of peace because as soon as one party to the agreement has relatively more political, military, or numerical power than the other, it becomes very tempting to break the same treaty and dominate the other. Rawls sees a *modus vivendi* as inherently unstable: "For Rawls, a *modus vivendi* is nothing more the grudging acceptance that under present circumstances one cannot compel others to live according to the tenets of his or her comprehensive doctrine. But should circumstances change, then such a person would no longer feel obliged to observe the terms of the *modus vivendi*."[57]

A *modus vivendi* conceived in this way is nothing other than a binding agreement for relative or momentary stability between irreducibly and incommensurably hostile doctrines. The duration of stability constituted on a *modus vivendi* is, according to Rawls, dependent upon the fortuitous conjunction of contingencies and vagaries of circumstances engendered by self-interest.[58] Rawls insists that the stability of the well-ordered society must transcend a mere *modus vivendi*, it must be stability spawned by the right moral reason, which the overlapping consensus on a political conception of justice makes possible. It must be stability whose strength is not dependent on happenstance or the balance of relative forces.

However, Rawls does not exclude a *modus vivendi* entirely from the stability thesis of his well-ordered society. A *modus vivendi* might be a viable, strategic step to stability for the right reasons, especially in situations when stability is desperately needed under unideal circumstances. Rawls argues that balance achieved in such conditions, on an initial basis as a *modus vivendi*, can still possibly progress from that standpoint to a constitutional consensus, and later to an overlapping consensus. A constitutional consensus recognizes certain principles of justice. Still, it does not require that society be a system of cooperation with a moral and political conception of persons and a shared public conception of justice.[59] Rawls hypothesizes that a society's journey to an *overlapping consensus* might begin with an initial *modus vivendi*.[60] He cites the example of the truce of the Reformation period to support this view. As the old truce between Catholics and Protestants can attest, people who initially enter into a peace accord on practical grounds for the cessation of hostilities may through their experience of living under a relatively peaceful society, come to appreciate the goods of peaceful coexistence and endorse their system for reasons that trump mere instrumental considerations:

> At least, explicit acceptance of this notion of minimal toleration would most likely be predicated on the notion that it was preferable to the alternative: sterile, destructive, costly and wasteful war. But Rawls's claim is that as the parties experienced the quality of life made possible by terms of the agreement, they were able to endorse the public principles of justice associated with it. Not only would these principles have a palpable instrumental value, it would also be possible for both sides to endorse them from within the conception of the good that defines each of the parties. (Milde 1995, 149)

## SKEPTICISM ABOUT RAWLS'S WELL-ORDERED SOCIETY AND STABILITY THESIS

Here we are to explore, first, Amartya Sen's critique of Rawls's idea of the well-ordered society of justice as fairness and, second, whether Rawls's stability thesis is feasible. John Horton (2017) in his essay "What Might it Mean for Political Theory to Be More 'Realistic'?"[61] writes that much of the recent normative political theory published in English resembles episodes from NBC Television's American serial political drama *The West Wing* because it "presents us with a highly idealised image of how political life should be that is basically at best an edifying fantasy" by ignoring "the motivational and practical complexities of political life."[62] However, in what seems to be a balanced analysis, or even an effort to rescue normative political theory from the garbage, Horton explains that the normativity of normative theory is indicative of its nature anchored in prescriptivism and idealization: "normative political theory is *normative*, which means that it is about ideals and prescription rather than mere description. It is about how politics ought to be, not about how it is; and, therefore, it is simply a mistake to confuse prescription with description."[63] But even at that, Horton insists that "normative political theory surely needs to be firmly rooted in an understanding of human experience and political possibility that is genuinely plausible, if it is to have something serious to say about politics, as we know it."[64]

In a similar mode, Amartya Sen (2009) criticizes Rawls's idea of the well-ordered society and, by extension, his theory as a whole for being what he calls "transcendentalist" and, therefore, irrelevant when it comes to dealing with the here and now injustices in our world. While I do not believe that Sen places Rawls's "justice as fairness" in the category of theories that Horton (2017) describes as "edifying fantasy," he does probably see Rawls's theory mostly from the angle of an economist, who for practical purposes of justice considers idealism not quite worthwhile. Sen doubts whether Rawls's theory would ever be useful in the debate about comparative justice in the real world: "Despite its own intellectual interest, the question 'what is a just society?' is not . . . a good starting-point for a useful theory of justice. . . . It may not be a plausible end-point either. A systematic theory of comparative justice does not need, nor does it necessarily yield, an answer to the question 'what is a just society?'"[65] For practical purposes, Sen (2009) concludes that policymakers searching for solutions to the myriads of problems associated with institutional injustices would find a transcendental theory of justice less useful:

> To be sure, members of any polity can imagine how a gigantic and totally comprehensive reorganization might be brought about, moving them at one go to the ideal of a fully just society. A no-nonsense transcendental theory can serve, in this sense, as something like the grand revolutionary's "one-shot handbook." But that marvelously radical handbook would not be much invoked in the actual debates on justice in which we are ever engaged. Questions on how to reduce the manifold injustices that characterize the world tend to define the domain of application of the analysis of justice; the jump to transcendental perfection does not belong here. (Sen 2009, 100)

However, I also think that ideals, quite often, call forth aspiration and practicality. Rawls's justice as fairness has been the subject of intense debate among policymakers and has served as the prism through which one can see whether a policy is fair or unfair for some lawmakers. For example, Richard A. Epstein's (2008) *Forbes* article, "The Risk-Free World of John Rawls," blames Rawls for the collapse of the financial markets, the failure of the housing market, and the raging debates about universal healthcare:

> His central insights have been construed in ways that have hastened the wreckage in the financial markets. . . . We are all grim witnesses to the downside of the Rawlsian approach when it translates into the determined insistence that no one should be removed from his home for nonpayment of mortgage. We see the same philosophical mindset play out in the urge for universal health care, so that no person in need should be forced to do without care.[66]

In the debates of real issues of justice, even on a comparative scale, Rawls's justice as fairness is as useful, impactful, and worthwhile. Another example to illustrate how Rawls's ideas are gradually entering into the consciousness of the average American and influencing their social, political, and economic decisions is Jerome Foss's piece (2016) in the *Heritage Foundation*, "The Hidden Influence of John Rawls on the American Mind." Foss writes:

> Few Americans outside of the academy have heard of John Rawls, yet his influence on the American mind is astounding. . . . Rawls's influence on contemporary America can be gauged by the extent to which many today think about and look at contemporary political matters, often unwittingly, through a Rawlsian prism. For instance: Many Americans think of themselves primarily in terms of the groups with which they identify. Some turn to a theoretical "consensus" rather than the Constitution to determine the government's power. Others refrain from referencing religion in the public square. Most turn to the Supreme Court of the United States as our political guide. . . . Mainstream America's growing sensitivity to political correctness finds its best theoretical defense in Rawls's work. He encourages us, especially judges, to adopt what he calls public reason, which sets a boundary for acceptable public statements and personal opinions.[67]

While Rawls's principles may appear utopian or futuristic, they are still useful yardsticks to test whether our moral judgments tally with the "oughts" of moral realism.

Rawls's principles of justice in *Political Liberalism (*1996), unlike, let us say, Kant's "categorical imperative," no longer aspire to apply universally and necessarily. Rawls's principles are not *apriori*. He takes into account the nature of liberal democratic polity and does not ignore anthropological, sociological, or political factors when making claims about liberal democracies.

Rawls's principles of justice, though ideal in nature, are nevertheless realizable within the liberal democratic setting. Thus, they cannot be easily dismissed as transcendental fantasy. As Freeman (2018) rightly counters:

> What is "perfectly just" about a well-ordered society is (1) that its *basic social institutions* are reasonably just . . . and (2) that all society's ("reasonable and rational") members accept the public conception of justice regulating these institution[s], and all have an effective sense of justice and willingness to comply with its demands, and they normally do so. (Freeman 2018, 259)

For the skepticism about Rawls's stability thesis, we are to look at two threads of thought: Rawls's moral psychology and the idea of an overlapping consensus. Although children's developmental psychology (Piaget/Kohlberg) has been subject to some controversies, the specific part of the cognitive development theory that Rawls adopts to explain how citizens acquire the sense of justice is not that contentious.[68] Nonetheless, the role model status given to parents and peers or fellow citizens, as the case may be, in the process leading to the acquisition of the sense of justice in the well-ordered society, may not always lead to the positive modeling of morality envisaged by Rawls. For example, McClennen (1999) argues that the developing child may acquire a sense of injustice instead of a sense of justice if the role model acts unjustly. Thus, the expected effect of role modeling can sometimes be counterproductive.[69] Considering the substantial rate of child abuse and other social ills recorded in today's family settings, it would not be unreasonable for someone to argue that the family as a part of the basic structure of society is not always just. An unjust family could habitually influence the growing child in negative ways. Depending on how prevalent these social ills manifest in a given society, a stability thesis arising from a psychology of the family could be called into question.

Furthermore, McClennen suggests that the problems associated with the presence of "free-riders" in modern society can also weaken Rawls's stability thesis:

> Consider now Rawls's suggestion that a sense of justice can serve to counterbalance the disposition to unilaterally defect. Suppose that a person has a well-developed sense of justice but finds that others have acted as free-riders. On Rawls's account, the sense of justice does not demand that we unconditionally continue to do our part. Those who have a sense of justice will be disposed to do their part only if they expect others, or sufficiently many of them, to do theirs. May we suppose, then, that when those who have a sense of justice anticipate that others will not do their part, rational self-interest takes over and determines what they shall do? (McClennen 1999, 149)

To counter the effects of blatant injustice in society, such as the "free-rider" phenomenon, Rawls proposes that public institutions provide adequate measures to minimize the violation of public trust: "The assurance problem as we have seen, is to maintain stability by removing temptations of the first kind, and since this is done by public institutions, those of the second kind also disappear, at least in the well-ordered society."[70]

Another Rawls skeptic is Jürgen Habermas, who in his 1995 article "Reconciliation Through the Use of Public Reason: Remarks on John Rawls's Political Liberalism" contends that Rawls's idea of an overlapping consensus is merely a pragmatic approach to the problem of stability in modern liberal societies, rather than a normative one. Habermas accuses Rawls of reducing the issues of stability in a liberal society to that of finding a workable political consensus without regard to the task of discovering adequate ethical or moral affirmation for such an agreement. In his view, since Rawls's political conception of justice, upon which comprehensive worldviews overlap, does not admit of "moral truth" but instead appeals to citizens' worldviews as a reasonable doctrine, "reasonableness" devoid of moral truth ought not to be a sufficient basis for political stability.

According to Habermas, the justification offered by Rawls for the political conception of justice is its acceptability—that is to say, that comprehensive worldview would endorse it:

> Because Rawls situates the "question of stability" in the foreground, the overlapping consensus merely expresses the functional contribution that the theory of justice can make to the peaceful institutionalization of social cooperation; but in this the intrinsic value of a *justified* theory must already be presupposed. From this functionalist perspective, the question of whether the theory can meet with public agreement—that is, from the perspective of different worldviews in the forum of the public use of reason—would lose an epistemic meaning essential to the theory itself. The overlapping consensus would then be merely an index of the utility, and no longer a confirmation of the correctness of the theory; it would no longer be of interest from the point of view of acceptability, and hence of validity, but only from that of acceptance, that is, of securing social stability. . . . When [Rawls] calls his conception of justice "*political*," his intention appears to be rather to collapse the distinction between its justified acceptability and its actual acceptance. (Habermas 1995, 122)

In support of Habermas's arguments, Krasnoff (1998) adds that the stability of a liberal democracy premised on practical convenience such as "acceptance or agreement" and not on normatively "justified acceptability" cannot be rightly called stability for the right moral reasons. Krasnoff asks, "Can agreement serve as the basis for a theory of justice? For Habermas, the answer is 'no,' because agreement lacks the normative content that any morally justified concept must have. For how good is agreement if what is agreed to lacks moral content?"[71] While it is not a bad idea to reach an agreement on political issues, Krasnoff argues that it has always been the task of the philosopher to look for normative grounds for a consensus.[72]

While it is conceivable from a pragmatic standpoint to regard some form of consensus as a prerequisite for lasting stability in liberal democracies, some skeptics still doubt whether Rawls's overlapping consensus can be suitable for it in the face of multiculturalism. Rawls's overlapping consensus, says Bohman (1995), can offer at most a minimal condition for stability, by providing a basis for the reconciliation of mild conflicts in a liberal democracy. Still, it is hardly a sufficient basis for the complex pluralism of our time. If we accept reasonable pluralism as an enduring feature of modern democracies, "then we must also wonder whether the scope of what is 'reasonable for all to accept' turns out to be so small as to be irrelevant for most political disagreements."[73]

Rawls's overlapping consensus utilizes an idea of reasonableness, which, according to Bohman, is conceptually narrow. A citizen's reasonableness is dependent upon a person's worldviews, religious or ideological inclinations. For this reason, it would be difficult for citizens under certain situations to acknowledge the comprehensive worldviews of their fellow citizens as equally reasonable, a condition set by Rawls's "burdens of judgment," and which defines reasonable persons. The presence of profound cultural, religious, or ideological conflicts renders the determination of what constitutes "reasonableness" in given occasions very difficult.[74] This problem leads Rawls's critics to believe that the majority of citizens of modern pluralistic liberal societies may not, after all, endorse his political conception of justice. The skeptics further argue that Rawls may have missed the point when he states that citizens of liberal democracies would subordinate their beliefs to his political conception of justice whenever there is a clash between the two. Critics claim that citizens who affirm the truth of moral or religious doctrines will not adjust or revise their allegiance to these divine or moral truths in favor of a political conception of justice, which is in itself devoid of such moral or metaphysical truths.

Critics also contest Rawls's claim that the majority of citizens of modern liberal democracies exhibit some laxity toward religious, moral, or philosophical doctrines. If such looseness is indeed the case, they argue, violence engulfing diverse cultural communities caused by conflicts of value or religion between Muslims, Christians, Jews, Hindus, and so on in several so-called liberal states would have been rare occurrences. Young (2000), for example, observes that the predisposition of citizens stands in opposition to Rawls's thesis. When confronted with conflicts between the political conception of justice and their religious or moral worldviews, citizens tend to withdraw their allegiance to the political conception, even if temporarily, instead of mending their faith.[75] It may not be unreasonable, after all, for people to accord preeminence to religious, secular, or cultural values, when convinced of their moral or divine truth, rather than to the "reasonableness" of a political conception of justice. To expect citizens of liberal democracy to share the same ordering of values, which gives priority to the political conception of justice over their comprehensive worldviews, would only lead to a "metaphysics of value" overshadowed by inherent complexities and controversies which Rawls's political liberalism has been trying to avoid from the very beginning.[76]

## NOTES

1. See Rawls 1971, part III; 1996, lecture 1, §6, etc.
2. See Daniels 2000, 132–33.
3. Rawls 1971, 5.
4. See also Barry 1995, 880.
5. See also Young 2000.
6. Rawls 1996, 68–69.
7. See Rawls 2001, 27.
8. Rawls 1996, 40–41.
9. See Rawls 2001, 18–19.
10. Rawls 1963, 28.
11. Rawls 1996, 141.
12. See also Hill 1994, 337.
13. See Rawls 2001, 196.
14. Rawls's moral psychology is extensively treated in *A Theory of Justice* (1971). Although, as I mentioned earlier, Rawls has recast that book. However, the moral psychology of *Theory* remains valid and provides the basis for the understanding of moral psychology in *Political Liberalism* (1996). Referring to his treatment of moral psychology, Rawls writes in a footnote in *Political Liberalism*, "How this happens I have discussed in [*A Theory of Justice* 1971], esp. chap. viii. I hope that account suffices, for our purpose here, to convey the main idea" (Rawls 1996, 143).
15. See Rawls 1963, 285; 1971, 461. See also Brennan and Noggle 2000, 58.
16. See Müller 1995, 278.
17. See Weinreich-Haste 1982, 182–83.
18. See Piaget and Inhelder 1969, 127.
19. See Weinreich-Haste 1982, 182–83.
20. See also Piaget and Inhelder 1969, 122–24.
21. See Petrovich 1986, 87.
22. Rawls, in an earlier writing before the publication of *A Theory of Justice* (1971), classified the three stages leading to the acquisition of the sense of justice in terms of feelings of guilt: "The psychological construction by which the sense of justice might develop consists of three parts representing the development of three forms of guilt feelings in this order: authority guilt, association guilt, and principle guilt" (Rawls 1963, 286).
23. See Brennan and Noggle 2000, 57.
24. Rawls 1971, 464.
25. Ibid., 466.
26. See Rawls 1971, 467.
27. Brennan and Noggle 2000, 58–59.
28. See Rawls 1971, 467–72.
29. Ibid.
30. See Rawls 1996, 43.
31. See also Rawls 2001, 33.
32. Habermas 1996, 99.
33. Rawls 1996, 144.

34. Reasonable views or doctrines are, roughly, views that in Rawls opinion are compatible with liberal democratic principles, even when some of such views may be themselves nonliberal. For Rawls on the notion of reasonable views and persons, see, for example, Rawls 1996, XXXIX, 58–66, etc.

35. See Rawls 1996, 134.
36. Freeman 1999, 430.
37. Rinderle 1998, 287.
38. See also Müller 1995, 293.
39. See Scheffler 1994, 9; Rinderle 1998. See also Rawls 1996, 170.
40. See Rawls 1987, 433–34.
41. Rawls 1996, 170.
42. See Scheffler 1994, 11–12.
43. See also Greenawalt 1994, 672; Scheffler 1994, 11–12; Weinstock 1994, 178.
44. See Rawls 1996, 139; 2001, 193.
45. See Mulhall and Swift 1997, 187.
46. See Rawls 1996, xlii.
47. Larmore 1996, 188.
48. See also Rawls 1996, 143; 2001, 185ff; Mulhall and Swift 1997, 185.
49. Some critics assume the contrary—namely, that Rawls's overlapping consensus is more pragmatic than normative. See, for example, Habermas 1995, Bohman 1995, and Mulhall and Swift 1997, 185.
50. Rawls 2001, 195.
51. See also Mills 2000, 197.
52. Kant 1964, 112–13.
53. Kant's reference to St. Pierre and Rousseau is to the Abbe de St. Pierre (1658–1743), who wrote after the Spanish war *Projet de Paix Perpetuelle* (Utrecht 1713), part of which Rousseau published in 1760. See also Kant 1964, 13.
54. Rawls 1987, 422.
55. See also Hershovitz 2000, 222.
56. Young 2000; Rawls 1987; 1996, xl–xli. A good example is the Peace of Augsburg of 1555.
57. Dauenhauer 2000, 207.
58. See Rawls 1987, 421; 1996, 147.
59. See also Hershovitz 2000, 228.
60. Rawls 1996, 158–68.
61. Horton 2017.
62. Ibid., 488.
63. Ibid.
64. Ibid.
65. Sen 2009, 105.
66. https://www.forbes.com/2008/10/13/rawls-risk-system-oped-cx_re_1013epstein.html#6ffcde7b4ccf.
67. https://www.heritage.org/progressivism/report/the-hidden-influence-john-rawls-the-american-mind.
68. See also Brennan and Noggle 2000, 60–61.
69. See McClennen 1999, 149.
70. Rawls 1971, 336.
71. Krasnoff 1998, 270.
72. Ibid.
73. Bohman 1995, 255.
74. See also Krasnoff 1998, 292; Bohman 1995, 255.
75. Here, Young refers to the views of Huemer 1996.
76. See Weinstock 1994, 179.

*Part III*

# Rawls's Global Justice and the Non-Western World

*Chapter Seven*

# Human Rights in *The Law of Peoples*

## ON THE POSSIBILITY OF GLOBAL JUSTICE[1]

In this age of modern technology, humans employ global positioning systems (GPS) and other technological means to demarcate borders in the air, at sea, and on land. By marking out territories for themselves, modern humans engage in an endless ordering of the environment as an exploitable good. With such an attitude, they abuse both nature and their fellow humans. Strong economies take advantage of weak ones, powerful nations overrun less powerful ones, worldviews compete with one another, cultures and civilizations clash, ethnic cleansing and genocide occur, and millions die of starvation each year in the global competition for resources and domination. As a result of the ensuing confusion and turmoil, walls emerge to determine boundaries and to carve out safe zones: walls of inclusion and exclusion that assume social, economic, religious, ethnic, racial, or even psychological postures. In the face of this confused and complicated human-made situation of the contemporary world, who can dare to raise questions about justice at the global level? What propositions can we advance to uncover the nature of such an idea of justice?

In today's world, global justice as a philosophical idea has a lot to do with globalization. Alberto Ruiz Méndez (2018) in "Who Are the Subjects of Justice in a Globalized World?" defines globalization as "a phenomenon of history in which relationships among countries, societies and people have soared, and time-space boundaries have been reduced through the flux of goods, services, products, knowledge and financial capital."[2] Beyond the apparent interconnectedness of the contemporary world, Méndez also points out something else at work with globalization: the interdependence of world peoples. As an example, he notes that "the economic measures that a country undertakes related to agriculture could affect the migrant workers and the families in their country of origin; or if a country decides to close its borders to legal or illegal migration, this would have consequences in diverse regions of the world."[3]

Even as we witness an unprecedented flow of cultures and peoples across the world, at present, a good number of political philosophers question the possibility of global justice in the absence of a global sovereign state. One such philosopher is Thomas Nagel:

> Every state has the boundaries and population it has for all sorts of accidental and historical reasons; but given that it exercises sovereign power over its citizens and in their name, those citizens have a duty of justice toward one another through the legal, social, and economic institutions that sovereign power makes possible. This duty is *sui generis*, and is not owed to everyone in the world, nor is it an indirect consequence of any other duty that may be owed to everyone in the world, such as a duty of humanity. Justice is something we owe through our shared institutions only to those with whom we stand in a strong political relation. It is, in the standard terminology, an *associative* obligation . . . the requirements of justice themselves do not . . . apply to the world as a whole, unless and until, as a result of historical developments not required by justice, the world comes to be governed by a unified sovereign power. . . .
>
> [T]he full standards of justice, though they can be known by moral reasoning, apply only within the boundaries of a sovereign state, however arbitrary those boundaries may be. Internationally, there may well be standards, but they do not merit the full name of justice. (Nagel 2005, 121–22)

Yet even the strongest supporters of global justice are wary of the dangers that might follow a colossal and super powerful world state. Such concerns are, most probably, the reason Rawls designates his theory of global justice as a "realistic utopia." Onora O'Neill (2016), in her book *Justice Across Boundaries: Whose Obligations?*, alerts us to the dangers that might accompany a world state: "I am at least partly skeptical about those attempts to realise cosmopolitan principles by means of global institutions without showing what is to prevent global governance from degenerating into global tyranny and global injustice. . . . Big may not always be beautiful."[4]

Looking at the history of the modern world, it is incontestably true that what happens within the closed borders of one country can create ripples around the globe. For example, the world as a whole is grappling right now with the outbreak of the coronavirus COVID-19. What probably started at the Huanan Seafood Wholesale Market in China in late 2019 was declared a global pandemic by the World Health Organization (WHO) on March 11, 2020. Thus, the difficulty of articulating the idea of global justice does not undermine the urgency with which we ought to respond to questions of justice and order across our borders if we are to prevent the next global pandemic, the next Holocaust, the next Biafran genocide, the next Cambodian genocide, or the next Rwandan genocide. On this note, Amartya Sen reminds us:

> The world beyond a country's border cannot but come into assessment of justice in a country for at least two distinct reasons.... First, what happens in this country, and how its institutions operate, cannot but have effects, sometimes huge consequences, on the rest of the world. This is obvious enough when we consider the operation of world terrorism or attempts to overcome their activities, or events such as the US-led invasion in Iraq, but the influences that go beyond national borders are altogether omnipresent in the world in which we live. Second, each country, or each society, may have parochial beliefs that call for more global examination and scrutiny, because it can broaden the class and type of questions that are considered in that scrutiny, and because the factual presumptions that lie behind particular ethical and political judgments can be questioned with the help of the experiences of other countries or societies. (Sen 2009, 71)

In 1999, Rawls published *The Law of Peoples*, which was his attempt to provide the diverse peoples of the world with practicable principles to begin a realistic dialogue on international justice and relations. My main interest in this chapter is to ascertain whether *The Law of Peoples* adequately addresses the question of justice in the contemporary world and whether Rawls's theory of global justice needs some addenda. Here, some items come to mind: How should liberal societies relate with nonliberal societies on economic matters and issues of justice in the international forum? In *The Law of Peoples*, Rawls asserts that the modern international standard of human rights, the Universal Declaration of Human Rights, hereafter UDHR, cannot achieve universal validity, owing to its biased and ethnocentric origins.[5]

As a subtle departure from Rawls's position, I will give serious consideration to the argument for the possibility of according retroactive cultural legitimacy to the international standard of the UDHR. Retrospective cultural-legitimacy thesis[6] refers to the search for legitimacy, validity, or acceptability for those UDHR norms imposed on some non-Western countries in 1948 by the United Nations, without being sensitive to the background cultures of these societies. It will require an investigation of these norms alongside the cultural specificities of some non-Western societies. Although Rawls may have already answered some of the questions that this chapter raises in *The Law of Peoples*, I think that his liberal internationalism consciously abandons liberal progressivism on the international stage in order to achieve broader acceptance among nonliberal societies. Critics fear that, for Rawls, acceptability has become a synonym for normative justification of moral principles.[7] An important issue that this chapter addresses is Rawls's attenuation of the existing international human rights norms (UDHR), which critics think is a means to avoid real or imagined, possible charges of ethnocentrism and cultural imperialism.[8] In this way, his idea of international justice rejects cross-cultural critiques, making itself susceptible to some of the conventional criticisms against culturalism and value relativism.[9]

## RAWLS'S GLOBAL JUSTICE AND COSMOPOLITANISM

In *A Theory of Justice* (1971), Rawls mentions in passing, "the law of nations," which seems like a model of an egalitarian system of international justice, especially as it relates to just war ethics.[10] This would prompt some of his faithful followers, such as Charles Beitz (1979)[11] and Thomas Pogge (1989, 1994a),[12] to propose a cosmopolitan restructuring of Rawls's justice as fairness. Such a cosmopolitan extension of Rawls's theory of justice would incorporate a global "original position."[13] For starters, let us recall that within the framework of a functioning Western, liberal society, Rawls's justice as fairness requires the implementation of the following principles of justice: "First: each person is to have an equal right to the most extensive basic liberty compatible with a similar liberty for others.[14] Second: social and economic inequalities are to be arranged so that they are both (a) reasonably expected to be to everyone's advantage, and (b) attached to positions and offices open to all."[15] The (a) section of the second principle, as I mentioned earlier in chapter 1, is known as the "difference principle."

On further examination, the difference principle can allow the state to tax the rich if doing so alleviates the situation of the worst-off members of the society. The rich, in turn, benefit from such a principle by living in relatively safe and less hostile neighborhoods. In the face of staggering inequality and unconscionable but preventable poverty around the globe, especially in developing countries, the cosmopolitan overhaul, which Beitz and Pogge advocate, would help to promote the idea of justice as fairness in the entire world. That way, justice as fairness would eliminate poverty in the world in no distant future, once and for all, and make the world safer and more habitable for everyone. The cosmopolitan aspiration is to see Rawls's justice as fairness morph into a full-blown egalitarian theory of global, redistributive justice:[16]

> As a consequence, cosmopolitanism claims that a global difference principle that allows not only redistribution between richer and poorer members, but also a correction of an unjust global structure, should be applied beyond national borders to counteract the arbitrariness of the territorial distribution of natural resources and to fight poverty. As a matter of principle, all unjust inequalities between persons as well as between nations should be eliminated, perhaps through global taxation. (Audard 2007, 69)

The position of Beitz and Pogge, as insiders privy to the imminent release of *The Law of Peoples* (1999), undoubtedly aims at persuading Rawls to change his line of thought on international justice, which many of his critics claim is in disagreement with his more rigorously articulated egalitarian, liberal principles of distributive justice at the domestic level.[17] David Gordon (2019), writing in the *Mises Wire*, asks:

> Why has Rawls restricted the difference principle to the least well-off class in a given society? Why not extend the scope of the principle to cover the least well-off class in the entire world? Even the worst-off in a prosperous society like the United States are much better off than those in most other countries. Isn't birth in the United States and not in a poor country also a matter of luck? If so, don't anti-luck arguments require us to extend the difference principle worldwide?[18]

The observed inconsistency lies primarily in the fact that Rawls "endorses normative individualism domestically, but rejects it internationally."[19] Beitz's and Pogge's cosmopolitan approach to the question of global justice opposes Rawls's nation-centric notion of international justice.

The cosmopolitan conception of global justice is, unlike Rawls's "law of peoples," an international conception of justice, which sees the individual person as a participating member of the international society and as a legitimate subject of global justice, irrespective of the contingent circumstances that define her origin, position in society, or biographical standpoint. The international society, according to cosmopolitanism, is a global union of societies or *cosmopolis*, and persons rather than nations or states are to form its proper constitutive elements.[20]

In *The Law of Peoples*, an extension of *Political Liberalism* to issues of international relations and global justice, Rawls presents a rather conservative theory of global justice and, in so doing, disappoints many of his enthusiasts.[21] There, he insists that the domain of international justice and relations among nations cannot accommodate the cosmopolitan ideal of redistributive justice because it presupposes the belief that liberal democracy is the only acceptable political system, and that persons as citizens should be the primary concern of international justice:

> To proceed in this way [global original position or liberal cosmopolitanism] . . . amounts to saying that all persons are to have the equal liberal rights of citizens in a constitutional democracy. On this account, the foreign policy of a liberal people—which it is our concern to elaborate—will be to act gradually to shape all not yet liberal societies in a liberal direction, until eventually (in the ideal case) all societies are liberal. But this foreign policy simply assumes that only a liberal democratic society can be acceptable. (Rawls 1999, 82–83)

In Rawls's defense, one might say that his critics may have misunderstood his original intent in presenting the "law of peoples" as a realistic utopia. Rawls's apparent conservatism at the international level is not conservatism in the real sense of the word, but rather a sign of respect for the religion, culture, and other values of the world's nonliberal peoples. Furthermore, the "law of peoples" is a pragmatic approach to international justice and relations, anchored in Rawls's belief that the rest of the non-Western world may not yet be ready to embrace in totality the liberal values of the West. Therefore, at the global level, Rawls does not think that social liberalism translates to progressive politics. To make progress at the international level, the dialogue between the West and the rest of the world must begin somewhere and somehow, but respectfully. At the very beginning of this international dialogue, Rawls thinks that liberal and nonliberal peoples must search for common grounds, recognize their differences, and take thorny and divisive issues off the table.

An excellent example to illustrate Rawls's position is the issue of same-sex marriage or the legal right of a woman to abortion in the United States. While the 1973 Supreme Court landmark case established the right to abortion, *Roe v. Wade*, the legalization of same-sex marriage by the Supreme Court is a recent event. In 2015, the U.S. Supreme Court, under the Fourteenth Amendment, ruled that the ban on same-sex marriage was unconstitutional across the fifty states and the District of Columbia. President Barack Obama hailed the ruling as "a victory for America" and advocated for LGBTQ rights worldwide. But as Alexandra Hutzler (2019) notes in a *Newsweek* article dated July 3, 2019, "Where Is Same-Sex Marriage Legal?":

> Marriage equality is still prohibited in much of the world—in fact there are more than 70 countries that criminalize homosexuality outright. No country in Central or Eastern Europe allows same-sex couples to marry. Even in Western Europe, Italy, Switzerland and Greece continue to prohibit full marriage equality. And among the 54 nations that make up Africa, only one—South Africa—recognizes gay couples' right to legally wed.[22]

While the United States and a few countries have legalized gay marriage, most countries of the world have not. Even within the United States itself, a large section of the population is still kicking against the Marriage Equality Act of 2015 that the Supreme Court passed under the watch of the Obama administration. Amy Chua (2018) writes in *Political Tribes* that "[f]or tens of millions of white Americans today, mainstream popular culture displays an un-Christian, minority-glorifying, LGBTQ America they can't and don't want to recognize as their country—an America that seems to exclude them, to treat them as the enemy."[23] For most countries that have not followed in the footsteps of America, the attempt by the Obama administration to promote the idea to them was seen as an assault on their values and beliefs. To these peoples, same-sex marriage depraves the traditional values of the family. Some of these countries, such as Uganda and Nigeria, which had no laws criminalizing LGBTQ expressions before now (except in the Islamic states of Northern Nigeria), quickly enacted punitive laws in their effort to criminalize homosexuality.

When the former Nigerian president Goodluck Jonathan signed into law the Same-Sex Marriage Prohibition Act in January 2014, the general secretary of the Christian Association of Nigeria, Rev. Musa Aseke, welcomed the development and took a swipe at some Western nations (especially the United States) for tying the legalization of homosexuality to their foreign policy and financial assistance: "We don't have to drift into a situation where we don't have moral values because someone is giving us money."[24] A month earlier, precisely in December 2013, Uganda had passed a draconian law against homosexuality, citing resistance to the U.S.-led efforts to spread gay ideology in Africa as the driving force behind the enactment of the law, "which imposes life imprisonment for some types of homosexual acts."[25]

Similarly, Russia re-criminalized homosexuality with the "Ban On Gay Propaganda Law" of 2013. On August 21, 2019, *Reuters* reported that "[l]imiting marriage to a relationship between a man and a woman will remain China's legal position . . . ruling out following neighboring Taiwan in allowing same-sex marriage, despite pressure from activists."[26] Would Rawls support the idea of criminalizing gay activities or imprisoning LGBTQ activists in the United States? Very unlikely! However, does the United States have the right, for example, to demand compliance with gay rights from Nigeria, Moscow, or China (or to demand conformity with abortion rights from the majority of countries in Latin America, Africa, the Middle East, and some parts Asia, including India, that consider unrestricted access to abortion an outright murder of the unborn) as a precondition for international cooperation and justice? Rawls would say no. In fact, he would see such an outright demand from the United States as not only counterproductive but also a recipe for political hostility and deadlock at the international level. Same-sex marriage and abortion rights are few examples among numerous others that, I think, Rawls believes could hamper initial progress at the international level. Once liberal and nonliberal peoples begin to relate mutually over time, Rawls believes, cultures and values will overflow naturally to the left, right, or center. His theory of international relations and justice recognizes the fact that liberal democracy is not the only acceptable political system of government or way of life.

I think that on the question of global justice, no one could have been more enthusiastic than Rawls to see the entire world become an egalitarian *cosmopolis*. The only problem here is that he does not believe in the feasibility of a cosmopolitan system of global justice now or in the nearest future. For Rawls, it is an ideal that is good in theory, but sure to fail in practice. This explains why he insists that the "law of peoples" remains a "realistic utopia." It is realistic because it sets forth a limited but practical goal for itself, which is "the elimination of the great evils of human history: unjust war and oppression, religious persecution and the denial of liberty of conscience, starvation and poverty, genocide and mass murder."[27] That said, the "law of peoples" is also utopian because to argue for its possibility is the same as believing that "individuals are not inevitably selfish or amoral, and that international relations can be more than merely a contest for power, wealth, and glory. Affirming the possibility of a just and peaceful future can inoculate us against a resignation or cynicism that might otherwise seem inevitable."[28] There are other issues in *The Law of Peoples* (1999) that I think are harder to defend and may need some tweaking to remain consistent with Rawls's central ideas. One of these is the subject matter of global justice.

Elizabeth De Castro (2018) in "Globalization, Inequalities and Justice" writes that "one of the consequences of the globalization process has been the crisis of the nation-state, which questions the traditional significances of sovereignty and citizenship that are implicated in it."[29] Thus, we may ask who or what the primary subject of global justice is in the face of globalization. It is essential to consider whether the entitlements of global justice are for persons or peoples since these two ways of viewing the subjects of international justice tend to generate differing results.[30]

## THE LAW OF PEOPLES

Considering the primary subjects of justice, Rawls's idea of global justice, as put forth in *The Law of Peoples*, ignores "persons" and settles for the notion of "peoples," understood as societies or nations. International justice so conceived hinges on the idea of cooperation among societies that are, in Rawls's view, internally well ordered. This form of collaboration is based on principles of nonaggression, adherence to the international law of peoples, and mutual aid to burdened societies—that is, societies lacking the required means to be well ordered.[31] Rawls's international law of peoples circumscribes the following:

1. Peoples are free and independent, and their freedom and independence are to be respected by other peoples.
2. Peoples are to observe treaties and undertakings.
3. Peoples are equal and are parties to the agreements that bind them.
4. Peoples are to observe a duty of non-intervention.
5. Peoples have the right of self-defense but no right to instigate war for reasons other than self-defense.
6. Peoples are to honor human rights.

7. Peoples are to observe certain specified restrictions in the conduct of war.
8. Peoples have a duty to assist other peoples living under unfavorable conditions that prevent their having a just or decent political and social regime (Rawls 1999, 37).

Noticeably absent in the "law of peoples" is any form of egalitarian principle reminiscent of the difference principle, designed to regulate the distribution of the burdens and benefits of socioeconomic cooperation among persons across nations. In Rawls's view, the application of the difference principle at the global level is not justifiable. Unlike the difference principle, which conceives liberal democratic citizens as equal persons, Rawls's theory of global justice or the "law of peoples" does not embody a concept of the person in this liberal sense. As Rawls puts it, "The Law of Peoples does not say, for example, that human beings are moral persons and have equal worth in the eyes of God, or that they have certain moral and intellectual powers that entitle them to these rights."[32]

Rawls thinks it will be unfair to nonliberal societies to introduce a liberal conception, such as the difference principle into the codex of international law and relations. This line of thought derives from the fact that decent hierarchical societies may have conceptions of citizenship that run parallel to liberal ideas. Hierarchical societies may not regard their citizens as individuals or equal and free persons, but rather conceptualize citizenship from communalistic or group-oriented perspectives.

For Rawls, the redistribution of global economic wealth to the benefit of developing countries, following the difference principle, is not permissible.[33] Rawls's central argument here derives from his conviction that cultural ties and feelings of affinity among world peoples are weak. Therefore, the moral psychology needed to generate a sense of justice and sentiments, which could give rise to distributive justice based on the liberal idea of the difference principle, is absent at the global level. Furthermore, as an additional argument against demands for global redistributive justice, Rawls maintains that the arbitrary distribution of natural resources in the world does not provide persuasive reasons to justify the global redistribution of wealth. His position conflicts with the view of the proponents of global distributive justice, who consider the unequal distribution of natural resources as unfavorable to many countries and thus a good reason to argue for the worldwide redistribution of wealth. For Rawls, it is neither the possession of natural resources nor the lack of natural resources that makes countries rich or poor.

The economic prowess of rich countries (for example, the liberal democratic societies of the West) lies among other things in their political culture, industriousness, and innovation, as well as in the religious, philosophical, and moral traditions that support the basic structure of their political and social institutions. The causes of backwardness, Rawls argues, are primarily the lack of sound political and cultural tradition in developing countries, the absence of necessary technological expertise, coupled with poor population policies, and the state's failure to uphold human rights. Therefore, he asserts, the arbitrariness of the distribution of natural resources is not responsible for a country's economic and social progress or lack of it.[34]

Rawls declares that there is no country in the world (except in rare cases), so lacking in natural resources as to prevent it from attaining the status of a well-ordered society, were it to be reasonably and rationally governed. The possession of natural resources in many instances, he says, has proved to make some countries less innovative and economically less successful than those that are lacking in them. Rawls succinctly expresses this view when he observes that "historical examples seem to indicate that resource-poor countries may do very well (e.g., Japan), while resource-rich countries may have serious difficulties (e.g., Argentina)."[35]

Accordingly, Rawls proceeds to enunciate what he believes constitutes a more viable conception of international justice—that is, one that embodies the notion of a "duty of assistance" to burdened societies. Societies that lack the political culture, historical traditions, and basic technological know-how to become either decent or liberal well-ordered societies on their own are, in his global justice theory, entitled to a transitional foreign aid. Such a "duty of assistance," however, terminates at the point where a burdened society becomes self-supporting. As Gillian Brock (2010) notes, "This defines the target of assistance. After it is achieved, further assistance is not required, even though the now well-ordered society may still be relatively poor. The aim is to realize and preserve just (or decent) institutions that are self-sustaining."[36]

From this perspective, arguments for the redistribution of global wealth in favor of developing countries appear to be non sequitur. Since each decent or liberal society is autonomous, and its level of economic development is dependent upon the sound articulation of its own policies, Rawls argues, the economic inequality emanating from the social or economic policies of one country when compared with those of another is the sole responsibility of the country in question. The burden of decisions freely made by a given liberal or decent society, he concludes, is to be borne entirely by both the present and the future generations of the given society alone.

To impose the consequences of free decisions of one society on another society, under the pretext of distributive egalitarian global justice, is for Rawls, not acceptable. Following Rawls's conception of peoples as autonomous, equal, and free, organized as liberal or decent societies, economic inequalities among peoples or nations have domestic origins. In economic terms, liberal and decent societies are thus masters of their own fate. Accordingly, a theory of global justice that envisages the redistribution of wealth among nations beyond the "duty of assistance"—that is, beyond minimal aid to developing burdened societies—is not justifiable.

In opposition to Rawls, his cosmopolitan critics argue that an in-depth empirical study of the current global situation renders his position contestable. Beitz (2000), for example, counters that a meticulous study of the global issue of poverty and underdevelopment suggests that the sources of economic backwardness are obviously not always attributable to internal factors or domestic policies of governments. The factors that underlie underdevelopment vary from one society to another, and thus, the relative importance of the general factors listed by Rawls is disputable.[37]

Advocates of cosmopolitanism contend that there are some serious points that Rawls seems to ignore in his discussion of global justice. Some of these issues inform the current global economic structure and, conversely, play a significant role in the development or underdevelopment of today's developing countries of the world. The factors that contribute to the poverty of developing nations include the role that transnational trade plays with its negative impacts on the economies of developing nations. Furthermore, the effects of globalized capitalist market structures and the debt policy of donor-rich countries contribute to the underdevelopment of poor Third World countries; as well as the role played by the international financial institutions such as the Paris Club, the International Monetary Fund (IMF), and the World Bank.

Considering these factors, Beitz argues that the causes of poverty are not easily distinguished:

> [A] society's integration into the world economy, reflected in its trade relations, dependence on capital markets, and vulnerability to the policies of international financial institutions, can have deep and lasting consequences for the domestic economic and political structure. Under these circumstances, it may not even be possible to distinguish between domestic and international influences on a society's economic condition. (Beitz 2000, 690)

Thus, for his cosmopolitan critics, Rawls's liberal internationalism of *The Law of Peoples* fails to provide adequate and fair principles for transnational trade and economic relations persuasive enough to justify his position on global justice. Rawls's idea of international justice requires that citizens (present and future generations) of liberal or decent societies be considered responsible for the costs incurred as a result of social or economic policies adopted by such societies. It is difficult, these cosmopolitan critics maintain, to accept as fair the idea of imposing the costs of possible imprudent choices of previous rulers and previous generations on the present or future generation of a poor society, who are citizens of such an unfortunate poor society only by accident.[38] For his cosmopolitan critics, this explains why Rawls's "duty of assistance" as the basis of global justice is insufficient and incapable of providing adequate solutions to the pressing issues of global justice facing our contemporary world. And in such a rapidly globalizing world, Michael W. Doyle (2006) infers, "*The Law of Peoples* may be signaling a tolerance for such large differences in material welfare that the solidarity we will need to meet global challenges will never be cultivated."[39]

## THE LIBERAL TOLERATION OF NONLIBERAL SOCIETIES

Another important matter discussed in some detail in *The Law of Peoples* is how liberal societies are to deal with decent but nonliberal societies in the international forum. Rawls demands that liberal societies tolerate decent societies in the international "society of peoples." Toleration of decent societies by liberal societies not only entails that liberal peoples refrain from using political or economic sanctions, military force, or diplomatic pressures to instigate political changes in decent societies but further demands that liberal societies recognize decent societies as members with certain rights and obligations, participating on an equal basis in the "society of peoples."[40]

Rawls's idea of toleration in *The Law of Peoples* follows from the same line of thought he developed in *Political Liberalism*. Just as citizens of liberal societies must respect one another's comprehensive religious, philosophical, and moral doctrines, liberal societies at the international level should respect the cultures, traditions, and values of other societies of the world (provided such societies honor the "law of peoples"). In addition, Rawls opines, since no society is static, decent societies should have the freedom to undergo internal reforms at their own pace.

The admittance of decent but nonliberal peoples into the "society of peoples" with the equality of status and respect mentioned above, Rawls believes, would quickly produce positive results in the direction of reforms that may lead decent societies to become liberal. When granted equal status, respect, and recognition by liberal societies, decent societies would experience the advantages of liberal democracy through years of cooperation and interaction with liberal societies and, as a result, would freely appropriate liberal values without external coercion.[41] Nevertheless, societies falling under the umbrella of "indecency" may face justifiable intolerance on the part of both decent and liberal societies. Such outlaw or rogue states have no place within the forum of the international society of peoples. In today's world, determining which country falls under the category of a rogue state is one thing, while the political will of the international community to deal with the rogue regime is a more significant challenge. For example, some might classify North Korea under the regime of Kim Jong-un, a rogue state following Rawls's criteria for decency. Still, the United Nations and even the Unit-

Human Rights in The Law of Peoples 141

ed States have minimal resources to confront a nuclear-armed and powerful North Korea.

If honoring human rights is a necessary condition for decency, it becomes reasonable to examine what for Rawls constitutes human rights precisely. "Decency," as appropriated by Rawls in his theory of global justice, is a condition for toleration. A decent society could be hierarchical or nonhierarchical. What stands as a necessary condition (though not a sufficient condition) for decency, he says, is that a decent society must honor the human rights inscribed in the international law of peoples.[42]

## HUMAN RIGHTS AND THE QUESTION OF RETROSPECTIVE CULTURAL LEGITIMACY[43]

Rawls designates human rights as "a special class of urgent rights."[44] This class is, in essence, a concise list of specific rights and liberties. It includes freedom from slavery, a sufficient measure of freedom of conscience and religion (excluding equal or full liberty of conscience) and the right of ethnic minorities to live without fear of massacre or genocide, right to personal property, and the notion of formal equality, which is quite different from the equality of persons as citizens in the liberal sense.

A quick look at Rawls's list of human rights confirms that he has adjusted the liberal principles of rights in order to accommodate the political interests of nonliberal societies. He believes that non-Western peoples will not reject human rights understood in its shortened form as politically parochial.[45] Thus, Rawls excludes from his liberal internationalism a substantial number of rights and liberties, the kind that the principles of liberal democracy guarantee and which he defended in *Political Liberalism*. Such rights include basic political liberties and freedom from discrimination based on religion, race, caste, ethnicity, or gender. This set of rights further includes freedom of opinion and expression, freedom of the press, and full and equal freedom of thought, conscience, and religion, including the freedom of apostasy—that is, the right to change one's faith or belief and the right to question the orthodox interpretation of religious doctrine.[46]

Rawls's list of human rights in this way also differs from the UDHR of 1948 and the subsequent covenants, such as the International Convention on Economic, Social, and Cultural Rights (adopted on December 16, 1966, and entered into force January 3, 1976), the International Covenant on Civil and Political Rights (adopted on December 16, 1966, and entered into force March 23, 1976), and the Convention on the Elimination of All Forms of Discrimination against Women (December 18, 1979), and other international and regional conventions, which together provide the present standard of internationally recognized norms of human rights.[47]

Examples of UDHR rights that Rawls purposefully removed from his lists of "urgent rights" are Articles 1 and 19. Article 1 states, "All human beings are born free and equal in dignity and rights. They are endowed with reason and conscience and should act toward one another in a spirit of brotherhood."[48] Article 19 stipulates that "Everyone has the right to freedom of opinion and expression; this right includes freedom to hold opinions without interference and to seek, receive and impart information and ideas through any media and regardless of frontiers."[49]

Comparatively, Rawls asserts that only Articles 3–18 of the UDHR embody human rights in the proper sense of the words. The remaining articles, in his view, express ethnocentric, Western, and liberal aspirations, which are culturally and historically contingent, and as such, incapable of achieving universal validity. Therefore, any broader and universally valid conceptualization of human rights must weaken the specific Western philosophical and cultural outlook of the UDHR, in order to fit into the space of reasonableness of non-Western decent societies.

The inherent liberal individualism expressed by the UDHR has to make way for peoples whose traditional and cultural practices do not recognize the value of liberal individualism, but rather define persons in terms of community or group. Therefore, in the international sphere, liberal peoples must narrow the conception of justice modeled on liberal individualism, in order to accommodate decent people's "common good" conception of justice. By dismissing particularly Article 1 of the UDHR, which grounds the normative importance of human rights on the dignity of persons as human beings, critics think that Rawls may have weakened the importance of UDHR norms in some corners of our world and their role in shaping the global order.[50]

The notion of a decent society given in *The Law of Peoples*, Rawls maintains, is consistent with a reasonable interpretation of Islamic political ideas. Consequently, Rawls's model of a decent hierarchical society is the fictive Islamic nation of Kazanistan: "In §9.3 I give an example of an imaginary decent hierarchical Muslim people whom I have named 'Kazanistan.' Kazanistan honors and respects human rights, and its basic structure contains a decent consultation hierarchy, thereby giving a substantial political role to its members in making political decisions."[51] Rawls's criteria for a decent hierarchical society, as exemplified by Kazanistan, allows such a society the freedom to adopt a comprehensive doctrine, secular or religious, for the regulation of its political institutions, provided the political aims of such a society exclude imperialist interests. Rawls also describes such a society as associationist in nature. This means that such a society views its members in public life as segments of different groups, where a body represents each group in the existing legal system and the consultation hierarchy.

The conception of justice existing in a decent hierarchical society is definable in terms of "common good"—that is, ideas of the good, priorities, or ends that the society sets for its members to attain. Rawls makes it a rule that there must be a sincere and reasonable conviction on the part of judges and officials, who administer the legal system that what they pronounce as judgment depends on a reasonable interpretation of this common good notion of justice. The system of law in a decent hierarchical society, according to Rawls, is to impose moral duties and obligations on citizens and to secure for all members of society what they generally regard as human rights.[52]

The basic human rights operative in such a society need not encompass anything more than a special class of urgent rights. The conception of person in a decent hierarchical society does not necessarily need to be liberal. A decent hierarchical society is under no obligation to treat its citizens as equal persons. Rather, it classifies citizens as responsible and cooperating members of, for example, an ethnic, caste, or religious group, with duties, obligations, and rights specific to each group.[53] Rawls's Kazanistan, as an ideal representative of a decent hierarchical society, fulfills the criteria of decency in several ways. First, a comprehensive religious doctrine informs the Kazanistani system of government. As Rawls explains that "Kazanistan's system of law does not institute the separation of church and state."[54] Therefore, it is plausible to conjecture that a specific interpretation of sharia or Islamic law forms the basis of the legal system governing the basic structure of Kazanistan. Rawls seems to confirm this assumption when he states that in Kazanistan Islam is the only favored religion, and only Muslims can hold upper positions of political authority or influence the policies of the government.[55]

Second, although there is no equal or full liberty of conscience in Kazanistan, the state guarantees a sufficient measure of liberty of conscience and religion. Furthermore, the state, in some specific sense, tolerates non-Islamic religions, and the members of such religions may practice their faith without fear of persecution. However, the state can deny members of non-Islamic religions some civic and religious rights in accordance with Islamic law.

Third, Rawls's Kazanistan also honors the "law of peoples" and hence is not expansionist. Unlike the jihadists of old, Rawls notes, Kazanistan does not give in to territorial expansion and the building of empires. This is because of an enlightened Islamic theology that flourishes in such a society, leading its Islamic scholars to interpret jihad in a moral and spiritual sense, rather than in terms of physical military battles.[56]

Fourth, Kazanistan's system of government embodies a consultation hierarchy and honors the basic human rights inscribed in the "law of peoples:" "I think it is also plausible to imagine Kazanistan as organized in a decent consultation hierarchy, which has been changed from time to time to make it more sensitive to the needs of its people and the many different groups represented by legal bodies in the consultation hierarchy."[57]

Rawls's hypothetical Islamic state of Kazanistan, with its common good conception of justice and a comprehensive religious doctrine regulating its basic structure, is compatible with many of the illiberal tendencies he condemned in his liberal conception of justice in *A Theory of Justice* (1971) and *Political Liberalism* (1996). Some of these tendencies are inequality of persons, which is tantamount to social and economic injustice, discrimination against women, and prejudice toward religious, ethnic, cultural, and other minorities.

Rawls, for instance, writes that there is a sufficient measure of liberty of conscience and freedom of religion and thought in Kazanistan, albeit without equal or full liberty of conscience.[58] Critics see this as mere rhetorical frippery, which masks the fact that the state can legally deny equal liberty of conscience to members of minority religions, despite their cultural integration into the mainstream Muslim society.[59] Rawls adds that minorities can practice their beliefs without fear of persecution or loss of most civic rights, except the right to hold higher political or judicial offices. This further suggests that besides the denial of the right to hold principal offices, the state can legitimately deny non-Muslims certain civic rights, based on nothing other than religious reasons. It could be reasonably assumed that Islamic rulers may employ the denial of such rights to demonstrate the gains accompanying being Muslim and thus facilitate the conversion process of non-Muslims.

On further analysis, since the state of Kazanistan does not guarantee complete freedom of conscience, thought, and religion to its citizens, a Kazanistani Muslim may not have the choice to change his or her religion without persecution nor have the right to question the orthodox interpretation of Islamic doctrine. Bassam Tibi (1990), interpreting the Islamic law or sharia, writes that "Muslims themselves are not allowed to retreat from Islam. A Muslim who repudiates his or her faith in Islam can be prosecuted as a *murtadd* (apostate)."[60]

Under Islamic law and the fragmented-group conception of citizens in the hypothetical state of Kazanistan, the state may legitimately subject women to unequal and unfair treatment. In Rawls's *Political Liberalism*, the political conception of justice exhibits the priority of the right over the good, but the "common good" conception of justice he assigns to decent societies in *The Law of Peoples* is compatible with intolerant and unjust policies of the government when judged from a liberal standpoint.

Since determining what counts as a common good in certain instances appears enigmatic, to ground the conception of justice solely on this notion is very dangerous. Acting according to the presumed ideal of the common good, critics fear that Rawls's decent hypothetical society of Kazanistan may legitimately sanction horrendous practices against groups, sects, or individuals perceived by the larger society as unproductive or prone to criminality. While Rawls's model of international justice could be successful in charting a pragmatic path for liberal and nonliberal peoples in international relation, it may also be inadvertently suggesting to hierarchical societies that some of their institutional practices, which most people in the West view as unacceptable or even evil, are equally good.

In an attempt to extend the principle of liberal toleration to nonliberal or illiberal societies, Rawls's liberal internationalism eschews cross-cultural criticism. By weakening the internationally recognized human rights standard of the UDHR, Rawls believes he has captured the moral intuition of both liberal and nonliberal societies on what form of rights are to be accorded the status of human rights and hence capable of attaining universal acceptability.

The fear of possible charges of moral imperialism in international justice and relations obviously influences Rawls's action of truncating the list of the UDHR. Thus, he joins forces with those who argue that the current standard of international human rights, with its liberal individualism and liberal conception of person, is alien to many non-Western cultures. Arguments of this kind are popular among those who oppose the application of the UDHR norms in some non-Western countries of the world, such as in Africa and Asia. Such arguments seem to emphasize that peoples in traditional non-Western societies are predominantly group or community-oriented rather than individualistic.

Furthermore, proponents of such views consider peoples in group-oriented societies as lacking in individualistic psychology, which grants persons the impetus to make individual claims of rights against their government.[61] Rawls and those who oppose the universal application of the UDHR norms conclude that since the existing international standard of human rights originated from within the framework of Western liberal individualism, it is complicated to implement this standard within the cultures of non-Western societies. Some non-Western traditions and customs may actually have ways of conceiving and expressing rights that may not fit well with Western tradition and culture. As Virginia A. Leary states, "The rich cultures of Asia and Africa express matters of human dignity in terms other than 'rights.' Many of these cultures, in contrast, value a sense of community and stress duties to family and community more than they emphasize individualism and rights."[62]

Nevertheless, as Rhonda. E. Howard (1990) argues, the existence of community-rooted ethics in African and Asian societies does not negate the role and importance of human rights to these societies. It will amount to a definist fallacy if human rights are defined in terms and meanings that exclude communalistic or communitarian conceptions of rights. The international human-rights norms are there to protect individuals against abuses, irrespective of whether these individuals are persons or groups (communities).[63] Therefore, we should not undermine the relevance of the existing international standard of human rights on the assumption that individualistic conceptions of rights are alien to non-Western cultures and traditions. Rather, we need a cross-cultural dialogue aimed at reinterpreting the liberal conception of person and right from the standpoint of group and community-rooted conception of human dignity.[64]

While I understand why Rawls would shorten the UDHR list to lower the hurdle of cooperation for non-Western, mostly Islamic nations or peoples to participate as equal partners in the society of peoples, I do think that he should have kept the UDHR articles intact at least up to the point of the initial debates. Although some countries do not honor all human rights; most countries do honor some human rights, which would be a good starting point for the public discourse in the "society of peoples." A more viable approach would have been to let nonliberal peoples investigate their cultures first as they relate to human rights in a way Abdullahi Ahmed An-Na'im (1990) describes as "retrospective cultural legitimacy."[65] Retrospective cultural legitimacy thesis is the search for universal validity and applicability of UDHR norms in a way that does not undermine a people's history or tradition, and not destabilize society. The retrospective cultural legitimacy argument calls for the reinterpretation of the UDHR norms from within the specific cultures, worldviews, and traditions of non-Western societies, where these norms are presently considered alien.[66]

The cultural-legitimacy thesis is to be informed by a sincere cross-cultural dialogue. Parekh (1999) elaborates:

> If universal values are to enjoy widespread support and democratic validation and be free of ethnocentric biases, they should arise out of an open and uncoerced cross-cultural dialogue. Such a dialogue should include every culture with a point of view to express. In so doing we show respect for them, and give them a motive to comply with the principle of holding a cross-cultural dialogue. We also ensure that such values as we arrive at are born out of different historical experiences and cultural sensibilities, free of ethnocentric biases, and thus genuinely universal. The dialogue occurs both in large international gatherings of governmental and non-governmental representatives and in small groups of academics and intellectuals. (Parekh 1999, 139)

The aim of such an intercultural dialogue is not to argue for the existence of natural, universal morality, since historical and other contingent circumstances shape people's traditions, religions, and moral conceptions. It is to aim, as Parekh suggests, not at discovering values but at reaching a consensus on already existing international norms.[67] Such an intercultural dialogue aimed at seeking retrospective cultural legitimacy for UDHR is tenable if done with respect toward other cultures and if adequate knowledge of local content informs the background discussions. This would also weaken any charges of ethnocentrism, imperialism, or neocolonialism.[68]

For example, a closer study of the concept of the person in Africa reveals that the predominance of the so-called group-oriented notion of self-identity among its peoples is contestable.[69] As such, liberal individualism may, after all, be compatible with some values and particular concepts of the person in non-Western philosophy.

## NOTES

1. Some earlier parts of this chapter were published in the *Mind's Eye* (2006).
2. Méndez 2018, 157.
3. Ibid., 157–58.
4. O'Neill 2016, 178.
5. Rawls 1999, 80.
6. See An-Na'im 1990.
7. See, for example, Habermas's (1995) criticism of Rawls earlier on in chapter 6.
8. See John Rawls—Check New World Order Tasiolus. Find page for the criticism of Rawls for attenuating UDHR.
9. Robert J. McShea writes in *Morality and Human Nature: A New Route to Ethical Theory* (1990, 91) that culturalism as a value theory sees culture as the only important bases for value judgment.
10. See Rawls 1971, 8, 108, 378, 457, and 379–82 for the law of nations in his discussion of the just war ethics.
11. See Beitz 1979 and 1999.
12. See Pogge 1989 and 1994a.
13. See also Sen 2009, 71.
14. Rawls's notion of basic liberty encapsulates the following: the right to vote and be eligible for public office, freedom of speech and assembly, liberty of conscience and freedom of thought, freedom from arbitrary arrest, the right of person, and the right to hold personal property (1971, 61).
15. Rawls 1971, 60.
16. Wenar 2001, 85.
17. See also Pogge 2007, 211.
18. Gordon 2019.
19. Pogge 2007, 211.
20. Nardin 1981, 234.
21. Beitz 1999, 515–29.
22. https://www.newsweek.com/where-gay-marriage-legal-1445268.
23. Chua 2018, 173.
24. See the *Washington Post*: https://www.washingtonpost.com/national/religion/nigerias-religious-leaders-welcome-controversial-anti-gay-law/2014/01/16/12485d88-7ef7-11e3-97d3-b9925ce2c57b_story.html.
25. Ibid.
26. https://www.reuters.com/article/us-china-lgbt-marriage/china-parliament-rules-out-allowing-same-sex-marriage-idUSKCN1VB09E.
27. https://plato.stanford.edu/entries/rawls/#OriPosPolCon.
28. Ibid.
29. De Castro 2018, 124.
30. See also Nardin 1981, 233.
31. Hinsch 2001, 58–78.
32. Rawls 1999, 68.
33. Hinsch 2001, 70.
34. See Rawls 1999, 107–10.
35. Ibid., 108.
36. Brock 2010, 87.
37. Beitz 2000, 669–96.
38. Ibid., 692.

39. Doyle 2006, 116.
40. Rawls 1999, 59.
41. Ibid., 59–62.
42. Ibid., 80.
43. I am indebted to Abdullahi Ahmed An-Na'im for the use of the term "retrospective cultural legitimacy" for human rights. See An-Na'im 1990, 20–21ff.
44. Rawls 1999, 79.
45. Ibid., 65.
46. Hayden 2002, 131–32.
47. See https://www.ohchr.org/EN/ProfessionalInterest/Pages/CEDAW.aspx.
48. See UDHR.
49. See UDHR.
50. See, for example, Patrick Hayden, "Rawls, Human Rights, and Cultural Pluralism: A Critique," *Theoria: A Journal of Social and Political Theory*, No. 92 (December 1998), 46–56.
51. Rawls 1999, 64.
52. Ibid., 64–67.
53. Tesón 1995, 295–315.
54. Rawls 1999, 75.
55. Ibid., 75–76.
56. Ibid., 76.
57. Ibid., 77.
58. Ibid., 65, 76.
59. Tasioulas 2002, 383.
60. Tibi 1990, 104.
61. Howard 1990, 165.
62. Leary 1990, 16.
63. Howard 1990, 165.
64. Ibid., 182.
65. An-Na'im 1990, 20–21, etc.
66. See An-Na'im 1990, 20–21, etc.
67. Parekh 1999, 140.
68. See also Tan 2000, 34, 55, 208; Mbiti 1999, 106.
69. See Nnodim 2015.

*Chapter Eight*

# Liberal Individualism and the Concept of the Person in African Philosophy

*Implications for Rawls's Basic Human Rights*[1]

## A COUNTER-COLONIAL NARRATIVE

*Apriori* conceptualization of persons in other cultures as different, Western versus non-Western binary views, comes with some extra philosophical baggage. Rawls's assessment of the concept of the person in hierarchical, non-Western societies as "associationist" and his claim that some articles of the Universal Declaration of Human Rights (UDHR), which emphasize the individualism and equality of persons, are nothing but liberal and Western aspirations, provide the backdrop for my investigation of the concept of the person in an African philosophical setting. Again, the goal is not to undermine Rawls's overall project of global justice, but in some ways to argue for a better understanding of the thoughts and values of non-Western peoples: that they are not, in every sense, fundamentally different and in binary opposition to the West. This way, we may be able to reconcile some of Rawls's ideas with the cultures and values of the "distant" others.

Academic and philosophical discourses on personhood and self-identity in Africa revolve predominantly around a communalistic understanding of the self. For example, Tom Mboya (1963) writes that "[a] person is an individual only to the extent that he is a member of a clan, a community or a family."[2] Likewise, John S. Mbiti (1999) states that "[t]he individual can only say: 'I am, because we are; and since we are, therefore I am.' This is a cardinal point in the understanding of the African view of man."[3] While this emphasis on the social features of self-identity is of great significance to the constitution of a specifically black African concept of the person, historically, it served another important function, albeit one with a subversive political nuance. In the 1950s and 1960s, for example, conceptualizing a cumbered self, enmeshed in the fabric of social life, as opposed to the presumably unencumbered self of Western liberal individualism, was of theoretical importance to the emerging black African politics of identity and representation. The goal of this politics was to reclaim human dignity for the colonized Africans.

The pan-African intellectual and political movements of the colonial era, whose primary goal was to decolonize the African mind, required the creation of counter-images to the European concept of the person. Consequently, the pan-African project consciously eschewed Eurocentric, egological reifications in the discussion of African identities, while re-defining difference in a positive sense. Accordingly, African philosophers writing about the African concept of the person during the colonial era had to distance themselves from Western liberal individualism. Thus, as Emmanuel Chukwudi Eze (1997) suggests, contemporary African philosophy may be considered a counter-colonial practice:

> The idea of "African philosophy" as a field of inquiry thus has its contemporary roots in the effort of African thinkers to combat political and economic exploitations, and to examine, question, and contest identities imposed upon them by Europeans. The claims and counter-claims, justifications, and alienations that characterize such historical and conceptual protests and contestations indelibly mark the discipline of African philosophy. (Eze 1997, 11–12)

Thus, it is not surprising today to see some African scholars, both local and international, continue to postulate and defend a "we existence" ontology of person, which overrides the primacy and subjectivity of the ego. In contrast to an independent, self-authenticating individual, a person in Africa, then, is a self only in relation to how he or she lives in the community. In my view, this concept of the person constitutes an overly narrow abstraction based on epistemically and metaphysically minimal foundations, which were once very useful for the enunciation of a specific politics of identity and representation.

Presently, unmeasured emphasis on group-oriented ideas of the person among Africans undermines the broader metaphysical dimensions of personhood existing in the thought systems of many traditional African societies. Bearing in mind the enigma that philosophers, psychologists, and scholars in the natural sciences encounter in defining the self even in the face of the simplest introspection, I do not intend to undermine the social character of personal identity or claim that the self is a fully independent entity in an inter-subjective world. Instead, I would like to suggest in this chapter that the social character of persons is one among other foundational properties of the human person in African thought. This social character, as important as it may be, is but one feature among others in the construction or acquisition of self-identity.

This chapter focuses on the concept of the person among the Igbo of southeastern Nigeria, to illustrate this multifaceted nature of personhood in African thoughts. Though Igbo thought and belief systems closely relate to those of the Yoruba, Efik, Akan, and some other groups in West Africa, nonetheless, the Igbo concept of the person or personal identity may not reflect the broader conceptions of personhood among other various groups and cultures across Africa. My discourse on the concept of the person in Igbo thought and belief systems cuts across the fields of philosophical anthropology, moral psychology, cosmology, and religion, since the concept of the person among the Igbo has both ontological and normative dimensions.

## DIMENSIONS OF PERSONHOOD

The Igbo word for a human being is *Mmadu*. The etymology of the word *Mmadu* goes back to two other Igbo words *mma* (beauty) and *ndu* (life). Thus, *Mmadu* literally means *the beauty of life*.[4] A closer study of the concept of *Mmadu* that transcends this literary meaning reveals a triadic composition of the human person: *Ahu*—the material human body, which includes the external body parts and internal organs; *Mmuo*—the non-material soul, mind or spirit, which undergoes the process of disembodiment at death; and *Chi*—creative essence, complementary spirit or destiny. *Chi* is a mystifying concept, which, by virtue of its ambiguous connotation, requires in-depth exploration.

From an intrinsic or ontological standpoint or what I call the existing human being per se, or being for oneself, the three elements *Ahu*, *Mmuo*, and *Chi* constitute a person, as opposed to non-persons (animals, plants, and so on), which may lack one or two of these aspects of being. There is also an extrinsic dimension of being human—that is, the normative aspect of personhood in the Igbo context. The extrinsic perspective appeals to the notion of being with or for others. The extrinsic or normative status of personhood among the Igbo is attained through the acquisition of morals in communality with other persons and things. In what follows, I will examine the intricate relationship between the (1) intrinsic or ontological and the (2) extrinsic or normative constitution of personhood in Igbo thought and belief systems.

## INTRINSIC OR ONTOLOGICAL DIMENSION OF PERSONHOOD

The intrinsic or ontological dimension of a person encompasses the body, mind or soul and what the Igbo refer to as *Chi*.

## The Body or *Ahu*

Joseph Therese Agbasiere (2000) notes that the human person in Igbo thought is a material and non-material composite being endowed with a life-force or vital breath known in the Igbo language as *Ume*. This life force is found in all living things. A person's material composition is known as *Ahu* or the body. The Igbo word *Ahu*, according to Agbasiere (2000), derives linguistically from the Igbo verb *hu*, which means to see. Thus, *Ahu* designates that part of the human being, which is visible. A person derives his or her biological nature from the parents, while the non-material constitution of the human being originates from the creative essence of God. The complexity of this composite nature of the human being places a person above other living creatures that lack such a configuration.[5]

In general, though the human body is not seen as external to a person or the self, it can nevertheless be objectified in an ontical sense. Thus, an Igbo can talk of his or her body as an object of observation: "*Nkea bu anu ahu m*" or "this is merely the flesh of my body." It is not surprising when asked "How are you?" to hear someone answer, "My body is fine (*ahu di m or akpa m ahu*), but I am not doing fine." While the state of the body conveys someone's health condition, it does not necessarily capture the ultimate state of a person's being. In talking about the body, an Igbo expresses both the factuality and the facticity of human existence through the reflective power of consciousness: I am aware of myself not only as a centered, unified conscious being but also as a substantial locus of empirical attributes that can be objectified.[6] In his or her capacity to objectify various modes of being, a person in the Igbo context is the center of activities that can be abstracted beyond mere physical interaction between the organism and the physical environment.

Though the human body can be objectified, it is nevertheless held sacred among the Igbo as the seat of the life force and the non-material soul. Thus, traditional Igbo ethics strictly forbids the wanton shedding of human blood. One is forbidden to shed the blood of kin and is discouraged from committing suicide. A very good example of this proscription is found in Chinua Achebe's highly acclaimed novel, *Things Fall Apart*. The protagonist, Okonkwo, inadvertently sheds the blood of a kinsman during the burial rites of one of the elders of the clan. He is exiled for seven years to his mother's kin and will not return to Umuofia, his home town, until the land is cleansed of the abomination:

> The drums and the dancing began again and reached fever-heat. Darkness was around the corner, and the burial was near. Guns fired the last salute and the cannon rent the sky. And then from the center of the delirious fury came a cry of agony and shouts of horror. It was as if spell had been cast. All was silent. In the center of the crowd a boy lay in a pool of blood. It was the dead man's

sixteen-year-old son, who with his brothers and half-brothers had been dancing the traditional farewell to their father. Okonkwo's gun had exploded and a piece of iron had pierced the boy's heart. The confusion that followed was without parallel in the tradition of Umuofia. Violent deaths were frequent, but nothing like this had ever happened. The only course open to Okonkwo was to flee from the clan. It is a crime against the earth goddess to kill a clansman, and a man who committed it must flee from the land. The crime is of two kinds, male and female. Okonkwo had committed the female, because it had been inadvertent. He could return to the clan after seven years. (Achebe, 1958, 109–10)

The second intrinsic or ontological component of a human person is the soul, known in Igbo as *Mmuo* or spirit.

## *Mmuo* or Spirit

Although *Mmuo* (or *muo*) is the generic term for immaterial beings, gods, ancestors, and ghosts, it also designates the immaterial nature of the human being. This demonstrates that in Igbo cosmology, a human person is thought of as partaking existentially in the being-ness of spirits.[7] Abstracting beyond mere physical appearance, the Igbo view the human person as half matter and half form.[8] The *Mmuo* or spirit is the cause or principle of life in the individual and the primary source of self-identity. The human soul or spirit is credited in the human person with originating activities such as thought, reflection, advanced consciousness, advanced self-consciousness, memory, deliberation, planning, execution of plans, imagination, and so forth. According to Theophilus Okere (1995), the idea of self or person in the Igbo context cannot be fully articulated in the absence of *Mmuo* or soul:

> The Muo or spirit in man is clearly conceived as the cause or principle of life in the individual because when someone dies it is often said that his spirit has left muo ya ahafula. Further usage of the notion of spirit shows that it is regarded as the seat of emotions. . . . It is the Muo in man that is responsible for the following activities without which the idea of Onwe/Self could neither emerge nor be sustained: (1) Uche, Iche echiche—Thinking, considering, reflecting with some anxiety over one's lot. . . . (2) Iru eruru to reflect deeply, usually on some sad, sombre, tragic subject. (3) Ncheta lit. to think out, to remember, recall. (4) Nghota—lit. to pluck, to grasp, to understand, to comprehend, to appreciate the full implications of. . . . (5) Izu—deliberation, consensus or wisdom and information resulting therefrom. . . . (6) Ako—Cleverness, Wisdom, Prudence. . . . (7) Ngenge, Igba Ngenge—Imagining, surmising; and finally (8) Atutu, Itu atutu—to plan, to project, to order the execution of a plan. These and all such are activities of the Muo or spirit in man. A dead man cannot do them. An animal or any being lacking spirit cannot do them. They are therefore typical of the self of which Muo is a

constituent part and it is from its aspect as Muo that the self can do them. (Okere 1995, IX)

## Chi

*Chi*, as a constitutive element of the human person, is not limited to the Igbo society. The same concept or similar concepts are found among some other African societies.[9] In the context of the colonial and missionary encounter in Igboland, and the urgency exhibited by Western missionary agents to understand local cultures, as well as to translate the Christian scripture into local languages, *Chi* hastily took the place of the Christian guardian angel. In reality, as Okere (1995) points out, "there is really no Western philosophical or theological equivalent."[10] In relation to the ontological structure of persons among the Igbo, *Chi* may be viewed as the creative essence of the Supreme Being (*Chi-ukwu*, great *Chi*, or God), complementary spirit, and personal destiny.

### Chi as Creative Essence of the Supreme Creator or Chi-ukwu

To understand the concept of *Chi* as a creative essence, one needs to revisit Igbo cosmology. According to John Anenechukwu Umeh (1997), Igbo see the universe as a deliberate act of a Supreme Being known as *Chi-ukwu* (great *Chi* or God). The Igbo word for the universe is *Uwa*, which for Umeh is an onomatopoeia for the fact that the universe came into being with a mystical sound ("Uuu . . . waaaa . . ."), and with this sound the universe "blazed forth like a flourish of light of the first sunshine at daybreak."[11] The creation of human beings within the universe follows the infinite, emanative essence of the Supreme Being through the idea of *Chi* or God's creative essence. Thus, "the spiritual [essence] and timeless essence of all in the universe and beyond are the respective *Chi*, which aggregate into *Chi-Ukwu* [great *Chi* or God], or part thereof."[12]

As is evident in Igbo cosmology, every individual person has an individual *Chi*, who created him or her. No two individuals share the same *Chi*. Chinua Achebe attributes the fierce egalitarianism among the Igbo to this unique role of *Chi* as a constitutive element of the Igbo self.[13] He writes, "But we should at least notice in passing the fierce egalitarianism . . . which was such a marked feature of Igbo political organization and may justifiably speculate on its possible derivation from this concept of every man's original and absolute uniqueness."[14]

*Chi* is the emanation of the Supreme Being in every individual person. The Igbo believe that when someone dies, his or her *Chi* returns to the great *Chi*, or Supreme Being (God). The individual, minuscule essence or *Chi* reunites with the infinite creative essence of the Supreme Being. The *Chi* of a deceased person does not cease to be. However, the individuality of that particular creative essence is lost in the great "sun" of essences of the Supreme Being. *Chi-ukwu*, or the Supreme Being, is the "Cosmic Unity as well as the Oneness of all that exist."[15]

## Chi as Complementary Spirit

The idea of the dualism of being is present in the Igbo worldview and plays a vital role in the concept of the person. This notion is expressed as "wherever something stands, something else will stand beside it. Nothing is absolute. . . . The world in which we live has its double and counterpart in the realm of spirits. A man lives here and his chi there."[16]

*Chi* in Igbo is not only immanent to the human person but also external to the self. For this reason, *Chi* is often translated in Igbo as personal deity, since an individual is free to erect a shrine for his personal *Chi*, worship or despise it.[17] Thus, just "being there" is not a sufficient ontological mode to categorize human existence in the Igbo context. The existence of the human person involves an intricate relationship between the corporeal and spiritual, visible, and invisible elements.[18]

## Chi as Destiny

*Chi*, as already noted, in many ways, depicts an unprecedented uniqueness and individualism of the human person in Igbo thought and religion. A happy and successful person in Igbo worldview is someone who is at peace with his or her *Chi*, or one whose *Chi* is active, awake, or good. If someone escapes a near-fatal accident, the Igbo will say that one's *Chi* is awake or active. A mad, unhappy human being or one who acts in ways antithetical to reason would be considered as someone who is in utter disharmony with his or her *Chi*. *Chi* is responsible for a person's destiny in the physical world.

*Chi* as destiny is not to be confused with an unalterable fatalism or predetermination.[19] Underlying the idea of *Chi* as destiny is the presence of choice and responsibility. An individual is fully responsible for his or her actions since everyone's *Chi* operates according to one's choices in life. This is expressed in Igbo as *onye kwe, chi ya ekwe*, which literally means that "when an individual says yes, his or her *Chi* will also say yes." The existentialist denunciation of "bad faith" is a sentiment shared by the Igbo. The Igbo conceive destiny as a maneuverable life path:

> Every individual has a distinct destiny, i.e., his allotted path in life, a path however, which is so delicately laid out that it has opportunities, failures and successes strewn along it. The individual's Chi enables, helps and collaborates with him in manipulating these possibilities for his self-realization. Hence the paradoxical juxtaposition of both limitation and enablement which connects the Chi idea with destiny in the sense of fatalism, but also makes it the very

agent enabling and prodding the individual towards success and achievement as he bursts the molds of fatalism. (Okere 1995, IX)

## THE EXTRINSIC OR NORMATIVE DIMENSION OF PERSONHOOD

My analysis of *Chi* as the mark of individuality in the Igbo concept of the person may falsely suggest that the Igbo conceive of an individual as an asocial, autonomous concentration of various indifferent conditions. This, of course, is not the case. A closer study of individuality in the Igbo setting clearly shows that various social dimensions of experience are constitutive of that very individuality.[20] Within Igbo society, self-identity is a relational and transactional category. Thus, a person is a creative articulation of his or her individuality within the matrix of the social community.[21] In a very fundamental sense, the community shapes identity.

The extrinsic or normative dimension of personhood is a procedural, status-oriented, self-realization of a human being, which individuals actualize in communality with other human beings and things in the world. Individuals achieve an extrinsic or normative status of personhood through the acquisition of morals. A child may be devoid of the extrinsic status of personhood, but is intrinsically speaking a human person. An individual acquires the normative status of a person through his or her being in time and space from childhood through elder-hood or even ancestor-hood. This fact is clearly expressed in this Igbo proverb, "what an old man sees sitting, a child does not see standing."[22] Normative personhood is neither a guaranteed status nor a permanent condition of an adult human being. An adult, whose moral psychology fails to appropriate the standard norms of his or her community, loses the extrinsic or normative status of personhood. In this sense, the normative concept of the person in Igbo traditional society hinges on a set of communalistic or communitarian ethics.

When the Igbo say *"nkea abughi mmadu"* or "this one is not a person," they demonstratively point to a human being who has not attained normative personhood or who has lost the extrinsic status of a person. *Nkea abughi mmadu*, or "this one is not a person," is a value judgment against someone whose behaviors are clearly anti-reason or anti-community. It points to the perversion of a normative persona or to some form of pathological disunity. Similar ideas exist among other African societies. For example, Placide Tempels (1959) in his ethnographic research among the Baluba group of the Democratic Republic of Congo (formerly Zaire) writes that "[t]he word 'muntu' [person] inherently includes an idea of excellence or plenitude. And thus the Baluba will speak of 'ke muntu po,' 'this is not a muntu,' of a man who behaves unworthily."[23]

Additionally, a person in the Igbo viewpoint functions as the center of a network of relationships. For example, a human being is a person in relation to being the grandson or granddaughter, son or daughter, brother or sister, father or mother, and so on of someone else in space and time. This network of relationships also serves as a channel of recognition for the individual. In this sense, the community grants meaning to the individual. This is expressed in Igbo as *umunna bu ike* or the community is my power or strength.

The strong communalism observed among African societies led some scholars of African studies to deny Africans a sense of individuality or to accord priority to the communal over the individual among Africans. This seems to be the case for the Belgian missionary, Placide Tempels (1906–1977), who lived among the Bantu people in former Zaire. Tempels in his work *La Philosophie Bantoue* (1945)[24] or *Bantu Philosophy* (1959) interprets the Baluba word *muntu*, or person, as a concept antonymous to the European notion of individualism or individuation:

> For the Bantu, man never appears in fact as an isolated individual, as an independent entity. Every man, every individual, forms a link in the chain of vital forces, a living link, active and passive, joined from above to the ascending line of his ancestry and sustaining below him the line of his descendants. It may be said that among Bantu the individual is necessarily an individual within the clan. (Tempels 1959, 108)

But does the importance of the community in the shaping of a person's identity result in the loss of individuality or to unanimism?[25]

The Igbo word for self is *onwe m*,[26] which derives from the verb "to possess." *Onwe m*, or *self*, literally means, "I am the possessor of myself." In his or her pure spontaneity, the self or *onwe m*, which is the deepest expression of awareness, knows itself. He or she is simply the owner of himself or herself. As much as we may try, one does not have direct memories of another person's experience nor takes direct hold of another's conscience and will.[27] Tempels (1959) seems to realize this when he talks about the notion of free will and conscience among the Bantu. He quotes a Bantu saying: "*Munda mwa mukwenu kemwelwa kuboko, nansya ulele nandi butanda bumo!* (None may put his arm into his neighbour's inside, not even when he shares his bed). The neighbour's conscience remains inviolable, even for his closest friend."[28]

The traditional Igbo, so to say, have no form of insurance outside the community. The community provides for the individual in times of disaster, while the individual must strive for integration and recognition. The community, with its historicity, culture, and spaces for creativity, becomes second nature to the human person and closes any existing subsistence gap generated by humanity's fundamental or basic nature. Therefore, the human person in the Igbo context is complete within the community.

# IMPLICATIONS FOR RAWLS'S THEORY OF GLOBAL JUSTICE

I will conclude by saying that while the Igbo concept of the person accentuates the critical role the community plays in shaping the identity of the individual, the notion of a person in Igbo, nevertheless, partly transcends the community. This partial transcendence of the social is compatible with communitarian ethics in Igbo or African societies because the individual remains a source of legitimate claims outside the group. The over-emphasis of the precedency of the communal over the individual may be rightly understood within the historical and political contexts of pan-Africanism.

Today, such emphasis has unacceptable social and political consequences within and beyond Africa. At the local level, for instance, it robs persons of the distinctiveness and independence needed to make rightful claims against oppressive regimes. Domestically and internationally, those eager to postpone the application of human rights in Africa evoke the apparent group-oriented nature or mentality of Africans, while vigorously claiming that the Universal Declaration of Human Rights (UDHR) is a secular version of Judeo-Christian values and Eurocentric extrapolation of Western liberal individualism. In as much as this claim cannot be easily dismissed, a closer study of the ontological and normative status of persons among Africans, as the Igbo case demonstrates, grants retrospective cultural legitimacy to most articles of the UDHR. A person has an intrinsic value in Igbo or African thought, whether as an individual or as a member of a group. While the Igbo may overcome egocentrism in the community, he or she is not egoless. Instead, the Igbo (or African) is a self-authenticating individual within a community of individuals. Therefore, the concept of the person among the Igbo (or Sub-Saharan Africans) is a much more complex system that defies the rather simplistic and predictably antagonistic schema: individualism versus communitarianism or the West versus Africa.

Much of the Igbo concept of the person avoids placing priority on either the community or the individual. An all-inclusive primacy of inalienable rights by individuals regardless of consequences, contrasted with a totalized subsuming of the individual by the community, misses the nuance of African moral order and concept of the person. Each individual within the community must acknowledge his or her responsibility to the community. This principle often gives the appearance of the dominance of communalism over individualism. While the individual ought to place the community at the forefront of moral and economic interests, this priority is nevertheless contextual. The individual is not eclipsed by his or her responsibilities toward the community, but is rather enriched by them.[29]

Rawls's idea of basic human rights is predicated on the claim that citizens of non-Western societies may not have a liberal conception of the self but may instead see themselves only as groups or segments of society. For this reason, they may not have the psychological disposition to make direct, legitimate claims on their government. In this sense, a class of human rights that includes articles 1 and 19 of the UDHR would, in Rawls's view, amount to ethnocentrism or imposition of Western values on non-Western peoples. Here, we may summon the courage to espouse a cross-cultural perspective that echoes the position of Amartya Sen that "respect for human rights and ideas of democracy are not simply Western values, but rather that substantial elements of these ideas can be found in all major cultures, religions, and traditions."[30]

Considering the interdependence of peoples, the dynamism and interconnectedness of world cultures, and the present trend of globalization, we could reasonably and optimistically say that achieving retrospective cultural legitimacy for UDHR, where the applicability of the existent international norms is not yet firmly rooted, is quite feasible. After all, the peoples of the world are always engaged in cultural exchange and the philosophical appropriation of the "other." In this modern age, world cultures are no longer isolated bubbles or the distant projections from travelers' tales. One can strongly contend that the schematic divides among peoples, such as individualism versus communalism, no longer define the foundational properties of personhood across the globe. What is strictly Western or African now collides with what was previously alien, and out of this confluence of ideas arises the *métissage* of cultures.

## NOTES

1. An earlier version of this chapter was presented as an invited talk at the "Life-Body" conference at Johannes Gutenberg University Mainz and published as a book chapter in *Life, Body, Person and Self: A Reconsideration of Core Concepts in Bioethics*, edited by Stephan Grätzel and Eberhard Guhe (Freiburg: Karl Aber Verlag, 2015).
2. Mboya 1963, 164–65.
3. Mbiti 1999, 106.
4. See also Agbasiere 2000, 65.
5. Ibid.
6. See also Deutsch 1992, 6.
7. See Okere 1995, IX.
8. Ibid.
9. *Ori* in Yoruba is very similar to the concept of *Chi* among the Igbo.
10. Okere 1995, IX.
11. Umeh 1997, 5.
12. Ibid., 6.
13. While the fierce egalitarianism Achebe writes about relates to the political culture of pre-colonial Igbo society, it is not obvious how the unique nature of every individual, predicated on the concept of *Chi*, translates to egalitarianism. The pre-colonial Igbo society had no kings or queens. However, it was a hierarchical society with a consultation forum made up of male elders and titled men.
14. Achebe 1998, 70.
15. Umeh 1997, 130.
16. Achebe 1998, 68.

17. Okere 1995, IX.
18. See Okolo 2003, 247–54.
19. See also Okere 1995, IX.
20. See also Deutsch 1992, 20.
21. Ibid., 3.
22. A similar Igbo proverb that deals with this topic says: *ana eji anya chara acha ahu ihe di na akpa dibia* ("it is with matured eyes that one sees what is concealed in the bag of the medicine man").
23. Tempels 1959, 101.
24. *La Philosophie Bantoue* is a translation of Rev. Placide Tempel's work from Dutch to French by Dr. A. Rubbens in 1945. It was first published by Lovania at Elizabethville in the Belgium Congo. See Tempels 1959, 10.
25. Bell, citing Hountondji, describes unanimism as "the illusion that all men and women in such societies speak with one voice and share the same opinion about fundamental issues." Bell 2002, 60.
26. See also Okere 1995, IX.
27. See also Deutsch 1992, 16–17; Okolo 2003.
28. Tempels 1959, 105.
29. Thanks to my 2016 student of African philosophy through literature, Devin Snell, for the discourse on the dichotomy between the individual and the community in African and Western philosophies.
30. Brock 2010, 90. See also Sen 1999, 147–48, 154–55.

# Epilogue

No sooner had the good philosopher celebrated with apodictic conviction the mastery of one philosophical problem than new ones disclosed themselves. Philosophy, it seems, is a perpetual aporetic investigation. Its joy and rewards lie in the inquiry itself, the fleeting triumphs of the human mind, and the fallibilism that knocks again and again at the door in no time. Whether one is a supporter or opponent of Rawls's idea of global justice, it is relevant to note that his theory of international justice, "the law of peoples," is only a realistic utopia. The fact that Rawls sets for his theory limited but pragmatic goals on the international stage means "that there will be much in the world to which Rawls's political philosophy offers no reconciliation."[1]

Although his account of global justice might suffer some setbacks at the moment or may not resonate with everyone's moral considerations, it is nevertheless a starting point in this all-important discourse. The debate must begin somewhere and somehow, and Rawls has given us the *prolegomena* to future discourses on justice. We now must connect the dots, fill in the blanks, and close the gaps by taking that debate to the next level while having as our framework the legal, economic, cultural, and religious complexities of our world. And perhaps, someday, we may realize a reformed model of Rawlsian global justice. Rawls has taken public philosophy a step further. Today, many of us in the field of social and political inquiry are his appreciative followers, even when we do not always agree with every aspect of his theory. Our sustained academic efforts must include finding ways to make our local and global communities, as well as the environment, better than we found them. And if, for any reason, we fall short of achieving the peace, stability, and sustainability that we hope for in our world, we should, nevertheless, remain grateful to Rawls for "deflecting us from worse alternatives."[2] And if someday, by either conscientious effort or sheer luck, we find ourselves beyond the frontiers of justice as fairness, we may conceptualize justice as fairness engendered by empathy, compassion, and love for our fellow humans and some other living beings.

## NOTES

1. https://plato.stanford.edu/entries/rawls/#OriPosPolCon.
2. http://harvardpress.typepad.com/hup_publicity/2013/04/john-rawls-a-theory-of-justice-1971.html.

# Bibliography

ACHEBE, C. (1995). *Things Fall Apart*. New York: Everyman's Library.
ACHEBE, C. (1998). "Chi in Igbo Cosmology." In: EZE, E. C. (ed.). *African Philosophy: An Anthology*. Malden: Blackwell Publishers, 67–72.
ACKERMAN, B. (1989). "Why Dialogue?" *The Journal of Philosophy*, Vol. lxxvi, No. 1. (January), 5–22.
AGBASIERE, J. T. (2000). *Women in Igbo Life and Thought*. London: Routledge.
ALEJANDRO, R. (1998). *The Limits of Rawlsian Justice*. London: The John Hopkins University Press.
AMAESHI, K., NNODIM, P., and OSUJI, O. (2012). *Corporate Social Responsibility, Entrepreneurship, and Innovation*. New York: Routledge, 2012.
AN-Na'im, A. A. (1990). "Problems of Universal Cultural Legitimacy for Human Rights." In: AN-Na'im, A. A and DENG, F. M. (eds.). *Human Rights in Africa: Cross-cultural Perspectives*. Washington, DC: Brookings Institution, 331–67.
AN-Na'im, A. A. (1992). "Toward a Cross-cultural Approach to Defining International Standards of Human Rights: The Meaning of Cruel, Inhuman, or Degrading Treatment or Punishment." In: AN-Na'im, A. A. (ed.). *Human Rights in Cross-cultural Perspectives: A Quest for Consensus*. Philadelphia: University of Pennsylvania Press, 19–43.
ARNESON, J. (2000) "Rawls Versus Utilitarianism in the Light of *Political Liberalism.*" In: DAVION, V. and WOLF, C. (eds.). *The Idea of Political Liberalism: Essays on Rawls*. Lanham, MD: Rowman & Littlefield, 231–51.
AUDARD, C. (1996). "Political Liberalism, Secular Republicanism: Two Answers to the Challenges of Pluralism." In: ARCHARD, D. (ed.). *Philosophy and Pluralism*. Cambridge: Cambridge University Press, 165–75.
AUDARD, C. (2007). "Cultural Imperialism and Democratic Peace." In: Martin R. and Reidy D. A. (eds.). *Rawls's Law of Peoples: A Realistic Utopia?* Malden: Blackwell Publishing, 59–75.
AUDARD, C. (2014). *John Rawls*. New York: Routledge.
AUDI, R. (1989). "The Separation of Church and State and the Obligations of Citizenship." *Philosophy and Public Affairs*, Vol. 18, No. 3.
AUDI, R. (2000). *Religious Commitment and Secular Reason*. Cambridge: Cambridge University Press.
AUDI, R. (2001). *The Architecture of Reason: The Structure and Substance of Rationality*. Oxford: Oxford University Press.
AUDI, R. and WOLTERSTORFF, N. (1997). *Religion in the Public Square*. Lanham, MD: Rowman & Littlefield.

AYBAR, J., HARLAN, J. D., and LEE, W. J. (1991). "John Rawls: For the Record." In: *Harvard Review of Philosophy*.
BARRY, B. (1995). "John Rawls and the Search for Stability." In: *Ethics*, 105, 874–915.
BEEM, C. (1998). *Pluralism and Consensus: Conceptions of the Good in the American Polity*. Chicago: Center for Scientific study of Religion.
BEITZ, C. R. (1999). "Social and Cosmopolitan Liberalism." *International Affairs*, Vol. 75, No. 3, 515–29.
BEITZ, C. R. (1979). *Political Theory and International Relations*. Princeton, NJ: Princeton University Press.
BEITZ, C. R. (2000). "Rawls Law of Peoples." In: *Ethics,* 110, 669–96.
BELL, R. H. (2002). *Understanding African Philosophy*. New York: Routledge.
BENTHAM, J. (1825). *The Rationale of Reward*. London: John and H. L. Hunt.
BENTHAM, J. (1970). *An Introduction to the Principles of Morals and Legislation*. BURNS, J. H. and HART, H. L. A. (eds.). London: The Athlone Press.
BERRY, B. J. (1982). *Hume, Hegel and Human Nature*. The Hague, Boston, and London: Martinus Nijhoff Publishers.
BIELEFELDT, H. (2000). "'Western' Versus 'Islamic' Human Rights Conceptions? A Critique of Cultural Essentialism in the Discussion on Human Rights." *Political Theory*, Vol. 28, No. 1, 90–121.
BLOCKER, G. H. and SMITH, E. H. (1980). *John Rawls Theory of Social Justice*. Athens: Ohio University Press.
BLOWFIELD, M. and MURRAY, A. (2008). *Corporate Responsibility: A Critical Introduction*. Oxford: Oxford University Press.
BOHMAN, J. (1995). "Public Reason and Cultural Pluralism: Political liberalism and the Problem of Moral Conflict." *Political Theory*, Vol. 23, No. 2, 253–79.
BRENNAN, S and NOGGLE, R. (2000). "Rawls Neglected Childhood: Reflections on the Original Position, Stability, and the Child's Sense of Justice." In: DAVION, V. and WOLF, C. (eds.). *The Idea of Political Liberalism: Essays on Rawls*. Lanham, MD: Rowman & Littlefield, 46–72.
BROCK, G. (2010). "Recent Works on Rawls's Law of Peoples: Critic versus Defenders." *American Philosophical Quarterly*, Vol. 47, No. 1, 85–101.
BRONNER, S. E. (1994). *Of Critical Theory and Its Theorists*. Oxford: Blackwell Publishers.
BUCHANAN, A. (2000). "Rawls's Law of Peoples: Rules for a Vanished Westphalian World." In: *Ethics*, 110, 697–721.
BUCKLEY, M. (2010). "The Structure of Justification in Political Constructivism." *Metaphilosophy*, Vol. 41, No. 5.
BYKVIST, K. (2010). *Utilitarianism: A Guide for the Perplexed*. New York: Continuum, 2010.
CALHOUN, C. (ed.). (1993). *Habermas and the Public Sphere*. Cambridge, MA: MIT Press.
CANEY, S. (1995). "Anti-Perfectionism and Rawlsian Liberalism." *Political Studies*, Vol. xliii, No. 2, 248–64.
CANEY, S. (2001). "Cosmopolitanism and the Law of Peoples." In: KUKATHAS, C. (ed.). (2003). *John Rawls: Critical Assessment of Leading Political Philosophers*. Vol. 4. London and New York: Routledge, 263–92.
CARD, C. (2000). "Individual Entitlements in Justice as Fairness." In: DAVION, V. and WOLF, C. (eds.). *The Idea of Political Liberalism: Essays on Rawls*. Lanham, MD: Rowman & Littlefield, 176–89.
CARTER, S. (1993). *The Culture of Disbelief*. New York: Basic Books.
CHOI, N. (2015). "Liberalism and the Interpretive Turn: Rival Approaches or Cross-Purposes?" *Review of Politics*, Vol. 77, No. 2, 243–70.
CHUA, A. (2018). *Political Tribes: Group Instinct and the Fate of Nations*. New York: Penguin Press.
CLARKE, M. J. (1996). "The Public Use of Reason in Kant's Political Philosophy." Michigan: UMI Dissertation Services.
CLARKE, S. (1999). "Contractarianism, Liberal Neutrality and Epistemology." *Political Studies*, Vol. xlviii, 627–42.

COHEN, J. (1999). "Moral Pluralism and Political Consensus." In: RICHARDSON, H. S. and WEITHMAN, P. J. (eds.). *The Philosophy of Rawls: A Collection of Essays*. Vol. 4. New York and London: Garland, 56–77.
D'AGOSTINO, F. (1996). *Free Public Reason*. New York; Oxford: Oxford University Press.
DANIELS, N. (ed.). (1989). *Reading Rawls*. Stanford: Stanford University Press.
DANIELS, N. (2000). "Reflective Equilibrium and Justice as Political." In: DAVION, V. and WOLF, C. (eds). *The Idea of Political Liberalism: Essays on Rawls*. Lanham, MD: Rowman & Littlefield, 127–54.
DAUENHAUER, B. P. (2000). "A Good Word for A Modus Vivendi" In: DAVION, V. and WOLF, C. (eds.). *The Idea of Political Liberalism: Essay on Rawls*. Lanham, MD: Rowman & Littlefield, 204–20.
DAVION, V. and WOLF, C. (eds.). (2000). "Introduction: From Comprehensive Justice to Political Liberalism." In: DAVION, V and WOLF, C. (eds.). *The Idea of Political Liberalism: Essays on Rawls*. Lanham, MD: Rowman & Littlefield, 1–15.
DE CASTRO, E. (2018). "Globalization, Inequalities and Justice." In: RUIZ, R. C. et al. (eds.). *Philosophy of Globalization*. Berlin: Walter de Gruyter.
DEUTSCH, E. *Creative Being: The Crafting of Person and World*. Honolulu: University of Hawaii Press, 1992.
DOMBROWSKI, D. A. and DELTETE, R. (2000). *A Brief, Liberal, Catholic Defense of Abortion*. Urbana and Chicago: University of Illinois Press.
DOMBROWSKI, D. A. (2001). *Rawls and Religion: The case of Political Liberalism*. Albany: State University of New York Press.
DOYLE, M. W. (2006). "One World, Many Peoples: International Justice in John Rawls's The Law of Peoples." *Perspectives on Politics*, Vol. 4, No. 1, 109–20.
DUSCHE, M. (2000). *Der Philosoph als Mediator*. Wien: Passagen Verlag.
DWORKIN, R. (1977). *Taking Rights Seriously*. London: Duckworth.
EJOBOWAH, J. B. (2001). *Competing Claims to Recognition in the Nigerian Public Sphere: A Liberal Argument about Justice in Plural Societies*. Lanham, MD: Lexington Books.
ESTLUND, D. (1998). "The Insularity of the Reasonable: Why Political Liberalism Must Admit the Truth." In: *Ethics*, 108, 252–75.
ESTLUND, D. (1999). "The Survival of Egalitarian Justice in John Rawls's Political Liberalism." In: RICHARDSON, H. S and WEITHMAN, P. J. (eds.). *The Philosophy of Rawls: A Collection of Essays*. Vol. 4. New York and London: Garland, 198–209.
EZE, E. C. (1997). "Introduction: Philosophy and the (Post)colonial." In: EZE, E. C. (ed.). *Postcolonial African Philosophy: A Critical Reader*. Cambridge: Blackwell.
FAGOTHEY, A. (1976). *Right and Reason: Ethics in Theory and Practice*, 6th ed. Saint Louis: C.V. Mosby.
FARK, R. (1992). "Cultural Foundations for the International Protection of Human Rights." In: AN-Na'im, A. A. (ed.). *Human Rights in Cross-cultural Perspectives: A Quest for Consensus*. Philadelphia: University of Pennsylvania Press, 44–64.
FINNIS, J. (2000). "Abortion, Natural Law, and Public Reason." In: GEORGE, R. P. and WOLFE, C. (eds.). *Natural Law and Public Reason*. Washington, DC: Georgetown University Press, 75–105.
FRANKEL, C. (2002). *The Case of Modern Liberalism*. New Brunswick, NJ: Transaction Publishers.
FRASER, N. (1998). "From Redistribution to Recognition? Dilemmas of Justice in a 'Post-Socialist Age.'" In: WILLETT, C. (ed.). *Theorizing Multiculturalism*. Malden and Oxford: Blackwell Publishers.
FRAZER, E. and LACEY, N. (1995). "Politics and the Public in Rawls' Political Liberalism." In: *Political Studies*, Vol. xliii, 233–47.
FREEMAN, S. (ed.). (1999). *John Rawls: Collected Papers*. Cambridge, MA: Harvard University Press.
FREEMAN, S. (2007a). *Justice and the Social Contract: Essays on Rawlsian Political Philosophy*. Oxford: Oxford University Press.
FREEMAN, S. (2007b). *Rawls*. New York: Routledge.

FREEMAN, S. (2018). *Liberalism and Distributive Justice*. New York: Oxford University Press.
FRIEDMAN, M. (1962). *Capitalism and Freedom*. Chicago: University of Chicago Press.
FRIEDMAN, M. and FRIEDMAN, R. (1979). *Free to Choose: A Personal Statement*. New York: Harcourt Brace and Company.
GALSTON, W. A. (1982). "Defending Liberalism." In: *American Political Science Review*, Vol. 72.
GALSTON, W. A. (1989). "Pluralism and Social Unity." In: *Ethics*, Vol. 99, 711–26.
GALSTON, W. A. (2018). *Antipluralism: The Populist Threat to Liberal Democracy*. New Haven, CT: Yale University Press.
GARGARELLA, R. (2000). *The Scepter of Reason*. Dordrecht: Kluwer Academic Publishers.
GARNER, T. R. and ROSEN, B. (1967). *Moral Philosophy: A Systematic Introduction to the Normative Ethics and Meta-ethics*. New York: Macmillan Company.
GAUS, G. F. (1996). *Justificatory Liberalism: An Essay on Epistemology and Political Theory*. New York and Oxford: Oxford University Press.
GAUS, G. F. (1999). "Reasonable Pluralism and the Domain of the Political: How the Weakness of John Rawls's Political Liberalism Can Be Overcome by a Justificatory Liberalism." In: *Inquiry*, Vol. 42, 259–84.
GAUS, G., COURTLAND, S. D. and SCHMIDTZ, D. (2018). "Liberalism." In: *Stanford Encyclopedia of Philosophy*. http://plato.stanford.edu/entries/liberalism/.
GAUTHIER, D. (1974). "Justice and Natural Endowment: Toward a Critique of Rawls' Ideological Framework." In: *Social Theory and Practice*, Vol. 3, 3–26.
GEORGE, R. P. and WOLFE, C. (2000) "Introduction." In: GEORGE, R. P. and WOLFE, C. (eds.). *Natural law and Public Reason*: Washington, DC: Georgetown University Press.
GORDON, D. (2019). "John Rawls's Unfortunate Notions of the Nation-State." *Mises Wire*, November 29, 2019. https://mises.org/wire/john-rawlss-unfortunate-notions-nation-state.
GRAY, J. (2000) "Pluralism and Toleration in Contemporary Political Philosophy." In: *Political Studies*, Vol. 48, 323–33.
GRCÍC, J. M. (1980). "John Rawls and the Social Contract Tradition." Dissertation, University of Notre Dame, Indiana.
GREENAWALT, K. (1994). "On Public Reason" In: *Chicago-Kent Law Review*, Vol. 69, 669–89.
HABERMAS, J. (1989). *The Structural Transformation of the Public Sphere*. Trans. BURGER, T. Cambridge: Polity Press.
HABERMAS, J. (1994). *Faktizität und Geltung: Beiträge zur Diskurstheorie des Rechts und des demokratischen Rechtsstaats*. Frankfurt a.M.: Suhrkamp.
HABERMAS, J. (1995). "Reconciliation Through the Use of Public Reason: Remarks on John Rawls's Political Liberalism." In: *Journal of Philosophy*, Vol. xcii, No. 3, 109–31.
HABERMAS, J. (1996). *Die Einbeziehung des Anderen: Studien zur politischen Theorie*. Frankfurt a.M.: Suhrkamp.
HABERMAS, J. (1999). *Wahrheit und Rechtfertigung: Philosophische Aufsätze*. Frankfurt a.M.: Suhrkamp.
HAMPTON, J. (1994). "The Common Faith of Liberalism" In: *Pacific Philosophical Quarterly*, Vol. 75, 186–216.
HART, H. L. A. (1989). "Rawls on Liberty and Its Priority." In: DANIELS, N. (ed.). *Reading Rawls: Critical Studies on Rawls' "A Theory of Justice"*. Stanford: Stanford University Press, 230–52.
HAYDEN, P. (2002). *John Rawls: Towards a Just World Order*. Cardiff: University of Wales Press.
HAZONY, Y. (2017). "Is 'Classical Liberalism' Conservative?" In: *Wall Street Journal*. New York: Dow Jones & Company. https://www.wsj.com/articles/is-classical-liberalism-conservative-1507931462.
HEGEL, F. W. (2008). *Outlines of the Philosophy of Right*. Oxford: Oxford University Press.
HEIDEGGER, M. (1993). *Sein und Zeit*. Tuebingen: Max Niemeyer Verlag, 1993.
HEIDEGGER, M. (2002). *Grundbegriffe der Aristotelischen Philosophie*. Frankfurt a.M.: Vittorio Klostermann Verlag.

HERSHOVITZ, S. (2000). "A Mere Modus Vivendi?" In: DAVION, V. and WOLF, C. (eds). *The Idea of Political Liberalism: Essays on Rawls*. Lanham, MD: Rowman & Littlefield, 221–30.
HILL, T. E. (1994). "The Stability Problem in *Political Liberalism*." In: *Pacific Philosophical Quarterly*, Vol. 75, 333–52.
HINSCH, W. (Hrsg.). (1994). *Die Idee des politischen Liberalismus: Aufsätze 1978–1989 / John Rawls*. Frankfurt a.M.: Suhrkamp.
HINSCH, W. (2001). "Global Distributive Justice." In: *Metaphilosophy*, Vol. 32, No. 1 / 2, 58–78.
HÖFFE, O. (1975). *Strategien der Humanität. Zur Ethik öffentlicher Entscheidungsprozesse*. Freiburg and München: Alber.
HÖFFE, O. (1977). "Kritische Einführung in Rawls' Theorie der Gerechtigkeit." In: HÖFFE, O. (Hrsg.). *Über John Rawls Theorie der Gerechtigkeit*. Frankfurt: Suhrkamp, 11–40.
HÖFFE, O. (Hrsg.). (1992a). *Einführung in die Utilitaristische Ethik*. Tübingen: Francke Verlag.
HÖFFE, O. (Hrsg.). (1992b). "Schwierigkeit des Utilitarismus mit der Gerechtigkeit." In: GÄHDE, U. und SCHWADER, H. W. (Hrsg.). *Der Klassische Utilitarismus*. Berlin: Akademie, 292–317.
HÖFFE, O. (1998). "Überlegungsgleichgewicht in Zeiten der Globalisierung." In: HÖFFE, O. (Hrsg.). *John Rawls: Eine Theorie der Gerechtigkeit*. Berlin: Akademie, 271–93.
HOLLAND, F. M. (1891). *Frederick Douglas: The Colored Orator*. New York: Funk and Wagnalls Company.
HOLLENBACH, D. (1993). "The Political Role of Religion." In: *San Diego Law Review*, Vol. 30, 877–901.
HÖLSCHER, L. (1997). *Öffentlichkeit und Geheimnis: Eine Begriffsgeschichtliche Untersuchung zur Entstehung der Öffentlichkeit in der frühen Neuzeit*. Stuttgart: Klett-Cotta.
HONNETH, A. (2002). "Liberal und Normativ." *Die Zeit* (28. November). Nr. 49, 39.
HORTON, J. (2003). "Rawls Public Reason and the Limits of Liberal Justification." In: *Contemporary Political Theory*, Vol. 2, No. 1, 5–23.
HORTON, J. (2017). "What Might It Mean for Political Theory to Be More 'Realistic'?" In: *Philosophia*, Vol. 45, Issue 2, 487–501.
HOWARD, R. E. (1990). "Group versus Individual Identity in the African Debate on Human Rights." In: AN-Na'im, A. A and DENG, F. M. (eds.). *Human Rights in Africa: Cross-Cultural Perspectives*. Washington, DC: Brookings Institution, 159–83.
HUDGSON, D. H. (1967). *Consequences of Utilitarianism: A Study in Normative Ethics and Legal Theory*. Oxford: Clarendon Press.
HUEMER, M. (1996). "Rawls's Problem of Stability." In: *Social Theory and Practice*, Vol. 22, 375–95. In: DAVION, V and WOLF, C. (eds.). *The Idea of Political Liberalism: Essays on Rawls*. Lanham, MD: Rowman & Littlefield, 231–51.
INGRAM, A. (1996). "Rawlsians, Pluralists, and Cosmopolitans." In: ARCHARD, D. (ed.). *Philosophy and Pluralism*. Cambridge: Cambridge University Press, 147–61.
JACKSON, B. (2005). "The Conceptual History of Social Justice." *Political Studies Review*, Vol. 3, No. 3, 356–73.
JEFFERSON, T. (2018). *Memoir, Correspondence, and Miscellanies, from the Papers of Thomas Jefferson*, Vol. II. Outlook Verlag.
JIM and BACH. "A Critique of Rawls's Hermeneutic as Translation." Department of Political Science, Maxwell School of Citizenship and Public Affairs, Syracuse University, New York: www.maxwell.syr.edu/maxpages/students/jsjosefs/ARTICLE3.HTM.
JONES, W. T. and SONTAG, F., et al. (eds.). (1969). *Approaches to Ethics*, 2nd ed. New York: McGraw-Hill Book Company.
KANT, I. (1964). *Kleinere Schriften zur Geschichtsphilosophie, Ethik und Politik*. VORLÄNDER, K. (Hrsg.). Hamburg: Verlag von Felix Meiner.
KANT, I. (1965). *Politische Schriften*. OTTO HEINRICH VON DER GABLENTZ (Hrsg.).
KANT, I. (1967). *Was ist Aufklärung? Aufsätze zur Geschichte und Philosophie*. ZEHBE, J. (Hrsg.). Göttingen: Vandenhoeck & Ruprecht.

KAUFFMANN, C. (2000). *Straus und Rawls: Das philosophische Dilemma der Politik.* Berlin: Duncker und Humblot.
KERSTING, W. (2001). *John Rawls zur Einführung.* Hamburg: Junius Verlag.
KISIEL, T. (1993). *The Genesis of Heidegger's Being and Time.* Berkeley: University of California Press.
KOHLBERG, L. (1984). *The Psychology of Moral Development.* San Francisco: Harper & Row.
KOLLER, P. (1987). *Neue Theorie des Sozial-Kontrakts.* Berlin: Duncker u. Humblot. Köln: Opladen: Westdeutscher Verlag.
KOLLER, P. (1998). "Die Grundsätze der Gerechtigkeit." In: HÖFFE, O. (Hrsg.). *John Rawls: Eine Theorie der Gerechtigkeit.* Berlin: Akademie Verlag, 45–69.
KRASNOFF, L. (1998). "Consensus, Stability and Normativity in Rawls's Political Liberalism." In: *Journal of Philosophy*, Vol. XLV, No. 6, 269–92.
KUKATHAS, C. (1997). "Cultural Toleration." In: SHAPIRO, I. and KYMLICKA, W. (eds.). *Ethnicity and Group Rights.* New York and London: New York University Press, 69–104.
KUKATHAS, C. and PETTIT, P. (1990). *Rawls: A Theory of Justice and Its Critics.* Cambridge: Polity Press.
KUMAR, R. (2015). "Utilitarianism." In: MANDLE, J. and REIDY, D. A. (eds.). *The Cambridge Rawls Lexicon.* Cambridge: Cambridge University Press, 858–65.
KUPER, A. (2000). "Rawlsian Global Justice: Beyond *The Law of Peoples* to a Cosmopolitan Law of Persons." In: *Political Theory*, Vol. 28, No. 5, 640–74.
KYMLICKA, W. (1989). "Liberal Individualism and Liberal Neutrality." In: *Ethics*, 99, 883–985.
KYMLICKA, W. (1990). *Contemporary Political Philosophy: An Introduction.* Oxford: Clarendon Press.
KYMLICKA, W. (1995). *Multicultural Citizenship: A Liberal Theory of Minority Rights.* Oxford: Oxford University Press.
KYMLICKA, W. (1997). *Politische Philosophie heute: Eine Einführung.* Frankfurt a.M. and New York: Campus.
KYMLICKA, W. (2000). *Multicultural Citizenship.* Oxford: Oxford University Press.
LABORDE, C. (2002). "The Reception of Rawls in Europe." In: *European Journal of Political Theory*, Vol. 1, No. 2, 133–46.
LAMBERT, F. (2010). *The Battle of Ole Miss: Civil Rights v. States' Rights*: New York: Oxford University Press.
LARGE, W. (2008). *Heidegger's Being and Time.* Bloomington: Indiana University Press.
LARMORE, C. (1987). *Patterns of Moral Complexity.* Cambridge: Cambridge University Press.
LARMORE, C. (1990). "Political Liberalism." In: *Political Theory*, Vol. 18, No. 3, 339–60.
LARMORE, C. (1996). *The Morals of Modernity.* Cambridge: Cambridge University Press.
LARMORE, C. (2003). "Public Reason." In: FREEMAN, S. (ed.). *The Cambridge Companion to Rawls.* Cambridge: Cambridge University Press.
LEARY, A. V. (1990). "The Effect of Western Perspectives on International Human Rights." In: AN-Na'im, A. A and DENG, F. M. (eds.). *Human Rights in Africa: Cross-cultural Perspectives.* Washington, DC: Brookings Institution, 15–30.
LEICHT, R. (2003). "Weil der Mensch vernünftig ist: über das Urvertrauen in die liberale Gesellschaft und über den Krieg: 'Das Recht der Völker von John Rawls, dem jüngst verstorbenen amerikanischen Philosophen der Gerechtigkeit." In: *Die Zeit* (20. Februar). Nr. 9, 46.
LITTLE, D. (1990). "A Christian Perspective on Human Rights." In: AN-Na'im, A. A. and DENG, F. M. (eds.). *Human Rights in Africa: Cross-cultural Perspectives.* Washington, DC: Brookings Institution, 59–103.
LUCAS, J. R. (1980). *On Justice.* New York: Oxford University Press.
LYONS, D. (1970). *Forms and Limits of Utilitarianism.* Oxford: Clarendon Press.
LYONS, D. (1984). *Ethics and the Rule of Law.* Cambridge: Cambridge University Press.
MACEDO, S. (1990). "The Politics of Justification" In: *Political Theory*, Vol. 18, No. 2, 280–304.

MACINTYRE, A. (1981). *After Virtue: A Study in Moral Theory*. Notre Dame: University of Notre Dame Press.
MACINTYRE, A. (1984). *After Virtue: A Study in Moral Theory*. 2nd Edition. Notre Dame: University of Notre Dame Press.
MACINTYRE, A. (1988). *Whose Justice? Which Rationality?* Notre Dame: University of Notre Dame Press.
MBITI, J. S. (1999). *African Religions and Philosophy*. Oxford: Heineman.
MBOYA, T. (1963). *Freedom and After*. London: Andre Deutsch.
MCCLENNEN, E. F. (1999). "Justice and the Problem of Stability." In: RICHARDSON, H. S. and WEITHMAN, P. J. (eds.). *The Philosophy of Rawls: A Collection of Essays*, Vol. 4. New York and London: Garland, 139–66.
MCSHEA, R. J. (1990). *Morality and Human Nature: A New Route to Ethical Theory*. Philadelphia: Temple University Press.
MÉNDEZ, A. R. (2018). "Who Are the Subjects of Justice in a Globalized World? From the 'Unidimensional Identity' to the 'Diversity of Identities.'" In: RUIZ, R. C. et al. (eds.). *Philosophy of Globalization*. Berlin: Walter de Gruyter, 153–66.
MENDUS, S. (1989). *Toleration and the Limits of Liberalism*. Atlantic Highlands, NJ: Humanities Press.
MILDE, M. (1995). "The Natural History of Overlapping Consensus." In: *Pacific Philosophical Quarterly*, Vol. 76, 142–58.
MILLER, D. (1999). *Principles of Social Justice*. Cambridge, MA: Harvard University Press.
MILL, J. S. (1968). *Utilitarianism and Other Writings*. WARNOCK, M. (Hrsg.). Cleveland and New York: Meridian Books.
MILLS, C. (2000). "'Not a Mere Modus Vivendi': The Bases for Allegiance to the Just State." In: DAVION, V. and WOLF, C. (eds.). *The Idea of Political Liberalism: Essays on Rawls*. Lanham, MD: Rowman & Littlefield, 190–203.
MOON, J. D. (1993). *Constructing Community: Moral Pluralism and Tragic Conflicts*. Princeton, NJ: Princeton University Press.
MULGAN, T. (2014). *Understanding Utilitarianism*. Hoboken, NJ: Routledge.
MULHALL, S. and SWIFT, A. (1997). *Liberals and Communitarians*, 2nd ed. Oxford and Malden: Blackwell Publishers.
MÜLLER, C. (1995). "Von der Gerechtigkeitstheorie zum politischen Liberalismus: Rawls-Libertarians-Communitarians-und wieder Rawls." In: *Zeitschrift für Politik*, Band XLII.
MÜLLER, J. (2002). "Rawls in Germany." In: *European Journal of Political Theory*, Vol. 1, No. 2, 163–79.
NAGEL, T. (1989). "Rawls on Justice." In: DANIELS, N. (ed.). *Reading Rawls: Critical studies on Rawls' "A Theory of Justice"*. Stanford: Stanford University Press, 1–16.
NAGEL, T. (1991). *Equality and Partiality*. New York: Oxford University Press.
NAGEL, T. (2005). "The Problem of Global Justice." *Philosophy & Public Affairs*, Vol. 33, No. 2 (Spring), 113–47.
NAILS, D. (2018). "Socrates." *Stanford Encyclopedia of Philosophy*. Stanford University, February 6, 2018. https://plato.stanford.edu/entries/socrates/.
NARDIN, T. (1981). "Distributive Justice and the Criticism of International law." In: *Political Studies*, Vol. XXIX, No. 2, 232–44.
NEAL, P. (1997). *Liberalism and Its Discontents*. London: Macmillan Press.
NICKEL, J. W. (2000). "Economic Liberties." In: DAVION, V. and WOLF, C. (eds.). *The Idea of Political Liberalism: Essays on Rawls*. Lanham, MD: Rowman & Littlefield, 155–75.
NIETZSCHE, F. (1994). *Jenseits von Gut und Böse*, 6. Aufl. Deutschland: Goldmann.
NIETZSCHE, F. (1997). *Twilight of Idols*. Indianapolis: Hackett Publishing Company.
NNODIM, P. (2004a). "Public Reason as a Form of Normative and Political Justification: A Study on Rawls's Idea of Public Reason and Kant's Notion of the Use of Public Reason in *What Is Enlightenment?*" In: *South African Journal of Philosophy*, Vol. 23, No. 2, 148–57.
NNODIM, P. (2004b). *Rawls' Theorie der Gerechtigkeit* Oberhausen: Athena.
NNODIM, P. (2006). "Global Justice and the Absence of Universal Morality: Rawlsian Perspectives on International Relations and Human Rights." In: *The Mind's Eye*.

NNODIM, P. (2015). "The Conception of Person in African Philosophy." In: GRAETZEL, S. and GUHE, E. (eds.). *Life, Body Person and Self: A Reconsideration of Core Concepts in Bioethics*. Freiburg: Karl Aber Verlag.
NNODIM, P. (2016). "Utilitarian Dilemmas in the Literature of Scapegoats." Thesis XII, MCLA Online Blog.
NORMAN, R. (1998). *The Moral Philosophers: An Introduction to Ethics*, 2nd ed. Oxford: Oxford University Press.
NOZICK, R. (1974). *Anarchy, State and Utopia*. Oxford: Blackwell.
O'NEILL, O. (1989). *Constructions of Reason: Explorations of Kant's Practical Philosophy*. Cambridge: Cambridge University Press.
O'NEILL, O. (1997) "Political Liberalism and Public Reason: A Critical Notice of John Rawls, Political Liberalism. In: *Philosophical Review*, Vol. 106, No. 3, 411–28.
O'NEILL, O. (2016). *Justice Across Boundaries: Whose Obligations?* Cambridge: Cambridge University Press.
O'NEILL, S. (1997). *Impartiality in Context: Grounding Justice in a Pluralist World*. Albany: State University of New York Press.
O'SULLIVAN, N. (1997). "Difference and the Concept of the Political in Contemporary Political Philosophy." In: *Political Studies*, Vol. xlv, 739–54.
OKERE, T. (1995). "The Structure of the Self in Igbo Thought." In: OKERE, T. (ed.). *Identity and Change: Nigerian Philosophical Studies*. Washington, DC: Council for Research in Values and Philosophy.
OKOLO, C. B. (2003). "Self as a Problem in African Philosophy." In: COETZEE, P. H. and ROUX, A. P. J. (ed.). *The African Philosophy Reader*. 2nd Edition. London: Routledge.
PAREKH, B. (1996). "Moral Philosophy and its Anti-Pluralist Bias." In: ARCHARD, D. (ed.). *Philosophy and Pluralism*. Cambridge: Cambridge University Press, 117–34.
PAREKH, B. (1999). In: DUNNE, T. and WHEELER, N. J. (eds.). *Human Rights in Global Polit ics*. Cambridge: Cambridge University Press.
PAREKH, B. (2000). *Rethinking Multiculturalism: Cultural Diversity and Political Theory*. New York: Palgrave.
PETROVICH, O. (1986). "Moral Autonomy and the Theory of Kohlberg." In: MODGIL, S. and MODGIL, C. (eds.). *Lawrence Kohlberg: Controversy and Consensus*. Philadelphia and London: Farmers Press, 85–106.
PETTIT, P. (1991). "Consequentialism." In: SINGER, P. (ed.). *A Companion to Ethics*. Oxford: Blackwell, 230–40.
PIAGET, J. and INHELDER, B. (1969). *The Psychology of the Child*. Translated by WEAVER, H. London: Routledge & Kegan Paul.
PIAGET, J. (1934). *The Moral Judgement of the Child*. Translated by GABAIN, M. London: Kegan Paul, Trench, Trubner.
PIAGET, J. (1983). *Das moralische Urteil beim Kinde*. GOLDMANN, L. (übers.). Stuttgart: Klett-Cotta.
PIES, I. (1996). "Der Primat des sozialen im politischen Liberalismus -von Mises, von Hayek, Rawls und Buchanan im Vergleich." In: *Diskussionsbeiträge* der *wirtschaftswissenschaftlichen Fakultät Ingolstadt der katholischen Universität Eichstadt*. Nr.74.
PLATO. (1992). *The Republic*. Translated by LINDSAY, A. D. New York: Everyman's Library.
POGGE, T. W. (1989). *Realizing Rawls*. Ithaca, NY: Cornell University Press.
POGGE, T. W. (1994a). "An Egalitarian Law of Peoples." *Philosophy and Public Affairs*, Vol. 23, No. 3, 195–224.
POGGE, T. W. (1994b). *John Rawls*. München: Verlag C. H. Beck.
POGGE, T. W. (2007). "Do Rawls's Two Theories of Justice Fit Together?" In: MARTIN, R. and REIDY, D. A. (eds.). *Rawls's Law of Peoples: A Realistic Utopia?* Malden: Blackwell, 206–25.
POGGE, T. W. (2001a). "Introduction: Global Justice." In: *Metaphilosophy*, Vol. 32, No. 1 / 2, 1–3.
POGGE, T. W. (2001b). "Priorities of Global Justice." In: *Metaphilosophy*, Vol. 32, No. 1 / 2, 6–24.

POGGE, T. W. (2001c). "Rawls on International Justice." In: *Philosophical Quarterly*, Vol. 51, No. 203, 246–53.
QUINN, P. L. (1997). "Political Liberalism and Their Exclusions of the Religious" In: WEITHMAN, P. *Religion and Contemporary Liberalism*. Notre Dame, IN: University of Notre Dame Press, 138–61.
RAJAN, N. (1998). *Secularism, Democracy, Justice: Implications of Rawlsian Principles in India*. New Delhi and London: Sage Publications.
RAMSAY, M. (1997). *What's Wrong with Liberalism? A Radical Critique of Liberal Political Philosophy*. London: Leicester University Press.
RAWLS, J. (1963). "The Sense of Justice.' In: *The Philosophical Review*, Vol. 72, 281–305.
RAWLS, J. (1971). *A Theory of Justice*. Oxford and Cambridge, MA: Harvard University Press/Belknap Press.
RAWLS, J. (1980). "Kantian Constructivism in Moral Theory." In: *Journal of Philosophy*, Vol. lxxviii, No. 9, 515–72.
RAWLS, J. (1982). "The Basic Liberties and Their Priorities." In: MCMURRIN, S. (ed.). (1983). *The Tanner Lectures on Human Values*, 3–87.
RAWLS, J. (1985). "Justice as Fairness: Political not Metaphysical." In: *Philosophy and Public Affairs*, Vol. 14, 223–52.
RAWLS, J. (1987a). "The Idea of an Overlapping Consensus." In: *Oxford Journal of Legal Studies*, Vol. 7/1, 1–25.
RAWLS, J. (1987b). "The Idea of an Overlapping Consensus." In: FREEMAN, S. (ed.). (1999). *John Rawls: Collected Papers*. Cambridge, MA: Harvard University Press, 421–48.
RAWLS, J. (1988). "The Priority of Right and Ideas of the Good." *Philosophy and Public Affairs*, Vol. 17, 251–76.
RAWLS, J. (1989). "The Domain of the Political and Overlapping Consensus." In: *New York University Law Review*, Vol. 64, 233–55.
RAWLS, J. (1993a). *Political Liberalism*. New York: Columbia University Press.
RAWLS, J. (1993b). "The Law of Peoples" In: SHUTE, S. and HURLEY, S. (eds.). *On Human Rights: The Oxford Amnesty Lectures*. New York: Basic, 41–82.
RAWLS, J. (1995). "Reply to Habermas." In: *Journal of Philosophy*, Vol. 92, 132–80.
RAWLS, J. (1996). *Political Liberalism*. New York: Columbia University Press.
RAWLS, J. (1997a). "The Idea of Public Reason Revisited." In: *University of Chicago Law Review*, Vol. 64, No. 3, 765–807.
RAWLS, J. (1997b). "Justice as Fairness." In: GOODIN, E. R. and PETTIT, P. (eds.). *Contemporary Political Philosophy: An Anthology*. Oxford: Blackwell.
RAWLS, J. (1998a). *Politischer Liberalismus*. HINSCH, W. (Übers.) Frankfurt a.M.: Suhrkamp.
RAWLS, J. (1998b) "Anhang: Über die für die deutsche Übersetzung veränderte Fassung der *Theorie der Gerechtigkeit*." In: HÖFFE, O. (Hrsg.). *John Rawls: Eine Theorie der Gerechtigkeit*. Berlin: Akademie Verlag, 295–301.
RAWLS, J. (1999). *The Law of Peoples*. Cambridge, MA: Harvard University Press.
RAWLS, J. (2000). *Lectures in the History of Moral Philosophy*. HERMAN, B. (ed.). Cambridge, MA: Harvard University Press.
RAWLS, J. (2001). *Justice as Fairness: A Restatement*. KELLY, E. (ed.). Cambridge, MA: Harvard University Press.
RAZ, J. (1990). "Facing Diversity: The Case of Epistemic Abstinence." In: KUKATHAS, C. (ed.). (2003). *John Rawls: Critical Assessment of Leading Political Philosophers*, Vol. 4. London and New York: Routledge, 395–431.
REIMAN, J. (2000). "Abortion, Natural Law, and the Liberal Discourse: A Response to John Finnis." In: GEORGE, R. P. and WOLFE, C. *Natural Law and Public Reason*. Washington, DC: Georgetown University Press, 107–24.
RICE, D. H. (1998). *A Guide to Plato's Republic*. New York: Oxford University Press.
RICOEUR, P. (1999). "On John Rawls' *A Theory of Justice*: Is a Pure Procedural Theory of Justice Possible?" In: RICHARDSON, H. and WEITHAM, P. J. (eds.). *The Philosophy of Rawls: A Collection of Essays*. New York and London: Garland, 133–44.

RINDERLE, P. (1998). *Politische Vernunft: Ihre Struktur und Dynamik.* Freiburg, München: Alber.
ROOSEVELT, T. (1920). *Roosevelt's Writings: Selections From the Writings of Theodore Roosevelt.* FULTON, G. M. (ed.). New York: Macmillan Company.
RYAN, A. (1993). *Justice.* Oxford: Oxford University Press.
SANDEL, M. (1982). *Liberalism and the Limits of Justice.* Cambridge: Cambridge University Press.
SANDEL, M. (1984). "The Procedural Republic and the Unencumbered Self." In: *Political Theory*, 81–96.
SANDEL, M. (2009). *Justice: What's the Right Thing to Do?* New York: Farrar, Straus and Giroux.
SANTAS, G. (2006). "Methods of Reasoning about Justice in Plato's Republic." In: SANTAS, G. (ed.). *Blackwell Guide to the Republic.* Malden: Blackwell, 129–32.
SCANLON, T. M. (1989). "Rawls's Theory of Justice." In: DANIELS, N. (ed.). *Reading Rawls.* Stanford: Stanford University Press, 169–205.
SCHEFFLER, S. (1994). "The Appeal of Political Liberalism." In *Ethics*, Vol. 105, 4–22.
SCHMIDT, J. (1989). "The Question of Enlightenment: Kant, Mendelssohn, and the Mittwochsgesellschaft." *Journal of the History of Ideas*, Vol. 50, No. 2 (April–June), 269–91.
SEN, A. (1999). *Development as Freedom.* Oxford: Oxford University Press.
SEN, A. (2009). *The Idea of Justice.* Cambridge, MA: Harvard University Press.
SHABER, T. (1991). *Globale Gerechtigkeit: Die Anwendung von Rawls' Theorie der Gerechtigkeit in den Internationalen Beziehung.* Frankfurt a.M.: Haag + Herchen.
SHAKESPEARE, W. (2010). *Julius Caesar.* BATE, J. and RASMUSSEN, E. (eds.). New York: Macmillan Publishers.
SIDGWICK, H. (1981). *The Methods of Ethics.* Indianapolis: Hackett Publishing Company.
SIMMONS, A. J. (2008). *Political Philosophy.* New York: Oxford University Press, 2008.
SLOTE, M. (1985). "Utilitarianism, Moral Dilemmas, and Moral Cost." *American Philosophical Quarterly*, Vol. 22, No. 2, 161–68.
SMART, J. J. C. and WILLIAMS, B. (1973). *Utilitarianism For and Against.* Cambridge: Cambridge University Press.
SOLUM, L. B. (1994). "Inclusive Public Reason." In: *Pacific Philosophical Quarterly*, Vol. 75, 217–31.
SOPER, P. (1984). *A Theory of Law.* Cambridge, MA, and London: Harvard University Press.
SPRIGGE, T. L. S. (1990). *The Rational Foundation of Ethics.* London and New York: Routledge and Kegan Paul.
STAUFFER, D. (2001). *Plato's Introduction to the Question of Justice.* Albany: State University of New York Press.
STERBA, J. P. (1998). *Social and Political Philosophy.* 2nd Edition. Belmont, CA: Wadsworth.
STERBA, J. P. (2000). "Rawls and Religion." In: DAVION, V. and WOLF, C. (eds.). *The Idea of Political Liberalism: Essays on Rawls.* Lanham, MD: Rowman & Littlefield.
STERBA, J. P. (2003). *Justice: Alternative Political Perspectives.* Boston: Wadsworth.
STURMA, D. (2000). "Universalismus und Neoaristotelismus." In: KERSTING, W. (Hrsg.). *Politische Philosophie des Sozialstaats.* Weilerwist: Velbrück Wissenschaften, 257–92.
SUGPURWALLA, R. (2006). "Plato's Defense of Justice in the *Republic.*" In: SANTAS, G. (ed.). *Blackwell Guide to the Republic.* Malden: Blackwell, 263–82.
SULLIVAN, R. T. (1989). *Immanuel Kant's Moral Theory.* Cambridge: Cambridge University Press.
SUNSTEIN, C. R. (1997). *Free Markets and Social Justice.* Oxford: Oxford University Press.
SWIFT, A. (2007). *Political Philosophy.* Cambridge: Polity.
TALISSE, R. B. (2001). *On Rawls: A Liberal Theory of justice and Justification.* Belmont, CA: Wadsworth.
TAN, K. (1998). "Liberal Toleration in Rawls's Law of Peoples." In: *Ethics*, Vol. 108, 276–95.
TAN, K. (2000). *Toleration, Diversity, and Global Justice.* University Park: Pennsylvania State University Press.

TASIOULAS, J. (2002) "From Utopia to Kazanistan: John Rawls and the Law of Peoples." In: *Oxford Journal of Legal Studies*, Vol. 22, No. 2, 367–96.
TEMPELS, P. (1959). *Bantu Philosophy*. Paris: Présence Africaine.
TESÒN, F. R. (1995). "The Rawlsian Theory of International Law." In: KUKATHAS, C. (ed.). (2003). *John Rawls: Critical Assessment of Leading Political Philosophers*, Vol. 4. London and New York: Routledge, 295–315.
THOMPSON, W. (2011). *Ideologies in the Age of Extremes Liberalism, Conservatism, Communism, Fascism, 1914 – 1991*. London: Pluto Press.
THORKILDSEN, T. A. (1995). "Conceptions of Social Justice." In: KURTINES, W. M. and GEWIRTZ, J. L. (eds.). *Moral Development: An Introduction*. Boston: Allyn and Bacon, 511–33.
TIBI, B. (1990). "The European Tradition of Human Rights and the Culture of Islam." In: AN-Na'im, A. A. and DENG, F. M. (eds.). *Human Rights in Africa: Cross-cultural Perspectives*. Washington, DC: Brookings Institution, 104–32.
TOMASI, J. (2001). *Liberalism beyond Justice: Citizens, Society and the Boundaries of Political Theory*. Princeton, NJ: Princeton University Press.
TOMBS, B. P. (1997). "Public Reason, Religion, and Politics." http://www3.sympatico.ca/toombs/rawls.html.
UMEH, J. A. (1997). *After God Is Dibia*. London: Karnak House.
Universal Declaration of Human Rights (UHDR). www. un.org/Overview/rights.html.
VESSEL, J. P. (2010). "Supererogation for Utilitarianism." In: *American Philosophical Quarterly*, Vol. 47, No. 4, 299–319.
WALDRON, J. (1987). "Theoretical Foundations of Liberalism." In: *Philosophical Quarterly*, Vol. 37, No. 147, 127–50.
WEINREICH-HASTE, H. (1982). "Piaget on Morality: A Critical Perspective." In: MODGIL, S. and MODGIL, C. (eds.). *Jean Piaget: Consensus and Controversy*. London: Holt, Rinehart and Winston, 181–206.
WEINSTEIN, D. (2007). *Utilitarianism and the New Liberalism*. Cambridge: Cambridge University Press.
WEINSTOCK, D, M. (1994). "The Justification of Political Liberalism." In: *Pacific Philosophical Quarterly*, Vol. 75, 165–85.
WEITHMAN, P. J. (ed.). (1997). *Religion and Contemporary Liberalism*. Notre Dame: University of Notre Dame Press.
WEITHMAN, P. J. (2009). "John Rawls and the Task of Political Philosophy." *Review of Politics*, Vol. 71, No. 1, 113–25.
WENAR, L. (1995). "Political Liberalism: An Internal Critique." In: *Ethics*, Vol. 106, No. 1, 32–62.
WENAR, L. (2001). "Contractualism and Global Economic Justice." In: *Metaphilosophy*, Vol. 32, No. 1 / 2, 79–94.
WILLIAMS, S. M. (1995) "Justice towards Groups: Political Not Juridical." In: *Political Theory*, Vol. 23, No. 1, 67–91.
WOLF, C. and HITTINGER, J. (eds.). (1994). *Liberalism at the Crossroads: An Introduction to Contemporary Political Theory and Its Critics*. Lanham, MD: Rowman & Littlefield.
WOOD, A. W. (1999). *Kant's Ethical Thought*. Cambridge: Cambridge University Press.
WOOD, A. W. (2001). *Basic Writings of Kant*. New York: Modern Library.
WRIGHT, D. (1982). "Piaget's Theory of Moral Development." In: MODGIL, S. and MODGIL, C. (eds.). *Jean Piaget: Consensus and Controversy*. London: Holt, Rinehart and Winston, 207–17.
YOUNG, S. P. (2000). "Political Stability and the Need for Moral Affirmation." *Minerva-An Internet Journal of Philosophy*, Vol. 4.
YOUNG, S. P. (2002). *Beyond Rawls: An Analysis of the Concept of Political Liberalism*. Lanham, MD: University Press of America.

# Index

Abbe de Saint-Pierre, 117
Achebe, Chinua, 152–153, 159n13
Ackerman, Bruce, 92
*Ahu*, 151, 152–153
An-Na'im, Abdullahi Ahmed, 146
Aristippus, 25

basic liberties, 17–18, 23, 33, 59, 91, 95, 114, 115
basic justice, matters/questions of, 52, 92, 94, 95
basic structure, of society, 14, 21, 23, 71–72, 86, 94, 105, 110, 112, 137–138, 142
Beitz, Charles, 132, 133, 139
Bentham, Jeremy, 13, 25–27, 115
Biester, Johann Erich, 88
Brock, Gillian, 138
Buckley, Michael, 52–53, 73–74
burdens of judgment, 82, 124

*Chi*, 151, 154–156
Choi, Naomi, 1, 13
Christianity/Christian, 43–44, 48, 50, 57, 68, 78, 118, 124, 158
Chua, Amy, 134
Cold War, 118
colonialism, 43–44
communitarianism, 57, 63n56, 74, 74–75, 79, 80, 145
constitutional essentials, 52, 92, 94–95

cosmopolitanism, 5, 132–136, 139–140
COVID-19 (coronavirus), 130

De Castro, Elizabeth, 136
deontological theories, 32
difference principle, 18, 19–20, 22, 71, 132, 137
Dombrowski, Daniel A., 42–43, 66, 71
Durkheim, Emile, 104
duty of assistance, 138, 139
Dworkin, Ronald, 13–14

Epicurus, 25
*epoché*, phenomenological, 3, 15
Enlightenment, 4, 45, 48, 85, 87–88, 90
Epstein, Richard A., 121
Eze, Emmanuel Chukwudi, 150

fair equality of opportunity, 17, 18, 23
Foss, Jerome, 121
Frazer, Elizabeth, 69, 70, 98
Freeman, Samuel, 14, 15, 17, 22, 42, 47, 86, 95, 122
"free-riders," 122–123
Friedrich the Great II, 91

Galston, William A., 20, 60, 69
globalization, 129–130, 136
global justice, 129–136, 139–140, 141, 158–159, 161
Gordon, David, 133

# Index

Gray, John, 43, 48

Habermas, Jürgen, 71, 81–82, 90, 113, 123
hedonistic calculus, 27
Heidegger, Martin, 2
Herder, Johann Gottfried, 45
Hobbes, Thomas, 5, 41, 62, 72, 104, 117–118
Horton, John, 119–120
Howard, Rhonda E., 145
Hume, David, 13, 25, 34
Hutzler, Alexandra, 134

Igbo, 151–157, 158, 159n13
intuitionism, 14, 33, 41, 54–55

Jefferson, Thomas, 9

Kant, Immanuel, 4, 13, 14–15, 41, 44–45, 46, 49, 54, 55–56, 72, 74, 85, 86–91, 98–99, 117, 121
Kohlberg, Lawrence, 5, 108, 122
Krasnoff, Larry, 123–124
Kymlicka, Will, 75–76

Lacey, Nicola, 69, 70, 98
*laissez-faire*, 16, 22, 47
law of nations, 132
law of peoples, 136–140, 161
Leary, Virginia A., 145
liberal individualism, 3, 142, 145, 147, 149–159
liberalism, classical/comprehensive, 3, 72, 74–75, 92, 114; departure from, 41–62
liberalism, political, 4, 5, 46–52, 53, 56–57, 58, 60, 61–62, 65, 71, 72, 73–74, 76, 78, 79, 81, 82, 85, 95–96, 99, 112, 113, 117, 118, 123, 125; goals of, 51–52
libertarianism, 16, 20–21
Locke, John, 13, 41, 44, 49, 72, 104

MacIntyre, Alasdair, 57, 58, 74–75
Mbiti, John S., 149
Mboya, Tom, 149
McClennen, Edward, 111, 122
Méndez, Alberto Ruiz, 129–130
Mendus, Susan, 75
Meredith, James, 10

Mill, John Stuart, 10, 27, 41, 44, 49, 72
*Mmadu*, 151
*Mmuo*, 151, 153–154
*modus vivendi*, 5, 116–119
Moon, Donald, 48, 76, 82
moral psychology, 5, 107, 108, 109, 122
moral universalism, normative, 65, 69
multiculturalism, 3, 48, 113, 124

Nagel, Thomas, 130
nonpublic reason, 95–96, 98
Nozick, Robert, 3–4, 13, 21–22

Obama, Barack, 9, 134
Okere, Theophilus, 153–154, 155–156
O'Neill, Onora, 98, 130
original position, 3, 16–17, 33, 67, 79, 115, 133
O'Sullivan, Noël, 56, 70
overlapping consensus, 5, 66, 68, 81, 107, 112–116, 117, 119, 122, 123, 124

pan-Africanism, 150, 158
Parekh, Bhikhu, 42, 43–44, 62, 146
perfectionism, 41, 91
Piaget, Jean, 5, 108–109, 111, 122
Poe, Edgar Allan, 29, 30
Pogge, Thomas, 132, 133
political conception of justice, 5, 50–51, 52, 56, 58, 59, 60, 62, 68–69, 71–81, 86, 91–92, 93, 94, 95, 97, 104, 105, 106, 107, 112–114, 115, 116, 117, 124–125
political constructivism, 52–56, 81
primary goods, 17, 59
principle of legitimacy, liberal/political, 4, 13, 93
priority of the right over the good, 79
private use of reason, 87, 89–91
property owning democracy, 22, 23
public political culture, 4, 70, 71, 73, 99, 115
public reason, 3, 4, 59, 82, 85–99, 116, 123; content of Rawls's, 91–94; forum of Rawls's, 94–96; limits of Rawls's, 96–98; meaning of, 85–87
public use of reason, 4, 81, 85, 87–91, 98–99
Prussia, 4, 90, 91

racism, 10–12
Rawls, John: background of, 1–2; *Justice as Fairness*, 58, 66; *The Law of Peoples*, 1, 5, 6, 129–147; *Political Liberalism*, 1, 4, 5, 18, 47–52, 53, 54–56, 58, 66, 67–69, 70, 71–74, 75, 80–81, 82, 85, 86–87, 96, 98, 99n4, 101n61, 103, 105, 112, 115, 121–122, 133, 140, 141, 144; *A Theory of Justice*, 1, 2, 3, 13, 14, 28, 32–36, 46, 58–59, 63n56, 65, 66–68, 69–71, 74, 75, 79, 80, 103, 104–105, 114, 125n14, 132, 144
reasonable pluralism, 5, 18, 48, 49–50, 55, 59, 62, 65, 68–69, 76, 80, 91, 99, 104, 107, 124
reciprocity of perspectives, 14, 22, 65
reflective equilibrium, 15
Rousseau, Jean Jacques, 13, 41, 104, 117

same-sex marriage, 134–135
Sandel, Michael, 12, 21–22, 30–31, 57, 58, 74
Sanders, Bernie, 16
Scheffler, Samuel, 115
Sen, Amartya, 1, 85, 119, 120, 131, 159
sense of justice, 5, 106, 107–109, 122, 125n22
Shakespeare, William, 2
Sidgwick, Henry, 27–28, 32, 53, 115
Simmons, John A., 35
Smith, Adam, 25, 34
social contract theory, 3, 15, 68, 69
Socrates, 27
Soviet Union, 118
stability for the right reasons, 5, 116
Sturma, Dieter, 75

Supreme Court, 95, 121, 134
Sunstein, Cass R., 18

Tan, Kor-Chor, 61
teleological theories, 32
Tempels, Placide, 156, 157
Tibi, Bassam, 144
Tomasi, John, 94
Trump, Donald, administration of, 15, 16
two principles of justice, 3, 17–19, 23, 71–72, 103, 115, 116. *See also* difference principle; fair equality of opportunity

Umeh, John Anenechukwu, 154
unencumbered self, 74
Universal Declaration of Human Rights (UDHR), 5–6, 131, 141–142, 145, 146, 158, 159
United Nations, 5, 131, 140–141
Ursula, Le Guin, 29–30
utilitarianism, 3, 11, 41, 49, 67, 114–115; classical, 25–28, 31–32; Rawls's objections to, 31–36; and scapegoat dilemmas, 28–31
utopia, realistic, 5, 130, 136

veil of ignorance, 3, 15, 16–17

Waldron, Jeremy, 93
Weithman, Paul, 96, 112
well-ordered society, 5, 31, 66, 68, 95, 103–125, 138
World War II, 1
Wright, D., 109

Zöllner, Johann Friedrich, 87–88

# About the Author

**Paul Nnodim** is professor of philosophy at Massachusetts College of Liberal Arts.

www.ingramcontent.com/pod-product-compliance
Lightning Source LLC
Chambersburg PA
CBHW050907300426
44111CB00010B/1421